S0-ADH-676

Frommer's™

Mallorca & Menorca
day BY day™

1st Edition

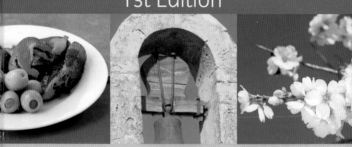

by Neil Edward Schlecht

WILEY

A John Wiley and Sons, Ltd, Publication

Contents

Copyright © 2010 John Wiley & Sons Ltd, The Atrium, Southern Gate, Chichester, West Sussex PO19 8SQ, England

Telephone (+44) 1243 779777

Email (for orders and customer service enquiries): cs-books@wiley.co.uk.

Visit our Home Page on www.wiley.com

All Rights Reserved. No part of this publication may be reproduced, stored in a retrieval system or transmitted in any form or by any means, electronic, mechanical, photocopying, recording, scanning or otherwise, except under the terms of the Copyright, Designs and Patents Act 1988 or under the terms of a licence issued by the Copyright Licensing Agency Ltd, Saffron House, 6-10 Kirby Street, London EC1N 8TS, UK, without the permission in writing of the Publisher. Requests to the Publisher should be addressed to the Permissions Department, John Wiley & Sons Ltd, The Atrium, Southern Gate, Chichester, West Sussex PO19 8SQ, England, or emailed to permreq@wiley.co.uk, or faxed to (+44) 1243 770620.

Designations used by companies to distinguish their products are often claimed as trademarks. All brand names and product names used in this book are trade names, service marks, trademarks or registered trademarks of their respective owners. The Publisher is not associated with any product or vendor mentioned in this book.

This publication is designed to provide accurate and authoritative information in regard to the subject matter covered. It is sold on the understanding that the Publisher is not engaged in rendering professional services. If professional advice or other expert assistance is required, the services of a competent professional should be sought.

UK Publisher: Sally Smith

Production Manager: Daniel Mersey

Commissioning Editor: Fiona Quinn

Development Editor: Marcus Waring

Content Editor: Erica Peters

Photo Research: Jill Emeny

Cartography: SY Cartographics

Wiley also publishes its books in a variety of electronic formats. Some content that appears in print may not be available in electronic books.

British Library Cataloguing in Publication Data

A catalogue record for this book is available from the British Library

ISBN: 978-0-470-72164-3

Typeset by Wiley Indianapolis Composition Services

Printed and bound in China by RR Donnelley

5 4 3 2 1

A Note from the Editorial Director

Organizing your time. That's what this guide is all about.

Other guides give you long lists of things to see and do and then expect you to fit the pieces together. The Day by Day guides are different. These guides tell you the best of everything, and then they show you how to see it *in the smartest, most time-efficient way*. Our authors have designed detailed itineraries organized by time, neighborhood, or special interest. And each tour comes with a bulleted map that takes you from stop to stop.

Hoping to see the best of Palma's Moorish and medieval architecture, lounge at some of the world's most splendid beaches, or discover local gastronomic specialities like *ensaïmades* and unique indigenous wines? Want to get to know the islands by bicycle or hiking among ancient villages along Mallorca's scenic northwest coast? Whatever your interest or schedule, the Day by Days give you the smartest routes to follow. Not only do we take you to the top attractions, hotels, and restaurants, but we also help you access those special moments that locals get to experience— those "finds" that turn tourists into travelers.

The Day by Days are also your top choice if you're looking for one complete guide for all your travel needs. The best hotels and restaurants for every budget, the greatest shopping values, the wildest nightlife—it's all here.

Why should you trust our judgment? Because our authors personally visit each place they write about. They're an independent lot who say what they think and would never include places they wouldn't recommend to their best friends. They're also open to suggestions from readers. If you'd like to contact them, please send your comments our way at feedback@frommers.com, and we'll pass them on.

Enjoy your Day by Day guide—the most helpful travel companion you can buy. And have the trip of a lifetime.

Warm regards,

Kelly Regan

Kelly Regan, Editorial Director
Frommer's Travel Guides

About the Author

Writer and photographer **Neil Edward Schlecht** first travelled to the Balearic Islands in the mid-1990s, while living and working in Barcelona. He was smitten by Mallorca's northwest coast—enough to ask his wife to marry him in a particularly magical spot there on a third trip to the island. He is equally enamoured of the quieter pleasures of Mallorca's smaller sister, Menorca, and his beloved Labrador Uisce hailed from a farm on Ibiza. Now living in New York City, Neil is the author of more than a dozen travel guides to places around the globe, including *Frommer's Barcelona Day by Day*, *Frommer's Peru*, and *Frommer's Buenos Aires Day by Day*, as well as articles on food and wine, tennis, contemporary art and antiques.

Acknowledgements

My sincerest thanks as always to Pilar Vico, of the Spanish Tourism Office in New York, and to David Sastre of IBATUR and Núria Sintes Llopis of Fundació Destí Menorca for assisting with local arrangements. My appreciation as well to Fiona Quinn, for her patient shepherding of this project.

An Additional Note

Please be advised that travel information is subject to change at any time—and this is especially true of prices. We therefore suggest that you write or call ahead for confirmation when making your travel plans. The authors, editors, and publisher cannot be held responsible for the experiences of readers while traveling. Your safety is important to us, however, so we encourage you to stay alert and be aware of your surroundings.

Star Ratings, Icons & Abbreviations

Every hotel, restaurant, and attraction listing in this guide has been ranked for quality, value, service, amenities, and special features using a **star-rating system.** Hotels, restaurants, attractions, shopping, and nightlife are rated on a scale of zero stars (recommended) to three stars (exceptional). In addition to the star-rating system, we also use a **kids** icon to point out the best bets for families. Within each tour, we recommend cafes, bars, or restaurants where you can take a break. Each of these stops appears in a shaded box marked with a coffee-cup-shaped bullet ☕.

The following **abbreviations** are used for credit cards:

AE	American Express	**DISC**	Discover	**V**	Visa
DC	Diners Club	**MC**	MasterCard		

Travel Resources at Frommers.com

Frommer's travel resources don't end with this guide. Frommer's website, **www.frommers.com**, has travel information on more than 4,000 destinations. We update features regularly, giving you access to the most current trip-planning information and the best airfare, lodging, and car-rental bargains. You can also listen to podcasts, connect with other Frommers.com members through our active-reader forums, share your travel photos, read blogs from guidebook editors and fellow travelers, and much more.

A Note on Prices

In the "Take a Break" and "Best Bets" sections of this book, we have used a system of dollar signs to show a range of costs for 1 night in a hotel (the price of a double-occupancy room) or the cost of a main course (entree) at a restaurant. Use the following table to decipher the dollar signs:

Cost	Hotels	Restaurants
$	under $100	under $10
$$	$100–$200	$10–$20
$$$	$200–$300	$20–$30
$$$$	$300–$400	$30–$40
$$$$$	over $400	over $40

How to Contact Us

In researching this book, we discovered many wonderful places—hotels, restaurants, shops, and more. We're sure you'll find others. Please tell us about them, so we can share the information with your fellow travellers in upcoming editions. If you were disappointed with a recommendation, we'd love to know that, too. Please write to:

Frommer's Mallorca & Menorca Day by Day, 1st Edition
Wiley Publishing, Inc. • 111 River St. • Hoboken, NJ 07030-5774

16 Favourite
Moments

16 Favourite **Moments**

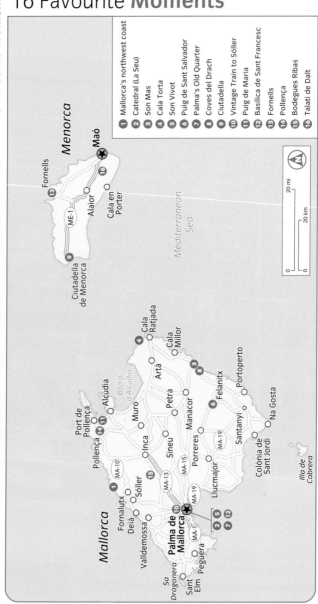

1. Mallorca's northwest coast
2. Catedral (La Seu)
3. Son Mas
4. Cala Torta
5. Son Vivot
6. Puig de Sant Salvador
7. Palma's Old Quarter
8. Coves del Drach
9. Ciutadella
10. Vintage Train to Sóller
11. Puig de Maria
12. Basílica de Sant Francesc
13. Fornells
14. Pollença
15. Bodegues Ribas
16. Talatí de Dalt

Previous page: Catedral (La Seu).

Mallorca is one of the Med's favourite summer playgrounds, and like its smaller cousin Menorca, it's a yearround destination. From outdoor sports and historic architecture to chic rural hotels, quiet coves and local wine trails, there's much more to the islands than vast hotels and long stretches of crowded sand. The following island experiences are some of my favourites.

The northwest coast of Mallorca.

1 Dropping your jaw along the northwest coast. The entire northwest coast of Mallorca, from Port de Andratx on the western tip to the Formentor peninsula jutting audaciously out into the sea, is a vertiginous landscape of sheared-off cliffs dropping to clear blue seas, strategic and camera-ready *miradors* (viewpoints), ancient hilltop villages amid agricultural terraces and secluded rocky coves. For me, it's one of the most picturesque places on the planet. *See p 88.*

2 Admiring Catedral (La Seu), inside and out. Palma's most majestic monument, which was started in the early 13th century, is one of the greatest Gothic cathedrals in the world. It's a mesmerising sight, viewed from below, illuminated and reflected in the wading pool at night. But the real treasures lie inside, in Antoni Gaudí's idiosyncratic canopy over the main altar and native son Miquel Barceló's wonderfully tactile modern-art chapel that depicts the creation of Mallorca. *See p 23.*

3 Staying at a rural boutique hotel. These hotels are the antithesis of the sprawling concrete beach hotels that began Mallorca's tourism boom (and gave it a bad name) and the latest trend. Historic farms, mansions and townhouses have been beautifully converted into intimate, often family-owned boutique hotels. You'll find them in cities, on coasts and in the mountains and they offer a chance to experience the islands at their most graceful. One of my favourites is **Son Mas,** on Mallorca's east coast. *See p 111.*

4 Scampering across the coastline to a deserted beach cove. Balearic beaches are world-famous,

Catedral (La Seu) at night.

Cycling around Mallorca.

but in summer finding one that's not wall-to-wall with people can be a fool's errand. The best bet on either island is to go where the masses can't easily reach. That means parking the car and setting out along paths through forested or rocky coastlines to spectacular beach coves, often devoid of humans (and, of course, facilities). Among my favourites are **Cala Torta** on Mallorca and **Cala Pregonda** on Menorca's north coast. *See p 126.*

Explore Palma's Old Quarter.

⑤ Sampling island gourmet specialities. Islanders have their own unique take on Mediterranean cuisine. Some of the homegrown items on the menu include *ensaïmades* (delicate and light, flaky spiral-bun pastries), *sobressada* (raw pork sausage) and Mahón cheese. See and sample them all at Palma's **Son Vivot.** *See p 80.*

⑥ Cycling Mallorca's flat plains and mountains. Mallorca is a cyclist's dream landscape. Every spring, professional and amateur teams travel from across Europe to train on its rural country roads in the interior *(Es Pla)* and the dramatic mountains along the northwest coast. You don't have to be a hardcore cyclist to enjoy two-wheeled cruising from village to village across Mallorca, but you might want to choose your routes carefully. **Puig de Sant Salvador** just outside Felanitx is a favourite of the strong-legged and lunged. *See p 132.*

⑦ Wandering the streets of Palma's old quarter. The Mallorcan capital's *Centre Històric* is an intoxicating mélange of small alleyways and Roman, Moorish, Medieval, Renaissance and Modernista (Catalan Art Nouveau) architecture, with dozens of stately churches and seigniorial palaces built around interior patios. With soaring palm trees fringing a wide bay, old Palma is like a more Mediterranean and laid-back version of Barcelona's Gothic quarter. *See p 46.*

8 **Descending into a 300-million-year-old cave.** Both islands are dotted with incredibly deep caves, full of fascinating stalactites and stalagmites formed slowly over time. Along Mallorca's east coast are the best-known and most accessible caves. At **Coves del Drach,** lighting and sound (and even live orchestras floating on subterranean lakes) enhance the experience: great fun for children. *See p 108.*

9 **Delighting in the early evening in Ciutadella.** Menorca's second city was the capital until the British moved it to Maó. The result is that this historic centre of 17th-century stone palaces and churches has been extraordinarily well preserved. At sundown, the old quarter turns golden, encouraging locals to turn out in their droves to stroll the beautifully illuminated streets and gaze at the sun setting over the port. *See p 20.*

10 **Hopping on the vintage train to Sóller.** Built to transport citrus from Sóller to Palma for export to the mainland, the vintage wooden cars of the 1912 narrow-gauge train still do the daily round trip between the two cities and make a wonderfully scenic journey through orange and lemon groves and the Serra de Tramuntana mountains. When you arrive in Sóller, you can then climb aboard the equally atmospheric vintage tram that travels through town and down to the harbour at Port de Sóller. *See p 11.*

11 **Trekking to the top of Puig de María.** Delightful walks and hikes abound on Mallorca, especially some multi-day treks in the Tramuntana range, but my favourite short trek is the climb up Puig de María, near Pollença. It's just a steep hour-long climb but the views on the way up and at the top of the Formentor peninsula and Pollença and Alcúdia bays are breathtaking. You can even spend the night at a cool 17th-century hermitage, now a refuge for walkers and cyclists. *See p 5.*

12 **Stumbling upon the organist rehearsing at Basílica de Sant Francesc.** The cloister of Palma's 13th-century basilica dedicated to St. Francis provides a wonderful, peaceful oasis in the old quarter. But if you duck inside the church on a weekday afternoon, you may just find the organist playing the colossal pipe organ, filling the cavernous space with music just for you. *See p 51.*

13 **Dining on *caldereta de llagosta* in Fornells.** The charming whitewashed fishing village of Fornells, on Menorca's north coast, has become a gastronome's paradise, with fresh seafood coming right off the boats and into restaurants facing the harbour. The dish that made

Hop on board the train to Sóller.

Via Crucis, Pollença.

Fornells famous is the rather pricey lobster stew (*caldereta de llagosta*), but you'll also find versions made with fresh fish or shellfish, as well as some delectable seafood paellas. *See p 148.*

⑭ Climbing and then strolling Pollença. After trudging up the 365 steps of the *Vía Crucis* (Way of the Cross) to the chapel of El Calvari, relax by strolling through the pleasant, pedestrian-only streets of old Pollença, long popular with British expats and celebrated citizens such as Agatha Christie and Winston Churchill. The distinctive 17th- and 18th-century architecture and clusters of sunny and relaxed cafés in open squares make it one of the more easygoing spots on the north coast, and one of the best for enjoying Mallorca's café culture. *See p 103.*

⑮ Sipping a wine unlike any other. Even among wine aficionados, few know much about Mallorcan wines, though the local wine industry dates back to the 15th century. Only recently have mainland Spain and a broader public begun to hear about the indigenous grapes produced only in the Balearics. Taste a substantial *manto negro* or brisk *prensal blanc* at one of a handful of wineries just outside Binissalem. My favourite is **Bodegues Ribas.** If you don't make it to a winery, make sure a well-stocked wine bar such as Palma's **Lo Di Vino** is on your itinerary. *See p 34 and p 80.*

⑯ Plunging into Menorcan history. For such a tiny island, Menorca has a huge history. Its prehistoric Talayotic period dates back to 2000 B.C. and is still very much in evidence, with perfectly preserved megalithic monuments (more than 1,500 still exist on the island) that include inscrutable stone structures called talayots, navetas and taulas. The whole of Menorca is crisscrossed by ancient *paredes secas*, stone walls that line old pathways and outline agricultural fields. Perhaps best for visitors is **Talatí de Dalt,** just outside the capital, Maó. *See p 150.* ●

Tour the wineries.

The Best of Mallorca
in **Three Days**

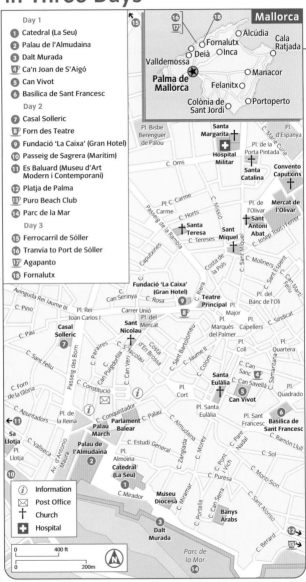

Mallorca

Alcúdia · Cala Ratjada
Fornalutx
Valldemossa · Deià · Inca
Palma de Mallorca · Manacor
Felanitx
Colònia de Sant Jordi · Portoperto

Pl. Bisbe Berenguer de Palou · Santa Margarita · Pl. d'Espanya
Pl. Marie Curie · Pl. de la Porta Pintada
C. Oms · Hospital Militar
Santa Catalina · Convento Caputxins

Pl. de l'Olivar · Mercat de l'Olivar
Pl. C. Carme · Sant Antoni Abat
Passeig de la Rambla · C. Horts · C. Missió
Santa Teresa · Sant Miquel · C. Josep Tous i Ferrer
C. Tereses
Costa de la Pols · C. Sant Miquel · C. Moliners · C. Sant Espert

Avinguda Rei Jaume III · Fundació 'La Caixa' (Gran Hotel)
Can Serinya · C. Rosa · C. Riera · Teatre Principal
Carrer Unió · Pl. del Mercat
C. Pino · Pl. Rei Joan Carlos I · Sant Nicolau · Pl. Major
C. Pau · Casal Solleric · C. S. Nicolau · Costa d'En Brossa · C. Sant Bartolomeu · Marquès del Palmer · Pl. Capellers · Pl. Sindicat
C. Sant Feliu · Passeig des Born · Pl. Coll · Pl. Quartera
C. Forn de la Glòria · C. Constitució · C. Jaume II · C. Colom · Santa Eulàlia · C. Can Sanç · Pl. Can Savellá · Pl. Quadrado
C. Apuntadors · Pl. de la Reina · C. Conquistador · Can Vivot · Pl. Santa Eulàlia
Sa Llotja · Parlament Balear · C. Palau · Pl. Cort · Pl. Sant Francesc · Basílica de Sant Francesc
C. Vallseca · Palau March · C. Almudaina · C. Ramón Llull
Pl. Llotja · Palau de l'Almudaina · Pl. Almoina · C. Estudi General · C. Zanglada · C. Morey · C. Pare Nadal · C. Sol
Catedral (La Seu) · C. Montí-Sion
C. Mirador · Museu Diocesà · C. Miramar · C. Puresa · C. Sant Alonso
Banys Àrabs · C. Portella · C. Can Serra
Dalt Murada · C. Berard
Parc de la Mar

i Information
✉ Post Office
✝ Church
✚ Hospital

0   400 ft
0   200m

Previous page: Cala Romàntica beach.

If you have just 3 days to enjoy Mallorca, you can still get a full taste of its beautiful capital, as well as sample the island's history and natural beauty. Staying in Palma, this tour does without the need to hire a car. It gives you 2 days in Palma followed by a vintage train excursion to the exceptionally beautiful northwest coast.
START: **Catedral (La Seu), Palma de Mallorca.**

Travel Tip

This tour assumes that you're staying in Palma. For recommended hotels in Palma, see p 70.

Day One

Spend your first day exploring Palma's *Centre Històric*: the old town that dates back to the Romans and when the Moors controlled Mallorca. It's a good walking tour, although you'll need sturdy shoes and may want to catch a taxi at the end.

1 ★★★ Catedral (La Seu). Start with the monument that dominates the city, the imposing Gothic cathedral (largely constructed during the 13th and 14th centuries) on the site of the Great Mosque that was the centrepiece of Moorish Mallorca. It's a visual feast, inside and out. ⏱ *1 hr. See p 47,* **1**.

2 ★★ Palau de l'Almudaina. Across from the cathedral is the Spanish royal palace. Originally a Moorish fortress, it was greatly expanded after the Christian Reconquest, with soaring salons, noble artwork and the small, ornate chapel of Santa Ana. ⏱ *1 hr. See p 47,* **2**.

3 ★ kids Dalt Murada. Segments of the original walls that once encircled medieval Palma still exist. This Renaissance-era wall is now a leisurely place to stroll, with marvellous views of waterfront parks and the cathedral. ⏱ *30 min. See p 48,* **3**.

4 ★★ kids Ca'n Joan de S'Aigó. Palma's oldest café, founded in 1697, is an ideal pitstop. It's classically Old World and known for its hot chocolate and pastries. *c/ Can Sanç, 10, Palma.* ☎ *971/71-07-59. $. See p 41.*

Palau de l'Almudaina.

Ca'n Joan de S'Aigó.

⑤ ★★ Can Vivot. The historic quarter is full of 17th- and 18th-century baronial mansions. Few are officially open to the public but you can peek into the handsome courtyards of several on a walk through the old town, including grand Can Vivot, with its elegant arches, columns and antique cars. ⏱ *1 hr. See p 50,* ❻.

❻ ★★ Basilica de Sant Francesc. After the cathedral, my second-favourite church to visit in Palma is this late 13th-century Gothic Franciscan basilica with a Renaissance façade and quiet cloisters. ⏱ *45 min. See p 51,* ⑫.

Day Two
Start out in the morning by visiting modern (19–20th century) Palma and its waterfront. In the afternoon, head out (by taxi or no. 25 bus) to a white-sand beach along the bay.

❼ ★ Casal Solleric. This 18th-century manor house has been transformed into a municipal art gallery; seize the opportunity to see inside one of the city's palatial mansions. ⏱ *45 min. See p 53,* ❸.

❽ ★ kids Forn des Teatre. One of Mallorca's most famous products is a delicate, spiral-bun pastry called

an *ensaïmada,* and the ones sold at this landmark Modernista (Catalan Art Nouveau) bakery are supposedly the King of Spain's favourites. *Pl. de Weyler, 9, Palma.* ☎ *971/71-52-54.* $.

❾ ★★ Fundació 'La Caixa' (Gran Hotel). Of Palma's Modernista buildings, the 1903 Gran Hotel, built by Gaudí's contemporary, Domènech i Muntaner, is the most ornate. Today it's a first-rate art exhibition space. ⏱ *1 hr. See p 54,* ❺.

Walk back towards the waterfront along Passeig d'es Born and turn right opposite Parc de la Mar.

❿ ★ kids Passeig de Sagrera (Marítim). After lunch, stroll along this wide promenade, a favourite of walkers and cyclists, under tall palm trees. ⏱ *30 min. See p 57,* ❶.

Continue west along Passeig de Sagrera; right on c/ Consolat and left on c/ Sant Pere.

Basilica de Sant Francesc.

⑪ ★★ kids Es Baluard (Museu d'Art Modern i Contemporani). This contemporary, and relatively young, art museum is architecturally adventurous. The best pieces are the outdoor sculptures surrounding the superb café, which offers sweeping views of the bay and much of Palma. ⏱ *1 hr. See p 58,* ④.

Take a taxi or bus no. 25, or cycle 8km (5 miles) southeast of Palma to:

⑫ ★ kids Platja de Palma. This urban beach can be alarmingly crowded with the young and scantily clad, but the wide stretch of sand that gently bends around the vast Bay of Palma is impressive. Families may prefer the more relaxed beaches at Cala Estancia, Ciutat Jardí or Es Portixol, closer to Palma. ⏱ *2 hr. See p 63,* ⑧.

⑬ ★★ Puro Beach Club. This hip beachside lounge club heats up at night, but in late afternoon can be a pleasant spot for a drink by the pool overlooking the sea. *c/ Pagell 1, Cala Estancia.* ☎ *971/74-47-44. www.purobeach.com. $$$.*

⑭ ★★ kids Parc de la Mar. As the sun fades, head back to the old town and the waterfront park of Parc de la Mar below the cathedral and Palau de l'Almudaina: both are illuminated at night. Their reflection in the pool below is one of Palma's most magical sights. ⏱ *30 min. See p 48,* ③.

Day Three
Head out of town to see a couple of highlights of Mallorca's northwest coast. Start early and make a full day of it. You can either return in the evening to Palma or arrange to spend the night in Sóller and catch the first train back to Palma in the morning.

Fundació 'La Caixa' (Gran Hotel).

⑮ ★★★ kids Ferrocarril de Sóller. Not driving is almost a blessing if you have the chance to hop aboard the 1912 narrow-gauge train from Palma. Built to facilitate transport for Mallorca's established citrus fruit trade, the original, polished wooden cars are charmingly retro. ⏱ *1¼ hr. See By Train, p 168.*

⑯ ★★ kids Tranvia to Port de Sóller. A vintage 1913 tram passes through Sóller on the way to the northwest coast's only natural harbour, travelling 5km (3 miles) through lemon and orange groves. At the other end of the line is a popular small resort. ⏱ *2 hr. See p 94,* ⑲.

⑰ ★ Agapanto. A stylish Mediterranean/seafood restaurant with a good vantage point looking over the harbour, this makes an enjoyable spot for lunch. *Camino del Faro, 2, Port de Sóller.* ☎ *971/63-38-60. $$.*

Take a taxi, or walk 3km (1.8 miles) from Sóller.

⑱ ★★ Fornalutx. Return to Sóller station on the tram and then head to one of Mallorca's most pristine small villages. Fornalutx (pronounced *fohrn-ah-looch*) is a scenic ensemble of medieval stone houses and cobblestone alleyways. ⏱ *1 hr. See p 95,* ㉑.

The Best of Mallorca in One Week

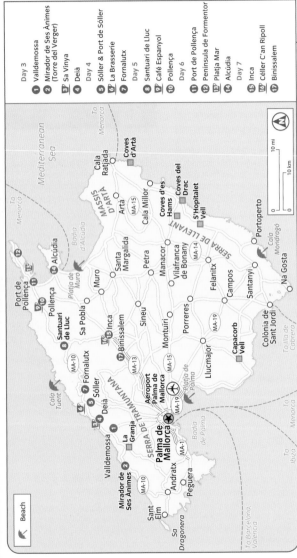

With 1 week in Mallorca, you have time to see a good cross-section of the island and some of its varied landscapes. This driving tour takes in the best of the capital, Palma, as well as the scenic northwest coast and the wide bays and capes of the northeast coast. START: **Valldemossa; from Palma, drive 24km (15 miles) north on MA-1130.**

Travel Tip

Hiring a car to get around the coasts beyond Palma is nearly essential, because public transportation from point to point is limited. A car allows you to make stops at viewpoints and small villages at your own pace. With rare exceptions, rental agencies (p 167) in Palma are located at the airport.

Days One & Two

For your first 2 days on Mallorca, follow Days One and Two of the Palma itinerary for 'The Best of Mallorca in Three Days', starting on p 9.

Day Three

1 ★★★ Valldemossa. A highlight of northwestern Mallorca, this historic village is best known for its monastery, **Reial Cartoixa** (often called *La Cartuja* in Spanish). The

The northwest coast's Torre del Verger.

The historic village of Valldemossa.

town also has 19th-century associations with composer Frédéric Chopin and his lover, the French writer George Sand. 🕐 *3 hr. See p 90,* 9 .

17km (10½ miles) northwest on MA-10, just beyond Banyalbufar.

2 ★★★ kids Mirador de Ses Ànimes (Torre del Verger). Several viewpoints (*miradors*) dot the coast with stupendous views of the sea crashing into the cliffs in both directions, but this is the winner. Climb the slender ladder to the top of a 16th-century tower for the most captivating views. 🕐 *1 hr. (including drive time). See p 90,* 7 .

25km (15½ miles) northeast on MA-10.

3 ★★ Sa Vinya. This laid-back restaurant, with a welcoming garden terrace, is the perfect place for a leisurely lunch of grilled fish, gazpacho or salads. *c/ Sa Vinya Vella, 3, Deià.* ☎ *971/63-95-00.*

④ ★★★ Deià. Famous for its pristine beauty and unrivalled location, as well as its literary and artistic associations, including the English poet and writer Robert Graves, Deià epitomises the northwest coast's incomparable allure. ⏲ *3 hr. See p 92,* **⑬**.

Day Four
11km (7 miles) east on MA-10 from Deià.

⑤ ★ Sóller & Port de Sóller. An historically prosperous town and attractive harbour set amid citrus groves in a mountain valley, with handsome Modernista architecture and a vintage train and tram. Take the latter down to the port. ⏲ *4 hr. See p 93 and 94,* **⑰** *&* **⑲**.

⑥ La Brasserie. This casual bistro within Hotel Los Geranios has good views of the port and serves well-prepared Mediterranean fare, perfect for a relaxed lunch. For something more formal and creative, head upstairs to the hotel restaurant s'àtic. *Pg. Platja, 15, Port de Sóller.* ☎ *971/63-14-40. $$.*

Port de Sóller.

⑦ ★★ Fornalutx. A gem of a mountain town a short drive (or 3km/1.8-mile walk) from Sóller, this is one of Mallorca's most enchanting towns, with clean mountain air and relaxing medieval beauty. ⏲ *1 hr. See p 95,* **㉑**.

Day Five
30km (19 miles) east on MA-10.

⑧ ★★ Santuari de Lluc. This monastery, treasured by Mallorcans and religious pilgrims, traces its roots back to the 13th century. Although the monastery is a must-see for many, for dedicated walkers the challenging hiking trails through the Tramuntana mountains connecting Lluc to the coast are even more alluring. ⏲ *1½ hr. See p 96,* **㉔**.

20km (12 miles) northeast on MA-10.

⑨ ★ Café Espanyol. There's plenty of people-watching on Pollença's main square, which is filled with cafés and bar terraces. Any of them will do, but Café Espanyol, right next to the church, is popular day and night. *Pl. Major, 2, Pollença.* ☎ *971/53-42-14. $.*

⑩ ★★ kids Pollença. A delightful resort town and a favourite of holidaying families for decades, Pollença is convenient for visiting the beaches of Pollença and Alcúdia bays as well as the spectacular scenery of Formentor. The pedestrian-only streets, stylish shops, cafés and appealing ambience make it an ideal place to stay overnight. ⏲ *3 hr. See p 103,* **❶**.

Day Six
7km (4 miles) northeast on MA-2200.

⑪ ★ kids Port de Pollença. This family-friendly beach resort, which grew out of an old fishing village, has a wide swathe of white sand and yet feels laid-back, even in summer. ⏱ *2 hr. See p 104,* ❹.

7km (4 miles) northeast on MA-2210.

⑫ ★★★ kids **Península de Formentor.** One of the most photographed sights on Mallorca is the otherworldly scenery of the Formentor cape jutting out into the Mediterranean. Beyond the *mirador* is a beautiful white-sand beach, Platja de Formentor, with panoramic views framing the Bay of Pollença. ⏱ *2 hr. See p 104,* ❺.

Alcúdia's old town.

⑬ ★ **Platja Mar.** Belonging to the 1930s' jet-set Hotel Formentor (see p 110), this casual restaurant and café is right on the beach, with more-than-acceptable Mediterranean cuisine. *Platja de Formentor, s/n, Formentor.* ☎ 971/89-91-00. $$.

15km (4 miles) southeast on MA-2220.

⑭ ★★ kids **Alcúdia.** One of the most historic towns in the Balearics, Alcúdia dates to the Phoenicians and Romans, who left behind stony elements of their settlement, Pol·lèntia, including an amphitheatre. Beach lovers can venture out towards Cap des Pinar on the peninsula for unspoiled coves or join the masses at Platja d'Alcúdia. ⏱ *3 hr. See p 105,* ❻.

Day Seven
27km (17 miles) southwest on MA-13A & MA-13.

⑮ **Inca.** Stop briefly for some discount shopping in the commercial capital of the Es Pla (interior), known for its leather industry and

shoes. Some of Mallorca's best-known shoe designers, including Camper, maintain factory outlets in the town they originated. ⏱ *1½ hr. See p 115,* ❷.

⑯ **Céller C'an Ripoll.** Have lunch in this historic *céller* (cellar/tavern) restaurant, which dates from the 17th and 18th centuries when Inca was all about wine production. The fare is hearty Mallorcan, and there's a good-value midday *menú.* *c/ Jaume Armengol, 4, Inca.* ☎ 971/50-00-24. $$.

8km (5 miles) on MA-13A.

⑰ ★ **Binissalem.** Around this small town, you'll find the epicentre of the resurgent Mallorcan wine industry. If you're interested in tasting unique local wines, you can visit a handful of friendly, down-to-earth wineries. ⏱ *2 hr. See p 115,* ❶.

Travel Tip

For information on recommended hotels within this tour, see p 96 for Deià, p 96 for Fornalutx, p 109 for Pollença and p 109 for Alcúdia.

The Best of Mallorca & Menorca in Two Weeks

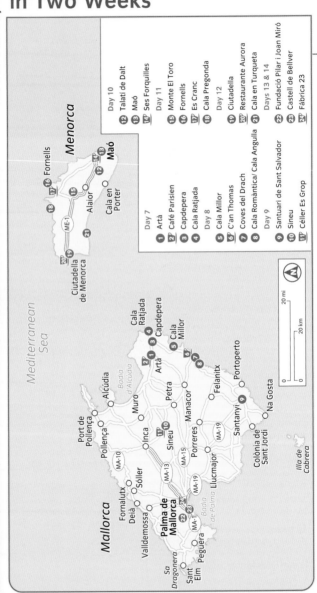

Day 7
1. Artà
27. Café Parisien
3. Capdepera
4. Cala Ratjada

Day 8
5. Cala Millor
6. C'an Thomas
7. Coves del Drach
8. Cala Romàntica/ Cala Anguila

Day 9
9. Santuari de Sant Salvador
10. Sineu
17. Céller Es Grop

Day 10
12. Talati de Dalt
13. Maó
14. Ses Forquilles

Day 11
15. Monte El Toro
16. Fornells
17. Es Cranc
18. Cala Pregonda

Day 12
19. Ciutadella
20. Restaurante Aurora
21. Cala en Turqueta

Days 13 & 14
22. Fundació Pilar i Joan Miró
23. Castell de Bellver
32. Fàbrica 23

To see a good deal of both **Mallorca and Menorca** and appreciate the islands' differences—as well as have time for some relaxation—you'll need about 2 weeks. For the first 6 days, follow 'The Best of Mallorca in One Week' tour (which begins on p 13). This driving tour of Mallorca includes flying to Menorca for a 3-day excursion. START: **Palma de Mallorca (week One).**

Day Seven
From Alcúdia, drive 33km (20 miles) southeast on MA-12 to Artà.

1 ★ **Artà.** A former Moorish stronghold, this unassuming town is distinguished by a fortified 14th-century, hilltop church, Santuari de Sant Salvador; as in Pollença, a *Vía Crucis* (Way of the Cross) leads to it and fine views of the surrounding countryside and coast. ⏱ *1 hr. See p 106,* **11**.

2 ★ **Café Parisien.** Grab a cappuccino at this French bistro, which has tables along Artà's restaurant row. *c/ Ciutat, 18, Artà.* ☎ *971/83-54-40. $$. See p 112.*

3 ★ **Capdepera.** A mini-version of Artà, crowned by a 14th-century castle built by King Jaume II. Hidden within the battlements is a tiny chapel. ⏱ *45 min. See p 106,* **14**.

4 ★ **kids Cala Ratjada.** This popular resort has a couple of pleasant

sandy beaches, the prettiest being Cala Gat, a protected cove. Beach aficionados in search of more seclusion head immediately south on Cap de Capdepera to the beaches at Cala Moltó and Cala Agulla, or north along walking trails to Cala Torta and Cala Mitjana. ⏱ *2 hr. See p 107,* **15**.

Travel Tip

The best option to avoid backtracking is to spend the night near Son Servera or Porto Cristo (see p 109 for accommodation).

Day Eight
5 **kids Cala Millor.** The longest sandy beach on the east coast—a sweep of more than 2km (1¼ miles) of fine sand and nearly 50m (165 ft) wide at most parts—Cala Millor has grown into a massive resort. The high-rise development and glut of shops detracts, but the beach remains spectacular. ⏱ *2 hr. See p 125.*

Cala Ratjada beach.

6 **C'an Thomas.** This homespun restaurant is a good place to escape the resort madness of the east coast. The menu is nothing too adventurous: just homemade pastas and tapas. *c/ de la Mar, 33, Porto Cristo. No phone. $$. See p 112.*

7 ★★ kids **Coves del Drach.** These celebrated 300-million-year-old caves have been transformed into a tourist-pleasing spectacle of illumination, sound and even musicians playing classical music as they float across the subterranean lake—something no other commercially exploited caves in Mallorca can boast. ⏱ *1½ hr. See p 108,* **21**.

8 **Cala Romàntica/Cala Angulla.** These two small, quiet beach coves are a welcome contrast to the tourist magnet of Cala Millor. Located just south of Porto Cristo, you can escape the crowds here even at the height of summer. ⏱ *2 hr. See p 129.*

Day Nine
20km (12 miles) southwest of Porto Cristo on MA-4020 and then MA-14 (on the outskirts of Felanitx).

The historic market town of Sineu.

Panoramic views from the summit of Sant Salvador.

9 ★★ **Santuari de Sant Salvador.** On top of Puig Sant Salvador, the highest peak of the Serra de Llevant foothills, this chapel and shrine date back to 1348. Hardcore cyclists and tourists (in the comfort of their cars) climb the 509m (1,700-ft) hill for commanding panoramic views from the summit. ⏱ *2 hr. See p 116,* **6**.

28km (17½ miles) northwest on MA-3300.

10 ★ **Sineu.** This historic market town south of Inca is perhaps interior Mallorca's most attractive, and the site of a 14th-century royal palace and lively traditional market on Wednesdays until 2pm. ⏱ *2 hr. See p 115,* **3**.

11 ★ **Céller Es Grop.** This antique cellar, full of huge wine vats, is a good taste of small-town, interior Mallorca. *c/ Major, 18, Sineu.* ☎ *971/52-01-87. $$. See p 122.*

Day Ten – Menorca

Travel Tip

Iberia (www.iberia.com) is the only airline that flies daily from Palma to Menorca (Maó); a roundtrip flight is the easiest way to spend a few days in Menorca.

Hire a car at the airport to get around Menorca, because public transportation is extremely limited.

En route from the airport, just off ME-1.

⑫ ★★ Talatí de Dalt. This megalithic site—one of hundreds across the island—is the perfect introduction to Menorca's enigmatic ancient history. The settlement, which dates from the end of the Bronze Age, around 1300 B.C., is one of Menorca's best preserved. 🕐 *30 min. See p 150,* ⑨.

⑬ ★ Maó. The Menorcan capital is a low-key, English-influenced port city known for its spectacularly deep natural harbour, which attracted the Spanish, French and British as a strategic military point in the Mediterranean. Among the city's highlights are fortresses, including the spectacular La Mola (which you should probably save to visit after lunch), left over from the island's various occupations. 🕐 *4 hr. See p 139,* ❸.

⑭' ★★ Ses Forquilles. A creative but low-key restaurant, popular for its tasting menus, tapas and great-value three-course lunch menu. *c/ Rovellada de Dalt, 20.* ☎ *971/35-27-11. $$$.*

Day Eleven
Take the main highway (ME-1) or the more tranquil old road (Cami d'en Kane)—commissioned by British governor General Richard Kane in 1722—to Es Mercadal.

⑮ ★ kids Monte El Toro. From Menorca's highest peak (357m (1,171 ft)), there are outstanding views, taking in everything from coast to coast. 🕐 *45 min. See p 148,* ❺.

9km (5½ miles) north of Es Mercadal on ME-15.

⑯ ★★★ kids Fornells. This picturesque fishing village built around a marina on a sheltered inlet is renowned for its seafood restaurants. 🕐 *2 hr. See p 148,* ❸.

⑰' ★★★ Es Cranc. My (and it seems, everyone else's) favourite Fornells restaurant is in the centre of the village, but you could also opt for a terrace and tapas at one of the restaurants overlooking the port. *c/ Escoles, 31, Fornells.* ☎ *971/37-64-42. $$$. See p 151.*

Maó, the low-key Menorcan capital.

15km (9 miles) west on ME-15 and Cf-3 and a 20-minute hike from the car park.

18 ★★★ kids Cala Pregonda. The beach of choice along the north coast for its dramatic scenery. The deep red sands and rock formations are completely unlike the gentle white sands, limestone and pine trees of the southern coast. 🕐 *2 hr. See p 148,* ❹.

Day Twelve
From Es Mercadal, 21km (13 miles) west on ME-1.

19 ★★★ kids Ciutadella. The gorgeous limestone old town and picturesque, slender port make Ciutadella the most captivating city in the Balearic Islands. The one-time capital of Menorca until the early 18th century (when the British moved it to Maó) is a delight to stroll, taking in the cathedral and magnificent 17th- and 18th-century manor houses. 🕐 *3 hr. See p 153,* ❷.

20 ★ Restaurante Aurora. This café on the eastern edge of the old quarter dates from 1893 and spills into the genial square, with tables for people-watching under an awning. *Pl. Alfons III, 3, Ciutadella.* ☎ *971/38-00-29. $.*

10km (6 miles) south of Ciutadella, along Camí Sant Joan de Missa (and a 10-minute walk from the car park).

21 ★★★ Cala en Turqueta. This cove is quite close to being the perfect beach. With limpid turquoise waters and brilliant white sand protected by pine woods and boulders, it's delightful. 🕐 *2 hr. See p 156,* ❼.

Days Thirteen & Fourteen
Head back to Maó (45km (28 miles)) on ME-1 to catch a return

Ciutadella's old town.

flight to Mallorca. Back in Palma, take a taxi or bus no. 3/6 to Cala Major, just west of downtown.

22 ★★★ Fundació Pilar i Joan Miró. This superb museum is the former home of the famous surrealist artist Joan Miró, who lived and worked in Mallorca for nearly three decades, and features his very lived-in studio. 🕐 *2 hr. See p 61,* ❶.

Taxi or bus no. 3 to Plaça Gomila (and a 15-minute walk uphill).

23 ★ kids Castell de Bellver. On a hillside overlooking the Bay of Palma, this 14th-century castle is a magnificent example of Gothic military architecture, although most people venture up here for the surrounding park and enchanting views. 🕐 *30 min. See p 59,* ❼.

24 ★ Fábrica 23. Santa Catalina, formerly a fishermen's quarter, is now one of Palma's most fashionable neighbourhoods for restaurants and bars. This foodie bistro has a market-based menu that changes daily. *c/ Cotoner, 42.* ☎ *971/45-31-25. $$.* ●

Art & Architecture

Day 1

1. Casal Solleric
2. Palau March Museu
3. Cappuccino Palau March
4. Catedral (La Seu)
5. Museu Diocesà (Palacio Episcopal)
6. Palatial Courtyards
7. Café La Caixa
8. Fundació 'La Caixa' (Gran Hotel)
9. Museu d'Art Espanyol Contemporani (Fundació Joan March)

Day 2

10. Sa Llotja
11. Es Baluard (Museu d'Art Modern i Contemporani)
12. BLD (Restaurant Bar Museu Es Baluard)
13. Fundació Pilar i Joan Miró

ℹ	Information
✉	Post Office
🚋	Train Station
†	Church
✚	Hospital

Previous page: Flowers of Deià.

Although you may not think of the Mallorcan capital as one of Europe's top art cities, it does have some fine museums and an interesting selection of largely Spanish contemporary artists on display. Architecture buffs will want to concentrate on Palma's Renaissance and 20th-century Modernista (Catalan Art Nouveau) buildings. START: **Palma de Mallorca. Trip length: 2 days.**

Day One

1 ★ Casal Solleric. A grand mid-18th-century Baroque mansion with an ornate balcony of five arches and a magnificent interior courtyard—something Palma's baronial houses are famous for—is now a beautifully designed municipal art space. It provides the venue for interesting contemporary and occasional avant-garde exhibitions, including sculpture and video installations. ⏱ *30 min. See p 53,* **3**.

2 ★ Palau March Museu. Crowding the courtyard of this 20th-century mansion are several large outdoor sculptures from some of the greatest Spanish and international names, including Moore, Rodin, Miró and Chillida, as well as Xavier Corberó's serpentine *Orgue del Mar* that slinks across the courtyard. ⏱ *30 min. See p 53,* **1**.

3 Cappuccino Palau March. This café at street level in the March Museum palace has a perfect terrace for people-watching: you can enjoy cappuccino and other coffees as well as light snacks and meals. *c/ Conquistador, 13, Palma.* ☎ *971/71-72-72. $$.*

4 ★★★ Catedral (La Seu). There is no greater piece of architecture in the Balearic Islands than this magnificent Gothic cathedral, begun in the 13th century. And although its graceful, soaring exterior is splendid, inside are two very unusual and idiosyncratic additions. Barcelona architect Antoni Gaudí enveloped the altar in a peculiar iron canopy, perhaps representing a crown of thorns, while Miquel Barceló (who came from the small Mallorcan town

Sculptures in the courtyard of the Palau March Museu.

Gaudí canopy, Catedral (La Seu).

of Felanitx (p 116, **6**) and went on to become one of Spain's most celebrated contemporary artists) transformed an entire chapel with a large-scale ceramic mural depicting the creation of the world. The rose window, with 1,236 pieces of stained glass, is one of the largest in the world. ⏲ *1 hr. See p 47,* **1**.

5 ★★ **Museu Diocesà (Palacio Episcopal).** Although a Diocesan Museum may not scream 'major attraction', for any fan of religious art this is one of Palma's finest museums, recently relocated to the handsome 17th-century Bishop's Palace. The 200-piece collection of largely Gothic, Renaissance and Baroque religious art includes the oldest relic in Mallorca and Gaudí's studies for the cathedral's stained-glass windows. ⏲ *1 hr. See p 48,* **4**.

6 ★★ **Palatial Courtyards.** The historic quarter's labyrinthine structure conceals a roster of 17th- and 18th-century baronial mansions, perhaps most notable for their interior patios (courtyards). A stroll through the neighbourhood usually presents several glimpses of these grand courtyards, which are windows looking back to an era of great wealth. Look for the impressive arches and staircase of **Can Oleza** on c/ d'en

Morey (no. 9), a 16th-century palace. ⏲ *30 min. See p 49,* **6**.

7 **Café La Caixa.** The Gran Hotel's sleek and popular bar at street level has huge floor-to-ceiling windows, perfect for watching the world go by as you have a coffee or light fare such as salads. *Pl. Weyler, 3, Palma.* ☎ *971/72-01-11. $$.*

8 ★★ **Fundació 'La Caixa' (Gran Hotel).** Palma's greatest Modernista building—with its intricately carved bay windows, Moorish-style mosaic tiles and wrought-iron balconies—is the former Gran Hotel, constructed in 1903 and designed by Lluís Domènech i Muntaner (who designed Barcelona's Palau de la Música concert hall). Not only can you visit the interior, but also this is one of the city's finest art spaces, hosting a permanent collection of the modernist Catalan painter Anglada Camarassa and shows organised by La Caixa. ⏲ *45 min. See p 54,* **5**.

Gaudí stained glass in the Museu Diocesà.

Fundació Pilar i Joan Miró.

⑨ ★★ Museu d'Art Espanyol Contemporani (Fundació Joan March). This small museum inhabits a handsome 18th-century mansion, surveying some of the biggest names in 20th-century Spanish art, including Picasso, Miró, Dalí, Julio González, Eduardo Chillida, Juan Gris, Antoni Tàpies and Mallorca's favourite son, Miquel Barceló (see also ④). 🕐 *1 hr. See p 55, ⑨.*

Day Two

⑩ ★★ Sa Llotja. This monumental example of Catalan Gothic architecture, and former site of the fish merchants' stock exchange in the 15th century, is currently undergoing restoration inside and out. I can't wait to see its delicate spiralling interior columns, vaulted ceiling and exterior sculptures after the work is done (probably not before 2011). The building will then return to its status as the city's most stately art exhibition space. 🕐 *30 min. See p 57, ②.*

⑪ ★★ Es Baluard (Museu d'Art Modern i Contemporani). A relatively new addition to the Palma art scene, this contemporary art museum, constructed of white poured concrete and carved out of Renaissance walls, was designed by a trio of local architects. Many of the highlights are

outdoors, including massive sculptures by the architect Santiago Calatrava (his site-specific *Bou*) and pieces by Jorge Oteiza and Rafael Canogar. The permanent collection needs time to bolster minor works by Miró and Picasso and other established European and American artists, but the museum hosts top-class itinerant exhibitions. 🕐 *1 hr. See p 58, ④.*

⑫ ★★ kids BLD (Restaurant Bar Museu Es Baluard). Have a drink or even lunch on the museum terrace, surrounded by the outdoor sculptures and overlooking the port. *Pl. Porta de Santa Catalina, 10.* ☎ *971/90-81-99. $$.*

⑬ ★★★ Fundació Pilar i Joan Miró. Just west of Palma is the summer home and studio of the Catalan surrealist painter and sculptor Joan Miró, to which the Pritzker Prize-winning architect Rafael Moneo added an angular museum. There are some 5,000 Miró works in the rotating collection, including the artist's signature enigmatic large canvasses, brightly coloured sculptures and works on paper. Miró's studio is preserved in time; it looks as though he's just taken a break for lunch. 🕐 *1½ hr. See p 61, ①.*

Romantic Mallorca

Day 1
1. Palacio Ca Sa Galesa
2. Dalt Murada
3. Abaco

Day 2
4. Valldemossa
5. Mirador de Ses Ànimes
6. Café Es Grau
7. Oleum

Day 3
8. Son Marroig
9. Deià
10. El Olivo

Day 4
11. Tranvia de Sóller
12. Península de Formentor
13. Pollença
14. Ca'n Costa

Beach

10 mi
10 km

speak from the heart about this tour—I proposed to my wife along the northwest coast of Mallorca a decade ago. But you don't have to make a life commitment to see the island's appeal for couples. From intimate boutique hotels and stylish restaurants to a scenic coast and isolated coves, Mallorca can bring out an amorous streak in anyone. START: **Palma. Trip length: 4 days.**

Travel Tip

I envision you enjoying this tour at a leisurely pace, with plenty of time for late starts, hanging around hotel pools, lingering at meals and taking relaxed walks without packing in lots of sightseeing. If you're up for a more active tour, feel free to add romantic sights in Palma's old quarter or additional towns along the northwest coast.

Day One

1 ★★★ **Palacio Ca Sa Galesa.** First on your romantic agenda should be checking into a beautiful, intimate boutique hotel, preferably in an exquisite old mansion in Palma's old quarter. Ca Sa Galesa is a secluded 15th-century palace with sumptuous salons, an underground Roman-bath-style pool and sauna, and a roof deck with views of the bay and cathedral. Those kind of elegant surroundings are pricey, though; more affordable is **Dalt Murada,** similarly full of Old World charm, with huge, elegant rooms and breakfast served on an interior patio, surrounded by lemon trees. *Palacio Ca Sa Galesa, see p 74; Dalt Murada, see p 48.*

2 ★★ **Dalt Murada.** Stroll hand-in-hand along the top of the old city ramparts, with handsome views of the Bay of Palma and the horizon. As the sun sets, the cathedral is bathed in an ethereal golden glow, and then the lights come on and its impressive shape is reflected in the pool below. At one end are the gardens of **S'Hort del Rei** (the King's

Orchard), where a pair of white swans idle about in the pond.
⏱ *1 hr. See p 48,* **3**.

3 ★★ **Abaco.** For a night out, this over-the-top cocktail lounge in the courtyard of a historic manor house oozes romance. Bursting with fresh flowers and burning candles, it has an interior patio that's ideal for a serious tête-à-tête. *See p 84.*

Day Two

From Palma, drive 23km (13 miles) north on MA-1130.

4 ★★★ **Valldemossa.** This exquisite village nestled in a mountain valley has become famous for the single winter (1838–39) that the composer Frédéric Chopin and his lover, the French writer George Sand, spent living in the Carthusian monastery. This was a romance

The elegant Palacio Ca Sa Galesa.

The northwest coast of Mallorca.

of great passions and withering illness—a Mallorcan version of *La Bohème*, later chronicled by Sand in *A Winter in Mallorca*. ⏱ *2 hr. See p 90,* **9**.

18km (11 miles) northwest on MA-10.

5 ★★★ **Mirador de Ses Ànimes.** The northwestern coast of Mallorca, where jagged cliffs tumble to the sea, makes for a superb drive and stunning landscape photographs. Just outside Banyalbufar, this historic viewpoint has a 16th-century tower, **Torre del Verger,** perched on a cliff. ⏱ *30 min. See p 90* **7**.

Explore the home of Robert Graves, Deià.

☕ **6** ★★ **Café Es Grau.** Sharing the same enviable perch along the coastline with Mirador de Ricardo Roca, this café boasts unbeatable views from its terrace. *Ctra Andratx-Estellencs/MA-10, km 98.* ☎ *971/61-85-27. $.*

19km (12 miles) northeast on MA-10 and then south on MA-1101 (signposted Puigpunyent).

7 ★★★ **Oleum.** The restaurant of the fairytale Gran Hotel Son Net (p 96), in a quiet mountain valley, is as romantic a setting as I can think, housed in a soaring old olive press with high-backed, red-velvet booths. The Mediterranean cooking is delectable and the wine cellar one of Mallorca's finest. If you can afford to stay, do. *See p 101.*

Day Three
Continue northeast through the Serra de Tramuntana, along the picturesque coastal road, MA-10.

8 ★ **Son Marroig.** With its impressive coastal views, this estate was much sought after by the Archduke Ludwig Salvator, the 19th-century Austrian aristocrat who was so in love with Mallorca's northwest coast that he went about acquiring as many properties as possible. Son Marroig is perched on a cliff above luxuriant gardens and the famous wind-eroded rock promontory Sa Foradada (a trail takes you down to the sea). ⏱ *1 hr. See p 92,* ⑫.

4km (2½ miles) east on MA-10.

⑨ ★★★ Deià. The English poet and writer Robert Graves was also deeply enamoured of the Mallorcan coast and this small town, so much so that he made it his permanent home at **Ca N'Alluny** (truly permanent—he's buried in the small cemetery next to the parish church at the top of the village). The writer's home is now open to the public, complete with his writing desk and bicycle, and you can venture down to the small beach cove, **Cala Deià,** where Graves found inspiration. ⏱ *3 hr. See p 92,* ⑬, ⑮ *&* ⑯.

⑩ ★★ Dinner at El Olivo. With candelabras burning like torches on the patio, dinner outside on the terrace at La Residencia (p 98), one of Mallorca's fanciest rural hotels, is a genuinely memorable, if pricey treat. *See p 100.*

Day Four
From Deià, continue 11km (7 miles) east on MA-10.

⑪ ★★ Tranvía de Sóller. Clamber aboard the vintage 1913 tram that rumbles through Sóller on its way down to the harbour, passing lemon and orange groves close enough to touch from the windows of the wooden cars. In **Port de Sóller,** enjoy a leisurely stroll along the promenade that lines the beach. ⏱ *2 hr. See p 94,* ⑲.

From Sóller, take the 64km (40 mile) long, picturesque mountain road, MA-10, stopping at *miradors* en route.

⑫ ★★★ Península de Formentor. The lunar landscape of this promontory plunging dramatically into the Mediterranean is a perfect spot for a couple's photograph. After that, head to the gentle waters and sweet, pine-shaded beach facing the wide Badia de Pollença. If old-school romance is your style, check into the legendary **Hotel Formentor** (p 110), whose guests have included Grace Kelly and F. Scott Fitzgerald. Otherwise, spend the night in nearby Pollença. ⏱ *3 hr. See p 104,* ⑤.

⑬ ★★ Pollença. The shops, cafés and restaurants of this genteel resort town make it a perfect place to enjoy a summer evening. Shop at the stylish boutiques lining the pedestrian-only streets before having a pre-dinner drink at Café Espanyol (p 103, ㉗) on Plaça Major. *See p 103,* ①.

⑭ Head to dinner at **Ca'n Costa,** in the 19th-century home of a well-regarded local poet. *See p 112.*

Beach facing the wide Badia de Pollença.

Gourmet Mallorca

Day 1

1. Forn des Teatre
2. Mercat de l'Olivar
3. La Favorita
4. Son Vivot
5. Confiteria Frasquet
6. Colmado Santo Domingo
7. Bar Mollet
8. Lo Di Vino
9. Fosh Food

Day 2

10. Wine Route
11. Céller C'an Ripoll
12. Jardins d'Alfabia Juice Bar
13. Béns d'Avall Restaurant

Day 3

14. Deià

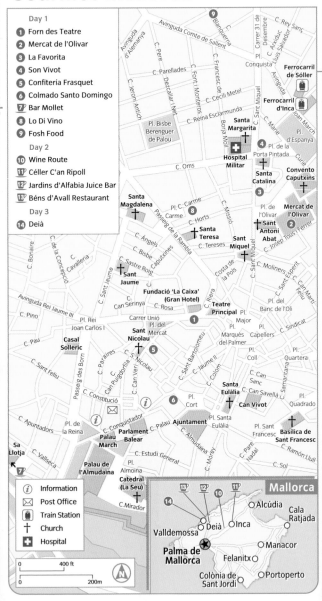

Information
Post Office
Train Station
Church
Hospital

Mallorca revels in what it does best: fresh fish from the Mediterranean, rustic peasant dishes and unique offerings that are indelibly associated with the Balearics, including home-grown wines that will surprise even the most knowledgeable oenophile. A gourmet tour of Mallorca is an eye-opening delight.

START: **Palma. Trip length: 3 days.**

Day One

1 ★★ **Forn des Teatre.** Start your morning off as most Mallorcans do: with an *ensaïmada*, the classic spiral-bun pastry that's as light as a feather. This bakery with a distinctive Modernista landmark shopfront has fiercely loyal *ensaïmada* customers. Most visitors not only try one while on the island, but also take several home in huge pastry boxes (you'll see them at the airport—it seems as if every passenger has one). Also worth a peek, just up the street, is **Forn Fondo** (c/ Unió, 15, ☎ 971/71-16-34), a bakery that has been churning out *ensaïmades* and more since 1745. ⏲ *30 min. Pl. de Weyler, 9.* ☎ *971/71-52-54.*

Fishmonger at the Mercat de l'Olivar.

2 ★★★ **Mercat de l'Olivar.** The epicentre of Palma's gastronomic scene is this sensational food market, the main supplier for restaurants and ordinary citizens. Arrive early to catch amiable fishmongers hawking their goods fresh from the boats in the port. From the sights and smells of exotic fish to meat and produce, this covered market, which has been around since 1941, is a delightful experience. After you have a look around, enjoy a snack at one of the kiosk bars inside the market and absorb the atmosphere. ⏲ *1 hr. See box, p 55.*

The Forn Fondo bakery has been trading since 1745.

Menorca for Gourmets: Drink

Menorca is also home to some unique drinking opportunities.
Menorcan Gin: British sailors in the 18th century brought gin to Menorca. A *pomada* (gin with lemonade) is the classic Menorcan cocktail. Pop into Maó's **Xoriguer Gin Distillery,** which has been in continuous operation since the 19th century, for free samples

of its gin and other herbaceous liqueurs (take home a bottle in a ceramic jug). See p 141, ❺.

Menorcan wine: For now there are only a handful of wineries on the island, but **Binifadet Winery** is banking on bigger and better things. The family-run operation has a cool modern winery on the outskirts of Sant Lluís, an outstanding steel-fermented chardonnay and a respectable bubbly. See p 141, ❽.

Menorcan Gin.

❸ ★ **La Favorita.** Palma has an abundance of inviting, old-school food purveyors selling the best indigenous island foods, such as *sobressada* (raw pork sausage),

A selection of old-school goods fill the shelves at La Favorita.

queso de Mahón (cheese from Menorca) and much more. This friendly and retro-style charcuterie emporium even has a patron saint overlooking the sausages. ⏱ *10 min. c/ Sant Miquel, 38A.* ☎ *971/71-37-40.*

❹ ★★★ **Son Vivot.** This foodie delight deceivingly looks like it has been around forever and sells everything from Mallorcan wines and olive oils to *sobressada*, with plenty of free tastings. ⏱ *30 min. See p 80.*

❺ ★ **Confiteria Frasquet.** Pick up some dark chocolates or *turrón* (a traditional Spanish almond nougat) at this Palma chocolate shop, which has been serving Mallorcans with a sweet tooth since 1697. ⏱ *15 min. See p 80.*

❻ ★★ **Colmado Santo Domingo.** A ridiculously tiny shop-front overstuffed with hanging meats and sausages. Ask politely before taking photos. ⏱ *15 min. c/ Santo Domingo, 1.* ☎ *971/71-48-87.*

7 ★★ **Bar Mollet.** After a morning of eyeing fish, produce and sweets, it's time for lunch—and where better than right in the port, next to the Llotja del Peix (fish market). This casual, classic seafood restaurant offers a good-value three-course lunch, but the market-priced fish, the way to go, will set you back a good deal more. *c/ Contramuelle Mollet, 2.* ☎ 971/71-98-71. $–$$.

8 ★★★ **Lo Di Vino.** By far Palma's most atmospheric wine shop, Lo Di Vino doubles as a wine bar/library and tapas restaurant. The stock of wines by the bottle is the star, but the snacks menu is surprising (you can easily construct a full meal over a few well-selected tapas and glasses of wine). Juanjo, the amiable owner, will open any bottle in the shop and charge you just a quarter of the bottle price for a glass. 🕘 *15 min. See p 80.*

9 ★★★ **Fosh Food.** For food-lovers, this innovative locale kills three fowl with one stone, being a gourmet food shop, a cooking school and a funky modern tasting-menu restaurant, with all kinds of

Foodies should head for Son Vivot.

surprises up its sleeves. The project is from the British chef Marc Fosh, who won a Michelin star at his previous restaurant in Mallorca (besides Fosh Food, he's also taken over the kitchen at the Hotel Convent de la Missió). Come for a class or one of the themed five-course (and common-table) dinners, which are excellent value and a fun time. 🕘 *15 min. See p 68.*

Foodie Festivals

Gastronomes may want to plan their trips around the following special events: **Mostra de Cuina Mallorquina** (Mallorcan Food Festival; www.mostradecuinamallorquina.com), which takes place in April and features special (and specially priced) menus at a number of restaurants in Palma and across the island, one region per week); and **Festa d'es Vermar** (Grape Harvest), a celebration of the annual grape harvest that transforms the town of Binissalem for nine days at the end of September and includes a 'grape fight' in the Plaça de l'Església (☎ 971/88-65-58; www.binissalem.org).

Jardins d'Alfabia Juice Bar.

Travel Tip

For recommended hotels in Palma, see p 72.

Day Two

From Palma, 27km (17 miles) northeast on MA-13A (the more scenic old road).

⑩ ★★ **Wine Route.** The wider wine-drinking world is only now discovering Mallorcan wines, even though the indigenous varietals are ancient. Those who aren't yet familiar with them will be thrilled to discover the extent of unique winemaking on this island. Several grapes are cultivated here and nowhere else, including *Callet*, *Manto Negro* and *Prensal Blanc*. You can visit a handful of wineries in and around Binissalem, just a half-hour north of Palma. The best to visit are: **Macià Batle,** in business since 1856 with a handsome

tunnelled cellar, film presentation, art collection and friendly tasting room; and **Bodegues Ribas,** a family-run venture since 1711 with a beautiful old cellar, producing some of the island's top reds, including the signature *Ribas de Cabrera*. If these whet your interest, see *www.binissalemdo.com* for information about visiting other nearby wineries, including **José Luis Ferrer** and **Finca Son Bordils**. *Macià Batle: Camí de Coanegra, s/n.* ☎ *971/51-00-14; www.maciabatle.com. Admission 8.60–11.60€. Mid-Jun to mid-Oct Mon–Fri 9am–7pm, mid-Oct to mid-Jun Mon–Fri 9am–6:30pm & Sat 9:30am–3pm. Bodegues Ribas: c/ Muntanya, 2, Consell.* ☎ *971/62-26-73; www.bodegaribas.com (by appointment only). José Luis Ferrer: Ctra. Palma-Alcúdia, Binissalem.* ☎ *971-51-10-50. Finca Son Bordils: Ctra. Inca-Sineu/MA-3240, km 4,1, Inca.* ☎ *971/18-22-00.*

7km (4 miles) northeast of Binissalem on MA-13A.

⑪ ★ **kids Céller C'an Ripoll.** The Mallorcan wine industry in the 17th and 18th centuries was centred in Inca, not Binissalem, and the legacy of that period is a handful of *céllers*, restaurants inhabiting former wine cellars. C'an Ripoll is one of the best examples, characterised by high ceilings, stone arches, huge wooden wine vats and a hearty menu that focuses on game and rustic vegetable dishes. *c/ Jaume Armengol, 4.* ☎ *971/50-00-24. $$.*

38km (24 miles) southwest on MA-13 and then north on MA-2040 and MA-11.

⑫ **Jardins d'Alfabia Juice Bar.** Although the enchanting gardens of Alfabia, on the other side of

Menorca for Gourmets: Food

Mallorca's smaller sister, Menorca, provides some unique opportunities for eating and drinking (also see box, Menorca for Gourmets: Drink, p 32).

Caldereta de Llagosta. The supreme gourmet destination in Menorca is **Fornells** (p 148, ③), which has earned a huge reputation for its fresh seafood, especially its *caldereta de llagosta* (a rich and pricey lobster stew). My favourite restaurant in town (and that of Spanish chef and TV personality José Andrés) is **Es Cranc** (p 151), where a kindly waiter may take you back to the kitchen to see the fish tanks. Although the restaurant is in the middle of the village, it has canals of fresh water that lead all the way to the port.

Queso de Mahón. The headquarters of the rich and creamy *queso de Mahón* cheese is **Alaior,** Menorca's third-largest city. Here you can visit two cheese factories. The cheese even has its own *denominació de origen* (Denomination of Origin). *See p 149.*

the mountain from Sóller, are the real draw, more than once I've been tempted to make the drive just to hang out at the relaxing juice bar tucked beneath soaring palm trees. So come for the gardens, but don't miss sitting on a bench amid ferns and palms, sipping some of the most delicious orange juice you're likely to have. *Ctra. Palma-Soller, km 17. No phone. $. See p 95, ㉑.*

Halfway between Sóller and Deià, off MA-10; the road wends for about 4km (2½ miles).

⓭ ★★★ **Béns d'Avall Restaurant.** The chef Benet Vicens has made a name for himself in an out-of-the-way spot in the mountains of the northwest coast. His creative Mediterranean cuisine is every bit as spectacular as the stunning views and sunsets: plan on an early dinner to take full advantage of the cliffside setting overlooking a bay, and opt for one of the tasting

menus. *Urb. Costa Deià/Ctra. Sóller-Deià, near Sóller.* ☎ *971/63-23-81. $$$.*

Travel Tip

For recommended hotels in Sóller, see p 96.

Day Three
From Sóller, 11km (7 miles) west on MA-10.

⓮ ★★★ **Deià.** Long the haunt of foreign artists and writers, this village has recently garnered a reputation as a foodie hangout. With just 800 residents, it supports half a dozen excellent restaurants. In fact, anyone interested in exploring Mallorca's gourmet scene would do well to base themselves in Deià. Among the outstanding restaurants for both lunch and dinner are **Restaurante Sebastián** *(p 101)*, **El Olivo** *(p 100)*, and the more casual **Sa Vinya** *(p 101)* and **El Barrigón Xelini** *(p 100)*.

Mallorca with Kids

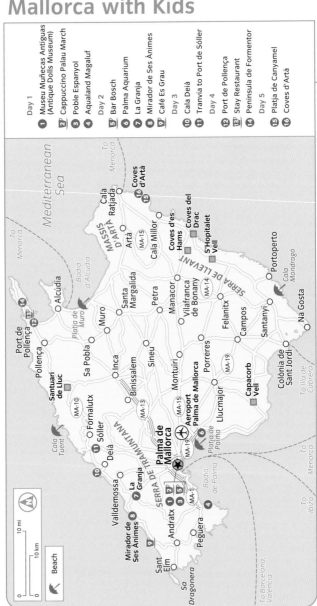

Although plenty of families just want to camp out on Mallorca's excellent beaches, some children will get restless without other diversions. Besides the predictable outings—waterparks and aquariums—there are other, more uniquely Mallorcan, attractions that make for a very enjoyable holiday for the entire family. START: **Palma. Trip length: 5 days.**

Travel Tip

For recommended hotels and restaurants in each town, please see Chapter 3 for Palma and Chapter 4 for towns outside of Palma.

Day One

1 Museu Muñecas Antiguas (Antique Dolls Museum). This small, quirky private museum, facing the cathedral, will entertain young girls (and perhaps some young boys, too). Up a flight of stairs are more than 500 19th- and early 20th-century antique dolls, including some rare and oddball items, such as the Kaiser baby, with the face of the German emperor. ⏱ 45 min. c/ Palau Reial, 27, Palma. ☎ 971/72-98-50. Admission 3.50€ adults; 2.50€ over 6. Tues–Sun 10am–6pm.

2 Cappuccino Palau March. An open-air café, this is a good spot for children to enjoy a milkshake, fruit juice or 'bubbling lollipop drink'. c/ Conquistador 13, Palma. ☎ 971/71-72-72. $$.

Take a taxi about 2km (1¼ miles) west of downtown or bus no. 29 to c/ de Andrea Doria.

3 Poble Espanyol. Just west of downtown, this Spanish village is an architectural theme park with miniature versions of classic Spanish buildings. It resembles an overgrown dollhouse, albeit with an Alhambra. ⏱ 1 hr. See p 59, 6.

The Alhambra, Poble Espanyol.

14km (9 miles) southwest along MA-1044.

4 Aqualand Magaluf. At this monstrously popular waterpark with a circular wave pool, multiple long water slides and rides like the Boomerang (a slide that flings you from one side to the other and back again) and the Tornado (a huge circular vortex slide), youngsters—and plenty of adults—are certain to be entertained as long as they stay wet. ⏱ 3 hr. Ctra. Cala Figuera, Magaluf. ☎ 971/13-08-11. Admission 19.50€ adults, 14€ children 3–12. Jun 10am–5pm, Jul–Aug 10am–6pm. Bus no. 3.

Day Two

5 ★ Bar Bosch. This family-friendly café has outdoor tables where children can be as noisy as they want, and the classic grilled sandwiches are sure to keep little people quiet. Pl. Rei Joan Carles I, Palma. ☎ 971/72-11-31. $.

Discover the folkier side to Mallorca at La Granja.

Take a taxi about 9km (6 miles) east of downtown or bus no. 25.

6 ★★ **Palma Aquarium.** With 55 tanks and some 8,000 sea creatures (representing 700 species from the deep and highlighting the Mediterranean), this is a must-do for families. Children love the sharks in the Gran Azul and the pirate ship with hidden treasures. ⏱ *2 hr. c/ Manuela de los Herreros I Soràm 21.* ☎ *971/74-61-04. www.palmaaquarium.com. Admission 19.50€ adults, 15€ children 4–12. Daily mid-Jun–Sep 10am–8pm, Apr–mid-Jun 10am–6pm, Jan–Mar 10am–4pm. Bus no. 25.*

17km (10 miles) north on MA-1040 from Palma to Esporles.

7 ★ **La Granja.** On the way to the northwest coast, this Mallorcan

finca (farm) aims to present traditional, agricultural Mallorca in a way that children can appreciate (even if some of the ethnographic exhibits might seem a little tedious), with farm animals, wooded grounds and regularly scheduled, costumed folkloric shows (Wed and Fri, 3:30–5pm). ⏱ *1½ hr. MA-1100 s/n.* ☎ *971/61-00-32; www.lagranja.net. Admission 9.50–11.50€ adults, 5€ children. Apr–Oct 10am–7pm, Nov–Mar 10am–6pm.*

8 ★★★ **Mirador de Ses Ànimes.** Older children are likely to appreciate the dramatic scenery of the northwestern coast. At this *mirador*, or historic viewpoint, just outside Banyalbufar, youngsters can scramble up a narrow ladder to the 16th-century tower (Torre del Verger) for unbeatable views. ⏱ *15 min. See p 90,* **7**.

9 ★★ **Café Es Grau.** Sharing the same enviable perch along the coastline with Mirador de Ricardo Roca (another 10km (6 miles) west along the coast), this café—where kids can have an early, light dinner—has incredible views from its terrace. *Ctra. Andratx-Estellencs/MA-10km, 98.* ☎ *971/61-85-27. $.*

Family enjoying the beach at Port de Pollença.

Day Three
Take a twisting 3km (1.8 miles) road just past Deià.

⑩ ★ Cala Deià. Promising the kids they'll get to go to the beach might be one way for you to spend some time in the enchanting village of Deià. This small, rocky cove and beach doesn't have much in the way of sand or facilities (though there's a restaurant-bar in summer), but it's still a very pretty spot with translucent water and cliffs to clamber on. ⏲ 2 hr. See p 93, ⑯.

12km (7 miles) east along MA-10.

⑪ ★ Tranvía to Port de Sóller. Hop aboard the vintage tram that connects Sóller to the port. The tram rumbles through town and citrus groves heaving with oranges and lemons. In Port de Sóller, children can get out and head for the beach. ⏲ 2 hr. See p 94, ⑲.

Day Four
A long drive of 59km (36 miles) on mountainous and curvy MA-10 (make sure youngsters are prepared for the journey).

⑫ ★★ Port de Pollença. This wide, sandy spot along the Bay of Pollença is one of the best beaches for families: easy-going, not frenetic with drinkers and gently sloped, making it ideal for swimming. ⏲ 2 hr. See p 104, ④.

⑬ ★★ Stay Restaurant. Parents will enjoy this relaxed modern seafood restaurant with views of the bay, and youngsters will like eating out on a pier floating over the water. Grab a seat under the awning if you've had too much sun and sample just-caught seafood. There are pastas, salads and fries for the children. Port de Pollença. ☎ 971/86-40-13. $$$.

⑭ ★★★ Península de Formentor. Take a late-afternoon drive up to this oddly lunar-looking promontory that juts out into the sea. Older children love seeing how the cliffs crash into the deep-blue sea below: it's a great spot for a memorable family photo. ⏲ 45 min. See p 104, ⑤.

Day Five
48km (30 miles) south on MA-12.

⑮ ★ Platja de Canyamel. This good swimming beach with golden sands isn't usually as crowded as the big resorts farther south on the east coast. There are pedalos and other facilities for youngsters, restaurants and hotels, and the beach looks across the bay to the some of the best caves on the coast, such as the Coves d'Artà (⑯). ⏲ 3 hr. See p 127.

⑯ ★★ kids Coves d'Artà. Cool off after a morning at the beach at these entrancing, 300-million-year-old caves. The chambers are dramatically lit, and there are all sorts of bizarre stalactite and stalagmite formations and caves that children can identify as the Hall of Flags, Purgatory and Inferno. ⏲ 1 hr. See p 107, ⑰.

Dramatically lit chambers, Coves d'Artà.

Island History & Culture

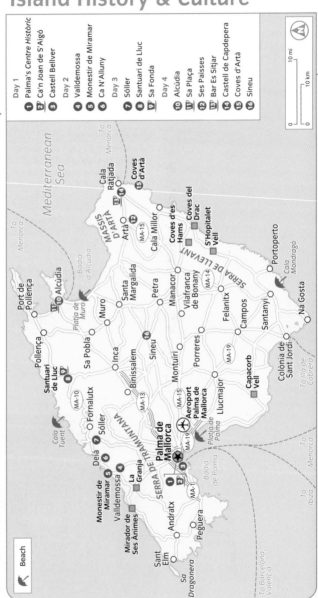

Day 1
1. Palma's *Centre Històric*
2. Ca'n Joan de S'Aigó
3. Castell Bellver

Day 2
4. Valldemossa
5. Monestir de Miramar
6. Ca N'Alluny

Day 3
7. Sóller
8. Santuari de Lluc
9. Sa Fonda

Day 4
10. Alcúdia
11. Sa Plaça
12. Ses Païsses
13. Bar Es Sitjar
14. Castell de Capdepera
15. Coves d'Artà
16. Sineu

🏖 Beach

Mediterranean Sea

To Menorca

To Menorca

To Menorca

To Ibiza

To Barcelona/Valencia

Cala Ràtjada
Coves d'Artà
Coves del Drac
MASSÍS D'ARTÀ
Artà
(MA-15)
Cala Millor
Coves d'es Hams
S'Hopitalet Vell
SERRA DE LLEVANT
Portopetro
Cala Mondragó
Na Gosta
Manacor
Vilafranca de Bonany
(MA-14)
Petra
Santa Margalida
Muro
Sa Pobla
Felanitx
Santanyí
Campos
(MA-19)
Colònia de Sant Jordi
Tolla de Cabrera
Port de Pollença
Alcúdia
Badia d'Alcúdia
Platja de Muro
Pollença
Santuari de Lluc
(MA-10)
Fornalutx
Deià
Sóller
Cala Tuent
Inca
Binissalem
(MA-13)
Sineu
Montuïri
Porreres
Llucmajor
Capacorb Vell
Monestir de Miramar
Valldemossa
La Granja
Mirador de Ses Ànimes
Sant Elm
Sa Dragonera
Andratx
Peguera
SERRA DE TRAMUNTANA
Aeroport Palma de Mallorca
Palma de Mallorca
(MA-1)
(MA-15)
(MA-19)
Platja de Palma
Badia de Palma

0 — 10 mi
0 — 10 km

The Balearic islands have rich histories stretching back millennia. Native peoples and conquerors, from Bronze-Age settlements to Roman and Moorish occupations, all left their various legacies. You can get a dose of history and culture even if you've come primarily to enjoy the beaches, because few sites of interest are far from the coast. START: **Palma. Trip Length: 4 days.**

TRAVEL TIP

For recommended hotels and restaurants in each town, please see Chapter 3 for Palma and Chapter 4 for towns outside of Palma.

Day One
① ★★★ Palma's *Centre Històric*. From its founding by the Romans in the 1st century B.C. to the Moors' transformation of the settlement into a significant medieval city, Palma's history is on view in the charming, medina-like old quarter. On foot, you can see an abbreviated version of it in less than a day, including: the Banys Àrabs, 12th-century Arab baths (c/ Serra, 7); La Seu, the great Gothic cathedral built in the 13th and 14th centuries on

the site of a Great Mosque (*Palau Reinal, s/n*); Palau de l'Almudaina (*Palau Reinal, s/n*), the Spanish royal palace that's itself a transformation of the former Moorish royal palace and fortress; and a dozen or more 17th- and 18th-century mansions and medieval and Renaissance churches. ⏱ *4 hr. See Chapter 3, Old Quarter, p 46.*

②★★ Ca'n Joan de S'Aigó. A number of shopfronts in Palma go back a century or more, but this is by far the city's oldest café, founded in 1697. The marble tables, antique chandeliers and tiled floors give it a genuine period feel and it makes an ideal stop for a hot chocolate and pastry. *c/ Can Sanç, 10 (Palma).* ☎ *971/71-07-59. $.*

Quiet courtyard in the old quarter of Palma.

Take a taxi 3km (2 miles) west of downtown or bus no. 3 to Plaça Gomila (and a 15-min walk uphill).

③ ★ kids Castell Bellver. To the west of the city, this 14th-century circular castle built by the order of King Jaume II served as a fortress, royal residence and then prison. Unfortunately, the museum of local history and archaeology within is only moderately interesting, even to history buffs—although you're unlikely to care with these sensational hilltop views of the Bay of Palma and the city. ⏱ *30 min. See p 59,* ⑦.

Decorative plaque, Valldemossa Monastery.

SANTA CATALINA THOMAS PREGAU PER NOSALTRES

Day Two
23km (14 miles) north of Palma along c/ de Valldemossa/ MA-1130.

Santuari de Lluc.

④ ★★★ Valldemossa. The 14th-century Carthusian monastery, **Reial Cartoixa,** at the centre of this beguiling town is now largely composed of neoclassical 17th- and 18th-century buildings. However, it's the early 19th-century association with the famed Polish composer Frédéric Chopin and his consort, the French writer George Sand—who spent an apparently pitiable winter (1838–39) in the monastery in an effort to improve Chopin's health—that appears to live on. Sand later chronicled the couple's disastrous stay in *A Winter in Mallorca.* Predating the Carthusian monks, in 1310 King Jaume II built a royal palace, the **Palau del Rei Sanxo,** on the site, now incorporated into the Cartoixa complex. Also of interest in town is the **Casa Natal de Santa Catalina Thomàs,** the birthplace of the 16th-century nun later beatified as Mallorca's only saint. ⏱ *2 hr. See p 90,* ⑨.

5km (3 miles) north on MA-10.

⑤ ★ Monestir de Miramar. This 13th-century monastery founded by the legendary Mallorcan mystic and philosopher, Ramón Llull, was acquired by the Archduke Ludwig Salvator, a 19th-century Austrian aristocrat. Although what remains of the monastery is little more than a few arches and pillars from the cloisters, the site is sensational—it's easy to see what attracted both Llull and Salvator. ⏱ *30 min. See p 92,* ⑪.

5km (3 miles) northeast on MA-10.

6 ★★★ **Ca N'Alluny.** Deià, an ancient and picturesque village, has been home to many an artist and writer over the years. Most celebrated was the long-time resident Robert Graves, the English poet and author of *I, Claudius*, who moved to the village in 1929 and essentially spent the rest of his life here, until his death in 1985. His home is now open as a museum. Graves's resting place, in the simple cemetery at the top of the village, and his house—frozen in time, exactly as he left it—is now open to the public. ⏱ *2 hr. See p 93,* **15**.

Day Three
11km (7 miles) east on MA-10.

7 ★★ **kids Sóller.** Although this prosperous town possesses a 16th-century Gothic church with a Modernista façade and several other notable Catalan Art Nouveau mansions, it's best known for the Ferrocarril de Sóller, the vintage 1912 narrow-gauge train established to transport citrus fruits from the Sóller valley to Palma for export. The cars are splendidly vintage, all original polished wooden panels, and the *estació de tren* (station) where they pull in is equally historic, adapted from a 17th-century manor house. For another trip back in time, hop aboard the 1913 tram that ambles through town and connects Sóller to the attractive natural port 4km (2½ miles) away. ⏱ *2 hr. See p 93,* **17**.

34km (21 miles) east on MA-10.

8 ★★ **Santuari de Lluc.** According to legend, back in the 13th century a carved, dark-skinned Madonna was found in the woods by a local shepherd boy, Lluc. More mystical appearances in the area led to the establishment of a monastery,

now a place of pilgrimage for 800 years. The handsome monastery that receives visitors today is mostly 17th- and 18th-century buildings, highlighted by the Baroque Basílica de la Mare de Deu de Lluc, which holds the famed, 15th-century version of the Virgin of Lluc. ⏱ *1½ hr. See p 96,* **24**.

9 ★ **Sa Fonda.** This old hall, with a high, wood-beamed ceiling, is the monks' former dining room. Where else would you want to grab a bite to eat in this most holy of places? *Santuari de Lluc.* ☎ *971/51-70-22. $$.*

Day Four
31km (20 miles) east on MA-10.

10 ★★ **kids Alcúdia.** Although the medieval-looking walls that surround the old town are mostly modern recreations, Alcúdia's history isn't in doubt. It dates back to the

The walls surrounding the old town, Alcúdia.

Phoenicians in the 8th century B.C.; the Romans then founded a settlement here around 70 B.C. Just beyond the fortifications are Mallorca's finest Roman ruins, from the original Pol·lèntia settlement, including the **Teatre Romà** (Roman Amphitheatre). See items unearthed there at the **Museu Monográfic** in the old town. ⏲ *3 hr. See p 105,* ⑥.

⑪ Sa Plaça. Grab a quick lunch at this restaurant with a terrace overlooking the main square within the old city walls. There's a varied and good-value, three-course fixed-price midday menu. *Plaça Constitutció, 1, Alcúdia.* ☎ *971/54-91-57. $$.*

34km (21 miles) south on MA-12.

⑫ ★ Ses Països. Although Mallorca pales in comparison with Menorca's collection of prehistoric ruins, this set of stony walls and a watchtower, a Talayotic village dating from 1300–800 B.C., is the larger island's finest. ⏲ *30 min. See p 106,* ⑬.

9km (6 miles) east on MA-15.

⑬ Bar Es Sitjar. This simple café near the Ajuntament (Town Hall) is a good place for a breather just before climbing up to the castle in Capdepera. *c/ Major, 26, Capdepera. No phone. $.*

⑭ ★ Castell de Capdepera. Mallorca was once vulnerable to marauding pirates circling the Mediterranean, and its coastline was dotted with watchtowers and fortified villages. The castle of Capdepera encircled King Jaume II's villa in the 14th century and still affords distant views over the surrounding countryside, all the way to the sea. ⏲ *45 min. See p 106,* ⑭.

9km (6 miles) southeast on MA-4040 and MA-4042.

⑮ ★★ kids Coves d'Artà. Talk about prehistory—these caves are at least 300 million years old, and their bizarrely shaped stalactite and stalagmite formations have evolved over many thousands of years. ⏲ *1 hr. See p 107,* ⑰.

48km (30 miles) west along MA-4040.

The Gothic Cross of the Dead at Sineu.

⑯ ★★ Sineu. On your way back to Palma, stop at one of the most historic small towns of *Es Pla*, the Mallorcan interior. King Jaume II built a royal palace here in 1309 (today it's a convent on carrer Major), while just paces away are an early 16th-century Gothic church and *Creu dels Morts* (Cross of the Dead), a 16th-century waymarker stone cross. ⏲ *1 hr. See p 115,* ③. ●

Old Quarter *(Centre Històric)*

1. Catedral (La Seu)
2. Palau de l'Almudaina
3. Dalt Murada/ Parc de la Mar
4. Museu Diocesà (Palacio Episcopal)
5. Banys Àrabs
6. Palatial Courtyards
7. Arc de l'Almudaina
8. Vidreres Gordiola
9. Plaça Cort/ Ajuntament
10. Café Moderno
11. Església de Santa Eulàlia
12. Basílica de Sant Francesc
13. Ca'n Joan de S'Aigó

Previous page: Catedral (La Seu).

The Romans founded Palmaria around the 1st century B.C., but it was the Moors who transformed the settlement into a major city. Although much of the city's Muslim past was destroyed by the Christian Reconquest and subsequently fire, Palma's old centre is still rich with medieval and Renaissance churches and historic manor houses. START: **Plaça de la Catedral.**

1 ★★★ **Catedral (La Seu).** This graceful yet imposing Gothic cathedral is one of Europe's great churches, and the greatest architectural achievement in the Balearic Islands; it was constructed 1229–1601 on the site of the Great Mosque, which was the centrepiece of Moorish Mallorca. With its soaring buttresses flanking a waterfront park and reflecting pool, it's an arresting sight. Inside are glorious Gothic *retablos* (altars), a huge stained-glass rose window (12m (40 ft) in diameter) and decidedly unexpected later artistic interventions. Antoni Gaudí's enigmatic *baldachin* is an iron canopy suspended over the principal altar and Miquel Barceló's shocking but sensuous 2007 ceramic mural represents Mallorca

Mural detail from the Barceló Chapel, Catedral (La Seu).

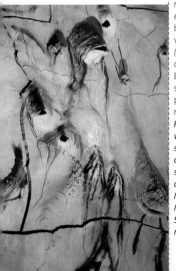

as the beginning of the world. The cathedral museum displays a rich collection of silver monstrances, candelabra and art from the School of Mallorcan Primitives. ⏱ *1 hr. Palau Reinal, s/n.* ☎ *971/72-31-30. www.catedraldemallorca.org. Admission 4€, free children under 10. Mon–Fri 10am–3:15pm, Sat 10am–2:15pm, Apr–May & Oct Mon–Fri 10am–5:15pm, Jun–Sep Mon–Fri 10am–6:15pm, Nov–Mar Mon–Fri 10am–3:15pm. Year-round Sat 10am–2:15pm. Bus no. 2. See also p 23,* **4** *.*

2 ★★ **Palau de l'Almudaina.** Facing the cathedral is the opulent Spanish royal palace, the official summer residence of King Juan Carlos and Queen Sofia, constructed on the site of the former Moorish royal palace and fortress. Transformed after the Christian Reconquest, it retains some distinctive Moorish elements, including vaulted Arab baths. Also notable are a stone-vaulted 13th-century *Saló Gòtic* (Gothic Room), numerous salons decorated with magnificent Baroque Flemish tapestries and the small but beautiful Santa Ana chapel, with its unusual pink-and-white marble Romanesque portal. ⏱ *1 hr. Palau Reinal, s/n.* ☎ *971/21-41-34. www.patrimoninacional.es. Admission 4€ adults guided tours; 3.20€ adults unguided; 2.30€ seniors & students; free children under 11; free on Wed for EU citizens. Apr–Sep Mon–Fri 10am–5:45pm, Oct–Mar Mon–Fri 10am–1:15pm & 4–5:15pm. Sat & holidays 10am–1:15pm. Bus no. 2.*

Palau de l'Almudaina.

③ ★ kids Dalt Murada/Parc de la Mar. Once a walled medieval city, Palma lost most of its remaining ramparts during a 19th-century expansion. The Dalt Murada, a replacement Renaissance-era wall, used to protect the city from the Mediterranean, though the sea has been pushed out to create room for the ring road and Passeig Marítim. Landscape designers added a long reflecting pool, fountain and parks running alongside it, making it one of Palma's prime public spaces. Take a stroll along the top for impressive views of the Cathedral and Bay of Palma. The western end of the wall passes just above the gardens of **S'Hort del Rei** (the King's Orchard) and grand **Arc del Wali,** the so-called Moorish governor's arch. ⏱ *45 min. Avda. Antoni Maura at Avda. Gabriel Roca.*

④ ★★ Museu Diocesà (Palacio Episcopal). One of the city's best-kept secrets is this relocated (since 2007) and handsomely designed museum of Gothic, Renaissance and Baroque religious art, housed in the extraordinary 17th-century Bishop's Palace. Key exhibits among more than 200 pieces include the late 12th-century *Christ of the Holy Sepulchre* (the oldest relic in Mallorca) and the remarkable central panel from the 15th-century Sant Jordi altarpiece by Pere Niçard, which depicts the city of Mallorca in the background. The Episcopal palace itself is key to Palma's early history,

Royal Palace Trivia

Although the Royal Family's official summer residence, the King and Queen are rarely found at Palau de l'Almudaina (see p 47, ②), preferring their summer home in Cala Major or boating around Port d'Andratx on the western tip. The Palau is used mainly for official acts, dinners and hosting of foreign dignitaries. Despite it being royal, regular citizens can have their weddings at the Gothic Capella de Santa Ana; they need only to request official permission from the state and pay the quite reasonable fee.

Courtyard (Patio) Tours

The Palma Tourism Office offers occasional guided tours of some of Palma's baronial mansions and their inner courtyards. Tours run for 2 hours, Monday–Saturday, 9am–6pm; cost 10€ per person. Call ☎ 971/72-07-20 or visit www.palmademallorca.es for additional information.

with its Roman walls and medieval elements including the rare Sant Pau Gothic chapel preserved in its original location. 🕐 *1 hr. c/ Mirador, 5.* ☎ *971/72-38-60. www.bisbatde mallorca.com. Admission 3€ adults, free children under 12. Mon–Sat 10am–2pm. Bus no. 2.*

5 ★ kids Banys Àrabs. One of Palma's few architectural remains of the city's Moorish domination, these 12th-century Arab baths may not be as impressive or well-preserved as some on the mainland (especially in Girona, Ronda and Granada), but they are still an evocative,

romantically dilapidated reminder of Mallorca's Muslim past. Set in a small courtyard garden in the heart of what was the Medina Majurka, a dozen slender columns support the domed ceiling of the main hot-bath chamber. 🕐 *20 min. c/ Serra, 7.* ☎ *971/72-15-49. Admission 2€, free children under 11, Daily 9am–6pm (until 7:30pm in summer). Bus no. 2.*

6 ★★ Palatial Courtyards. Fire destroyed much of medieval Palma and many original Gothic buildings, but a significant number of 17th- and 18th-century baronial mansions, built around majestic interior

Enjoy a stroll around the Dalt Murada.

A reminder of Mallorca's Moorish past at Banys Àrabs.

courtyards, are still intact (more than 100 manor houses populate old Palma). Although most aren't open to the public, it's usually possible to peek in at their stately courtyards. Among the best to take a look at are: **Can Oleza,** a 16th-century palace with large arches and a grand staircase; **Can Bordils,** one of Palma's oldest mansions, with Gothic features dating to the 13th century, and now home to a municipal building hosting occasional art exhibits; **Can Vivot,** a spectacular 18th-century mansion often open during the day and showing off antique cars in the courtyard, where coaches were once parked; and **Can Catlar,** with a Gothic courtyard. **Can Marquès** largely dates to the 18th century and is one of the few period mansions that's open to the public, although its architecture is a hodgepodge of periods and styles and admission is oddly double that of greater attractions. ⏱ *45 min. Can Oleza: c/ d'en Morey, 9; Can Bordils: c/ de l'Almudaina, 33; Can Vivot: c/ de Can Savellà, 4; Can Catlar: c/ Can Savellà, 15; Can Marquès: c/ Zanglada, 2.* ☎ *971/ 716-247; Admission 6€; Mon–Fri 10am–3pm. www.canmarques.net. Bus no. 2.*

❼ Arc de l'Almudaina. Little remains of old Palma's extensive original fortifications. This medieval-looking and much-modified arch is considered to date back to the Moorish occupation of Palma, although some experts contend that it was built on top of a 5th-century Roman wall. ⏱ *15 min. c/ de l'Almudaina s/n. Bus no. 2.*

❽ kids Vidreres Gordiola. Mallorca has long embraced the art of glassmaking and this family-owned shop is one of the island's oldest (since 1719) and still one of the most traditional. Peer at the clear and tinted bowls, glasses, vases and exquisite art glass, including chandeliers to rival Murano. ⏱ *30 min. c/ de la Victoria, 2.* ☎ *971/71-15-41. www.gordiola.com. Free admission. Mon–Fri 10am–2pm & 4:30–8pm, Sat 10am–2pm. Bus no. 2.*

❾ ★ Plaça Cort/ Ajuntament. Palma's 17th-century Town Hall, with its late Renaissance façade featuring 7 large windows, antique glass and a 19th-century French clock known as *En Figuera,* presides over the Plaça Cort and its large, gnarly olive tree. Peek in the Gothic entrance and grand foyer, where you'll be likely to spot a few *gegants,* the gigantic carnival folk figures paraded through the streets during popular celebrations. ⏱ *15 min. Not open to the public. Pl. Cort, 1. Bus no. 2.*

❿ Café Moderno. The perfect location on a sunny day for a coffee or beer on the terrace of this 1914 café facing Santa Eulàlia church. It's a popular hangout, usually teeming with locals whiling away the afternoon. *Pl. de Santa Eulàlia, 5, Palma.* ☎ *971/71-32-04. Bus no. 2.*

⓫ ★ Església de Santa Eulàlia. This Gothic church, built in the mid-13th century just after the

huge organ are highlights, but they take a back seat to the ethereal, two-storey Gothic cloisters and their delicately sculpted columns and fragrant orange and lemon trees. 🕐 *45 min. Pl. de Sant Francesc, s/n.* ☎ *971/71-46-25. Admission 1€ adults; free children under 10. Mon–Sat 9:30am–12:30pm & 3:30–6pm, Sun 9:30am–12:30pm. Bus no. 2.*

13 ★★ **kids Ca'n Joan de S'Aigó.** Palma's oldest café—founded in 1697—is busy with both tourists and locals. Technically, it's a *granja*, or milk bar, tucked away on a side street. With marble-topped tables, antique chandeliers and tiled floors, try the house speciality—hot chocolate with a flaky *ensaïmada* (feather-light pastry, see p 30) or quarts, a sponge cake served with almond ice cream (a big hit with children). *c/ Can Sanç, 10, Palma.* ☎ *971/71-07-59. $.*

Café Moderno.

Reconquest, has cartoon-like gargoyles projecting from the rafters, but the dark interior bursts forth with a wildly Baroque altarpiece. Santa Eulàlia is known for a dark episode in Mallorcan history—in 1435, Jews were forcibly baptised and converted to Catholicism or faced being burned at the stake. 🕐 *30 min. Pl. de Santa Eulàlia, s/n.* ☎ *971/71-46-25. Free admission. Daily 8–10:30am & 5–8pm. Bus no. 2.*

12 ★★ **Basilica de Sant Francesc.** A Franciscan basilica built in the Gothic style beginning in 1281 (the Plateresque portal wasn't added until the 17th century). Standing watch over it is a statue of Juníper Serra, the native Mallorcan who founded Franciscan missions in California and Baja California in the 18th century. A chapel holds the remains of the 13th-century Mallorcan philosopher and mystic Ramón Llull. The early-18th-century altarpiece and

The decorative façade of the Basilica de Sant Francesc.

19th- & 20th-Century **Palma**

1 Palau March Museu
2 Passeig d'es Born
3 Casal Solleric
4 Plaça Mercat/Can Casasayas
5 Fundació 'La Caixa' (Gran Hotel)
6 Forn des Teatre
7 Plaça Major
8 Carrer Sant Miquel
9 Museu d'Art Espanyol Contemporani (Fundació Joan March)
10 Gran Café Cappuccino

Information
Post Office
Train Station
Church
Hospital

Extending north from Palma's medieval heart is the city's modern expansion, which began in the 19th century. The lively core of the commercial centre, it has the city's best shopping, markets and examples of 18th- and 19th-century development, including several Modernista (Catalan Art Nouveau) architectural masterpieces, wide avenues and pedestrianised promenades. START: **Plaça de la Reina (Av. Antoni Maura at Conquistador).**

The decorative facades of Can Casasayas.

❶ ★ Palau March Museu. This mid-20th-century mansion, built on the site of a former convent, now houses a robust collection of open-air contemporary sculpture. Some of the greatest Spanish and international figures are represented, including Henry Moore, Auguste Rodin, Joan Miró and Eduardo Chillida. The Catalan sculptor Xavier Corberó's audacious, slinky-like *Orgue del Mar* slithers across the courtyard. The Catalan painter and designer Josep Maria Sert transformed the interior of the museum into a work of art. ⏲ *45 min. c/ de Palau Reial, 18.* ☎ *971/71-11-22. www.fundbmarch.es. Admission 3.60€ adults, 2.90€ seniors &*

students, free children under 12. Apr–Oct Mon–Fri 10am–6:30pm & Sat 10am–2pm, Nov–Mar Mon–Fri 10am–5pm & Sat 10am–2pm. Bus no. 2.

❷ Passeig d'es Born. This leafy and lovely pedestrian-only boulevard is book-ended by stone sphinxes, a reminder that it was once the site of jousting tournaments in the 17th century. Today it's lined on either side by cafés and upscale shopping boutiques, and is a favourite strolling ground for locals in the early evening. ⏲ *20 min. Between Pl. de la Reina & Pl. Joan Carles I. Bus no. 2.*

❸ ★ Casal Solleric. One of Palma's grandest Baroque mansions, this 1763 Italianate manor house (*casal*), built for a wealthy oil merchant family, was acquired by the town council in 1975 and converted into an exhibition space in 1985. It features a majestic courtyard with four huge stone arches and sculpted marble columns. Upstairs floors are now well-designed gallery spaces, hosting itinerant exhibits of contemporary sculpture and paintings. ⏲ *45 min. Passeig des Born, 27.* ☎ *971/72-20-92. Admission free. Mon–Sat 10am–2pm & 5–9pm, Sun 10am–1:30pm. Bus no. 2.*

❹ Plaça Mercat/Can Casasayas. This small square, joining carrer Unió and Plaça Weyler, is most notable for twin Modernista apartment buildings, commissioned by a wealthy merchant in 1908 from the architects Guillem Reynés i Font and Francesc Roca. Their decorative

Fom des Teatre.

6 ★ kids **Forn des Teatre.** A small bakery with a vivid green Modernista façade that's made it a historic landmark. Sit outside and enjoy a coffee and an *ensaïmada* pastry, or go next door to the tapas bar, which is an extension of the bakery, for heartier dishes. *Pl. de Weyler, 9.* ☎ *971/71-52-54. $.*

façades, which seem plucked from Barcelona's famed L'Eixample district, are especially alluring when illuminated after dark. ⏲ *10 min. Pl. Mercat, 13–14. Bus no. 2.*

5 ★★ **Fundació 'La Caixa' (Gran Hotel).** The grandest of Palma's Modernista buildings is the ornate former Gran Hotel, constructed in 1903. It was built by the famed Catalan architect Lluís Domènech i Muntaner (a rival of Gaudi), who also designed Barcelona's inspirational Palau de la Música concert hall. Today the building is owned by *La Caixa* bank, and functions as one of the city's best exhibition spaces, with interesting art shows, including a permanent collection of more than 500 romantic and vividly coloured modernist paintings by the Catalan painter Anglada Camarasa (1872–1959), who was from Barcelona but died in Pollença. ⏲ *1 hr. Pl. Weyler, 3.* ☎ *971/17-85-00. www.lacaixa.es/obrasocial. Admission free. Mon–Sat 10am–9pm, Sun 10am–2pm. Bus no. 2.*

7 **Plaça Major.** Palma's principal square, once the produce and fish market, is pale yellow and green, with symmetrical porticoes on all sides. Today it's lined with café terraces and is a magnet for street performers hoping to liberate tourists from a few extra euros. The square used to be the site of something far more sinister, though—the local office of the Spanish Inquisition in the late 15th century. ⏲ *30 min. c/ Sindicat at c/ Forn del Racó. Bus no. 2.*

8 ★ **Carrer Sant Miquel.** Heading north from the Plaça Major is Palma's one-size-fits-all, pedestrian-only shopping street, packed with

Plaça Major, Palma's principal square.

Mercat de l'Olivar: Palma's Lively Food Market

If you have another day in Palma, it's worth coming back this way early in the morning to see the city's fresh fish, meat and produce covered market at its most boisterous. The Mercat, dating to 1941, is a cook's (and photographer's) dream, teeming with beautiful vegetables, fruit and an amazing range of exotic fish still nearly wriggling, brought straight from the harbour. The sights, sounds of women fishmongers selling their goods, and of course smells are a delight for the senses. You might also pop in on a Saturday around noon, when you can have a snack and glass of wine at one of the kiosk bars inside the market and take it all in. *Plaça Olivar, s/n.* ☎ *971/72-03-14.* Free admission. Daily 7am–2pm.

fashion boutiques, old-school food purveyors (such as La Favorita; see p 80), occasional Renaissance mansions and decidedly non-commercial interests, such as the **Església de Sant Miquel,** a 14th-century Catalan Gothic church with a masterful Baroque altarpiece and striking murals. 🕐 *1 hr. Extending north from Pl. Major. Bus no. 2.*

⑨ ★★ Museu d'Art Espanyol Contemporani (Fundació Joan March). Inside a luxurious 18th-century mansion is a comprehensive collection of 20th-century Spanish contemporary and avant-garde art, including all the major names known in Spain and abroad: Picasso, Miró, Dalí, Julio González, Eduardo Chillida, Juan Gris, Antoni Tàpies and of course Mallorcan favourite son Miquel Barceló. 🕐 *1½ hr. c/ Sant Miquel, 11.* ☎ *971/71-35-15. www.march.es/arte/palma. Admission free. Mon–Fri 10am–6:30pm, Sat 10:30am–2pm. Bus no. 2.*

🔟 ★ kids Gran Café Cappuccino. With leafy plants and marble tables inhabiting an airy, classic 18th-century Palma manor house

courtyard, this atmospheric and antique café-bar-restaurant is a good option for a snack and beverage (or even a full meal); the coffee and pastries are first-rate (if a bit steep in price). *c/ Sant Miquel, 53.* ☎ *971/71-97-64. $$.*

The lavish décor of Església de Sant Miquel.

Western **Palma**

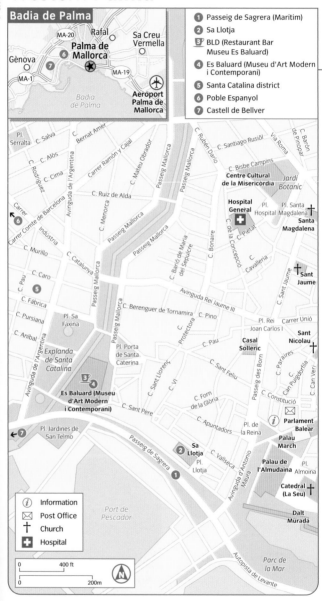

Badia de Palma

MA-20 Rafal Sa Creu
Palma de Vermella
Gènova Mallorca
MA-1 MA-19

Badia Aeroport
de Palma Palma de
Mallorca

1 Passeig de Sagrera (Maritim)
2 Sa Llotja
3 BLD (Restaurant Bar Museu Es Baluard)
4 Es Baluard (Museu d'Art Modern i Contemporani)
5 Santa Catalina district
6 Poble Espanyol
7 Castell de Bellver

Pl. Serralta
C. Salva
Bernat Amer
C. Albs
C. Rodríguez
C. Cima
Avinguda de l'Argentina
Carrer Ramón y Cajal
C. Mateu Obrador
Passeig Mallorca
Passeig Mallorca
C. Rubén Darío
C. Santiago Rusiñol
Via Roma
C. Baró de Pinopar

C. Ruiz de Alda
C. Bisbe Campins

Centre Cultural de la Misericordia
Jardí Botànic

Carrer Comte de Barcelona
Industria
C. Menorca
Passeig Mallorca
Passeig Mallorca
C. Catalunya
Passeig Mallorca
C. Baró de Maria del Sepulcre
C. Bonaire
C. de la Concepció
C. Pietat
Hospital General
Pl. Hospital
Pl. Santa Magdalena
Santa Magdalena

C. Murillo
C. Pau
C. Caro
C. Cavalleria
Sant Jaume
C. Sant Jaume

C. Fábrica
Avinguda Rei Jaume III
C. Pursiana
C. Berenguer de Tornamira
C. Pino
Pl. Rei Joan Carlos I
Carrer Unió
Sant Nicolau

C. Anibal
Pl. Sa Faxina
C. Protectora
C. Pau
Casal Solleric
Passeig des Born
C. Paraires
C. Can Puigdorfila
C. Can Veri

Avinguda de l'Argentina
Explanda de Santa Catalina
Pl. Porta de Santa Caterina
C. Sant Llorenç
C. VI
C. Sant Feliu
C. Constitució
Sant Nicolau

Es Baluard (Museu d'Art Modern i Contemporani)
C. Forn de la Gloria
Parlament Balear

C. Sant Pere
C. Apuntadors
Pl. de la Reina
Palau March

Pl. Jardines de San Telmo
Passeig de Sagrera
Sa Llotja
Pl. Llotja
C. Vallseca
Avinguda d'Antonio Maura
Palau de l'Almudaina
Pl. Almoina

Catedral (La Seu)

Dalt Murada

(i) Information
✉ Post Office
† Church
✚ Hospital

Port de Pescador

Parc de la Mar

0   400 ft
0   200m

Autopista de Levante

The city extends along the seafront promenade and port, west of Passeig d'es Born, in an area known as Sant Pere to some, though most call it Sa Llotja after an important 15th-century landmark. Either way, it's most identified with its maritime past and present and is now home to a major art museum, green spaces and walking and cycling paths. START: **Avda. Antoni Maura at Passeig de Sagrera.**

Passeig de Sagrera.

① ★ kids **Passeig de Sagrera (Marítim).** Directly across from the port (from which there are superb views over fishing boats towards La Seu rising above the city rooftops) is this delightful promenade dotted with tall, leafy palm trees. Passeig de Sagrera eventually becomes Av. Gabriel Roca, better known to locals as Passeig Marítim, as it bends around the harbour. ⏱ *30 min. Between Avda. Antoni Maura and Avda. de l'Argentina. Bus no. 1.*

② ★★ **Sa Llotja.** Just west along the seafront promenade is this emblematic Catalan Gothic building, which housed the fish merchants' stock exchange in the mid-15th century. Currently undergoing a lengthy restoration, it is one of the finest examples of civic Gothic architecture in Spain. Built by the sculptor

Biking Palma

Although most people who come to cycle in Mallorca head out for the interior or northwest coast, Palma and the Badia de Palma are great for gentle bicycling. The most popular spot in the city is the set of lanes that line Passeig Marítim, fanning out from downtown, but a bike is also a good way to get around the *Centre Històric*. You can easily bike to the major beaches southeast of the city (Platja de Palma and S'Arenal); there are designated bike lanes from Porto Pi to S'Arenal. **PalmaOnBike.com** (Avda. Gabriel Roca 15, or Salvador Coll 8; ☎ 971/91-89-88 or 971/71-80-62; www.palmaonbike.com) offers guided tours by bike as well as city, mountain and road bike (and inline skate) rentals (15€ per day to 50€ for a week). **Belori Bike** (c/ Marbella 22, local 34; ☎ 971/49-03-58; www.belori-bike.com), between Sometimes and Las Maravillas beaches, has road and mountain-bike rentals and organised excursions.

④ ★★ **Es Baluard (Museu d'Art Modern i Contemporani).** This contemporary art museum with an airy, Mediterranean feel, is a delight—even if more than half the reason for enjoying it is on the outside. Its large terrace is graced by a half-dozen large outdoor sculptures (including the famed Spanish architect Santiago Calatrava's site-specific *Bou*). The well-designed museum is a minimalist, avant-garde space of pale, poured concrete carved out of the city's original Renaissance walls and corner bastion, affording rooftop views of Palma and the bay. The permanent collection is rather small—the museum is relatively young, inaugurated only in 2004—although there are several minor works by Miró and Picasso as well as up-and-coming Spanish and Mediterranean artists. ⏱ *1 hr. Pl. Porta de Santa Catalina, 10.* ☎ *971/90-82-00. www.esbaluard. org. Admission 6€ adults, 4.50€ seniors & students, free children under 12; Fridays 'You Decide' (pay what you wish). Oct to mid-June Tues–Sun 10am–8pm, mid-Jun through Sep, Tues–Sun 10am–10pm. Bus no. 1.*

⑤ **Santa Catalina district.** Until several years ago, this former fishing quarter was a somewhat rough-around-the-edges middle-class neighbourhood, but today it's a

Terrace café-restaurant BLD.

responsible for the remarkable Mirador portal of the Cathedral, Guillem Sagrera, Sa Llotja (La Lonja in Spanish) includes beautiful gargoyle sculptures on the exterior (most notable is the *Guardian Angel* by Claus Sluter that presides over the main portal), corner turrets and delicate, arched windows. Inside, six slender columns spiral towards the vaulted ceiling. ⏱ *30 min. Pg. de Sagrera s/n.* ☎ *971/71-17-05. Free admission. Tues–Sat 11am–2pm, Sun 11am–1:30pm. Bus no. 1.*

③ ★★ kids **BLD (Restaurant Bar Museu Es Baluard).** This delightful, expansive terrace café-restaurant, attached to the Es Baluard Art Museum (④), is one of the most relaxing locations in the city. Hang out on the terrace, surrounded by monumental contemporary sculptures overlooking the harbour, with panoramic views of Palma and the sea. *Pl. Porta de Santa Catalina, 10.* ☎ *971/90-81-99. $$. See p 66.*

Discover mini-versions of famous Spanish buildings at Poble Espanyol.

View over the Bay of Palma from the Castell de Bellver.

good indication both of Palma's recent past and its future. Many of Santa Catalina's squat two- and three-storey buildings have been renovated and the tree-lined district is now one of Palma's most thriving for restaurants and bars; in fact, the principal reason to visit is for a meal or cocktail. The **Mercat de Santa Catalina,** the neighbourhood's indoor fish, meat and produce market, rivals better-known Mercat de l'Olivar (see box p 55). 🕐 *1hr. Mercat de Santa Catalina: Pl. Navegació s/n.* 📞 *971/45-50–79, Bus no. 1.*

⑥ kids Poble Espanyol. Built during the Franco era to represent a 'Spanish village' as a patriotic embodiment of the great Spanish nation, this kitsch architectural theme park contains scaled-down replicas of some of Spain's most notable and typical buildings (including churches, palaces, fortresses, plazas, shops and bars). I think its mini-version of Granada's wondrous Alhambra is surprisingly well-executed. The park is enjoyable for youngsters and anyone who's not had the opportunity to travel elsewhere in Spain. 🕐 *1 hr. Son Dureta,*

39. 📞 *971/73-70-75. Admission 5€ adults, 3€ children, students & seniors. Apr–Sep daily 9am–7pm, Oct–Mar daily 9am–6pm. Bus no. 29 to Av. de Andrea Doria.*

⑦ ★ kids Castell de Bellver. South of the Poble Espanyol, on a hill with towering views of the Bay of Palma and the city, this 14th-century circular castle was commissioned by King Jaume II. Obsolete as a fortress soon after its construction, it became a royal residence and then a prison. The castle, with a circular courtyard and ingenious elements, such as a sloping roof that channels rainwater into a massive cistern, is a superb example of Gothic military architecture. Inside is a rather uninteresting and label-free museum of local history and archaeology, but it's the pleasant park area, pine trees and commanding views that most people—especially families, who need a place for children to blow off steam—come for, especially at sunset. 🕐 *45 min. c/ Camilo José Cela, 17.* 📞 *971/73-06-57. Admission 2€, free children under 13. Apr–Sep daily 10am–7pm, Oct–Mar daily 10am–5pm. Bus no. 3 to Pl. Gomila (and a 15-min walk uphill).*

Badia de **Palma**

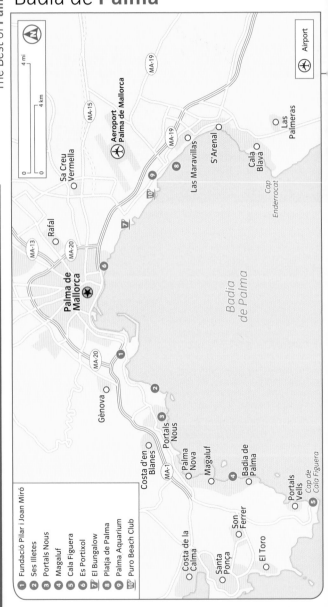

1. Fundació Pilar i Joan Miró
2. Ses Illetes
3. Portals Nous
4. Magaluf
5. Cala Figuera
6. Es Portixol
7. El Bungalow
8. Platja de Palma
9. Palma Aquarium
10. Puro Beach Club

Airport

MA-19

MA-15

Aeroport
Palma de Mallorca

Sa Creu
Vermella

Las
Palmeras

S'Arenal

Calà
Blava

Las Maravillas

Cap
Enderrocat

MA-13

Rafal

MA-20

Palma de
Mallorca

Badia
de Palma

Gènova

MA-20

Costa d'en
Blanes

MA-1

Portals
Nous

Palma
Nova

Magaluf

Badia de
Palma

Portals
Vells

Cap de
Cala Figuera

Son
Ferrer

Costa de la
Calma

Santa
Ponça

El Toro

Palma's port and wide bay transformed **Mallorca** from a Mediterranean backwater to a major European city. However, the long coastline was also crucial in another transformation—the tourism boom of the 1960s and 1970s. Besides resorts, the Bay also hides small coves, and the summer home and studio of the legendary artist, Joan Miró. START: **Taxi or bus no. 3 or 6 to Cala Major.**

1 ★★★ **Fundació Pilar i Joan Miró.** The Catalan surrealist painter and sculptor Joan Miró, who created his own colourful artistic language of erotically charged blips and squiggles, moved to Mallorca in 1956 and remained there until his death in 1983. The noted Spanish architect, Rafael Moneo, designed the angular main museum, which displays a rotating selection of some 5,000 Miró works in the collection. The studio (*El Taller*) is exactly as the artist left it, with easels, brushes, half-finished canvases and stacked paintings crowding the light-filled space. ⏱ *2 hr. c/ Joan de Saridakis, 29, Cala Major.* ☎ *971/ 70-14-20. miro.palmademallorca.es. Admission 6€ adults, 3€ students & seniors, free admission children under 16. Free admission Sat.*

The untouched studio of Surrealist painter Joan Miró.

Bay of Palma Beaches

The famed beaches that fan out around the Bay of Palma— some 30km (19 miles) of sand—are the most popular in the Balearics, a tourist magnet that drove the development of Mallorca in the 1970s into a major Mediterranean destination and created demand for the concrete masses of high-rise hotels and condos along the coast. They are also responsible for the island's overheated package-holiday and party reputation. That said, there are certainly some fine, pretty beaches and clear swimming waters amid the resorts, as long as you are willing to brave the crowds, noise and, shall we say, relaxed holiday attitudes. To the west of Palma, the beaches tend to be large coves and immaculate white sands, frequented largely by British holidaymakers; to the east, the longer stretches of sands attract predominantly German package tourists.

Yacht, Portals Nous.

Mid-May–mid-Sep Tues–Sat 10am–7pm, Sun 10am–3pm, winter, Tues–Sat 10am–6pm. Bus 3 or 46.

13km (8 miles) southwest of Palma on Autovia de Poniente/MA-1; or take a taxi or bus no. 3.

② ★ **Ses Illetes.** A jumble of residences and hotels clustered around a couple of coves with beaches, including **Platja Cala Comtessa**, one of the better beaches within easy reach of Palma. ⏲ *2 hr.*

4km (2½ miles) southwest of Ses Illetes on MA-1. Bus no. 3.

③ **Portals Nous.** One of the ritziest enclaves west of Palma, this area overflows with mansions, spacious flats and pricey restaurants overlooking the marina, where you'll find some of the Mediterranean's flashiest mega-yachts and summering international elite. ⏲ *1½ hr.*

9km (6 miles) southwest of Portals Nous on MA-1. Bus no. 3.

④ **Magaluf.** Long the haunt of package-holidaying British families

and rowdy bar-hopping sun-worshippers, Magaluf is one of the tackiest and most overbuilt resort areas on the coast. Although the government has tried to clean it up, it's still an unsightly mess of concrete and British-style pubs and fish 'n' chip shops. That said, the main beaches between Magaluf and Palmanova are fine stretches of white sand, and it's easy to see how they manage to attract such hordes year after year. ⏲ *1 hr.*

12km (7 miles) south of Magaluf on Ctra. de Cala Figuera. Bus no. 3.

⑤ **Cala Figuera.** Past the villas and restaurants of Portals Vells, the extreme southwestern tip of the island is marked by rocky cliffs, clear blue waters, a disused military zone and a lighthouse that's marked as private property. Although officially off-limits, plenty of people seem keen to disregard the postings and walk the 1½ km (1 mile) through the woods to see it. ⏲ *30 min.*

Walk or take a taxi along MA-19 east of Palma for 3km (2 miles) or bus no. 15.

⑥ ★ kids **Es Portixol.** The Passeig Marítim (and its cycling and walking paths) leads a couple of kilometres east of the centre of Palma and past an artificial beach, **Platja de Ca'n Pere Antoni,** to this fishing village. Its name means 'the little port', and it has a small bay and beach. Relatively relaxed, popular with Mallorcan families and touted as an example of smart beach development and neighbourhood renovation, it's home to a very sophisticated hotel, Portixol (see p 75), and a growing number of seaside restaurants here and in Es Molinar and Ciutat Jardí nearby. ⏲ *1 hr.*

Platja de Palma.

7 ★ **kids** **El Bungalow.** This fashionable seafood restaurant sports a much-coveted terrace overlooking the beach; relax with a lunch of *dorada a la sal* (sea bass cooked in salt) and a brisk white wine from Mallorca. Children are likely to be pacified by the water views. *c/ d'Esculls, 2, Ciutat Jardí.* ☎ *971/26-27-38. $$.*

8km (5 miles) southeast of Palma along MA-19. Bus no. 25.

8 ★ **kids** **Platja de Palma.** The vast package-holiday centre and coastal partying zone east of Palma focuses on one of the island's longest stretches of sand (nearly 5km (3 miles)). Grouped together as the 'Beach of Palma' are contiguous and largely indistinguishable resort areas. **Ca'n Pastilla** is popular with windsurfers, small **Cala Estancia** draws families and **S'Arenal** (along with **Sometimes** and **Ses Maravelles**) are the stomping grounds of roasting, scantily clad bodies involved in an annual ritual of binge drinking and pick-up games. ⏲ *2 hr. Avda. de Bartolomeu Ruitort.*

9 ★ **kids** **Palma Aquarium.** A favourite of families dodging the tanning beach and its lively occupants, the 55 tanks here show off more than 8,000 sea creatures. ⏲ *1½ hr. See p 38,* **6**.

10 ★★ **Puro Beach Club.** This super-chic lounge club is a place to strut if you're feeling confident in your coolness and wardrobe. Have a cocktail overlooking the bay, take a yoga class in the morning, or have a leisurely lunch or dinner and then stretch out among the beautiful people at the seriously sexy waterfront pool. *Pagell, 1 (Cala Estancia).* ☎ *971/74-47-44. www.purobeach. com. $$$.*

Dining Best Bets

Fosh Food.

Best **Tapas**
★★ La Bóveda $$ *c/ Botería, 3*
(p 68)

Best **Seafood Direct from the Port**
★★ Bar Mollet $$ *c/ Contramuelle Mollet, 2 (p 66)*; and ★★ Ca'n Eduardo (Sa Llonja des Peix) $$$ *c/ Contramuelle Mollet, 4 (p 66)*

Best **Homemade-style Cucina Mallorquina**
★★ Celler Pagès $ *Felip Bauza, 2*
(p 66)

Best for **Kids**
★ Gran Café Cappuccino $$ *c/ Sant Miquel, 53 (p 55)*

Best **Food as a Religious Experience**
★★★ Simply Fosh $$$ *c/ de la Missió 7A (Hotel Convent de la Missió) (p 69)*

Best **Asian Fusion**
★ Living $$ *Cotoner, 47 (p 69)*

Best **Wine Bar Food**
★★ Lo Di Vino $ *Carmen, 19 (p 80)*; and ★★ Taverna El Burladero $$ *Concepció, 3B (p 69)*

Best **Views of Palma & the Port**
★★ BLD (Restaurant Bar Museu Es Baluard) $$ *Pl. Porta de Santa Catalina, 10 (p 66)*

Best **Participatory Cooking Show**
★★★ Fosh Food $$ *c/ Blanquerna, 6*
(p 68)

Palma Dining

Bar Bosch 1
Bar Mollet 2
BLD (Restaurant Bar Museu Es Baluard) 3
Ca'n Carlos 4
Ca'n Eduardo (Sa Llonja des Peix) 5
Celler Pagès 6
Celler Sa Premsa 7
Fábrica 23 8
Forn de Sant Joan 9
Fosh Food 10
La Bóveda 11
La Taberna del Caracol 12
Living 13
Orient Express 14
Simply Fosh 15
Taberna de la Bóveda 16
Taverna El Burladero 17

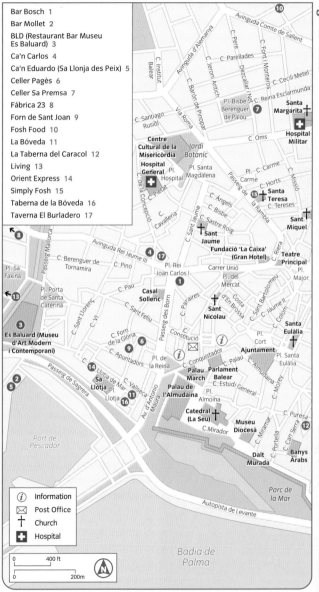

Palma Dining **A to Z**

★ kids **Bar Bosch** PLAÇA MAJOR & ENVIRONS *TAPAS* A long-time choice for locals, this simple establishment is known for its excellent grilled sandwiches called *llagostes*. The best place for lunch is on the terrace. *Pl. Rei Joan Carles I.* ☎ *971/ 72-11-31. Main course 4–12€. MC, V. Breakfast, lunch & dinner daily. Bus no. 2. Map p 65.*

★★ **Bar Mollet** PASSEIG MARÍTIM *SEAFOOD* This bustling seafood restaurant is right in the marina, just a few metres from the boats that bring in the day's catch. It's one of the best places in Palma to order market-priced fresh fish, or opt for the simple, good-value three-course lunch for just 11€. *c/ Contramuelle Mollet, 2.* ☎ *971/71-98-71. Main course 9–30€. MC, V. Lunch & dinner Mon–Sat; lunch only Sun. Closed dinner in winter. Bus no. 1. Map p 65.*

★ kids **BLD (Restaurant Bar Museu Es Baluard)** PASSEIG MARÍTIM *INTERNATIONAL/ASIAN* Although it's not considered the culinary destination it once was, BLD is still popular, not least for the

Taste freshly caught fish at Bar Mollet by the marina.

all-encompassing sea and city views from the sublime terrace. Lunch includes seafood salads and double-decker sandwiches, and dinner in the minimalist glass cube is largely Thai and other Asian-influenced dishes. *Pl. Porta de Santa Catalina, 10.* ☎ *971/90-81-99. www.bld-restaurant.com. Main course 12–19€. AE, DC, MC, V. Breakfast, lunch & dinner Tues–Sun. Bus no. 1. See also p 58. Map p 65.*

★ **Ca'n Carlos** PLAÇA MAJOR & ENVIRONS *MALLORCAN* This amiable restaurant, hidden on a small alleyway off the shopping thoroughfare of Jaume III, is a dependable place to try traditional Mallorcan dishes. Snails in a tasty broth and suckling pig are house specialities. *S'Aigua, 5 (Travesia Jaume III).* ☎ *971/71-38-69. Main course 14–21€. AE, DC, MC, V. Lunch & dinner Tues–Sat. Bus no. 2. Map p 65.*

★★ **Ca'n Eduardo (Sa Llonja des Peix)** PASSEIG MARÍTIM *SEAFOOD* Directly above the fish market, this traditional fish restaurant isn't fancy, but there are views of the marina. If you can afford it, try the seafood platter, lobster paella or *caldereta de llagosta* (lobster stew). *c/ Contramuelle Mollet, 4.* ☎ *971/71-65-74. Main course 15–35€. MC, V. Lunch & dinner Tues–Sat; lunch only Sun. Closed last week Dec & 1st 3 weeks Jan. Map p 65. Bus no. 1.*

★★ kids **Celler Pagès** SA LLOTJA *MALLORCAN* A charmingly old-school Mallorcan restaurant, this inexpensive, family-style venue has been serving first-rate hardy Mallorcan fare since 1956. Specialities include *sopes mallorquines* (hearty bread-and-vegetable stew), *croquetas* (croquettes) with seared peppers and squash stuffed with shellfish. *c/ Felip Bauza, 2.* ☎ *971/72-60-36. Main course 11–18€. MC, V. Lunch & dinner Tues–Sat; lunch only Mon. Bus no. 2. Map p 65.*

kids Celler Sa Premsa PLAÇA MAJOR & ENVIRONS *MALLORCAN* A local institution, this dining hall features traditional Mallorcan cooking. It may be touristy and noisy but it's also a classic, and everyone seems to visit here at least once. Like the cavernous old wine-cellar restaurants in Inca, it's a large tavern decorated with massive wine barrels. *Pl. del Bisbe Berenguer de Palou, 8.* ☎ *971/72-35-29. Main course 9–17€. MC, V. Lunch & dinner Mon–Sat; July–Aug, lunch & dinner Mon–Fri. Bus no. 2. Map p 65.*

★★ Fábrica 23 SANTA CATALINA *MEDITERRANEAN* This friendly bistro run by two brothers makes use of fresh fish and produce from the nearby Santa Catalina market—so much so that the menu changes every day based on what's best. That might mean smoked salmon and avocado salad for starters and grilled cod for a main. The weekday three-course meal, including wine, is a steal for just 15€, and Sunday lunch is a roast-beef fest that draws plenty of regulars. *c/ de Cotoner, 42, Santa Catalina.* ☎ *971/45-31-25. www.fabrica23.com. Main course 14–24€. AE, MC, V. Lunch & dinner*

Old school dining at Cellar Pagès.

Tues–Sat; lunch only Sun. Bus no. 2. Map p 65.

★★ Forn de Sant Joan SA LLOTJA *TAPAS/MEDITERRANEAN* A chic but unpretentious restaurant near Sa Llotja, which has intimate dining spaces on four levels. There's a long list of creative tapas and main courses of homemade pasta and fresh fish. Although this place attracts as many tourists as the unimaginative places nearby that pack them in, it's much higher quality here. *c/ Sant Joan, 4.* ☎ *971/72-84-22. www.forndesantjoan.net.*

Dining Tips

Like their mainland counterparts, Mallorcans eat dinner quite late. Many fashionable restaurants only start filling up for dinner around 10 or 11pm, even on weekdays. At smarter restaurants, your bill will include a *cubierto* (also called *servicio de mesa*) of about 1–3€. Essentially, this is the price to sit down at a table and receive your silverware, napkin and bread; the gratuity is extra, usually around 10%.

Sample Spanish and Basque tapas at the busy La Bóveda.

Main course 13–28€. AE, MC, V. Dinner daily. Bus no. 2. Map p 65.

★★★ Fosh Food PLAÇA MAJOR & ENVIRONS *HAUTE INTERNATIONAL/ MEDITERRANEAN* This innovative project—combined gourmet food shop, cooking school and chic, modern tasting-menu restaurant—is the brainchild of British chef Marc Fosh. The three-course fixed-price menu at lunch is a steal, but the best time to come is for one of the themed five-course dinners, which are also superb value at around 37€. Come for dinner, chat with the friendly English-speaking kitchen staff and you'll likely want to return for a cooking class. Reservations are a must. *c/ Blanquerna, 6.* ☎ *971/29-01-08. www.foshfood.com. Menus 15–40€. AE, DC, MC, V. Lunch & dinner Mon–Fri; dinner only Sat. Bus no. 2. Map p 65.*

★★ La Bóveda SA LLOTJA *TAPAS/ SPANISH* This restaurant is one of Palma's most enduringly popular, where queues spill out of the door every night. It's a lively place, with an extensive menu of Spanish and Basque tapas and *raciones* (larger portions). The casual interior looks like a classic Andalucian tavern, with gregarious regulars and tourists sampling tapas and knocking back carafes of wine. *c/ Botería, 3.* ☎ *971/71-48-63. www.restaurant elaboveda.com. Main course 8–28€. MC, V. Lunch & dinner Mon–Sat. Closed Feb. Bus no. 2. Map p 65.*

★★ La Taberna del Caracol OLD QUARTER *TAPAS/SPANISH* Tucked away among the warren of narrow alleyways of the old Jewish quarter, this warm and rustic tavern with impossibly high arched ceilings and wooden beams is a real crowd pleaser. It does a host of Spanish tapas very well, from *pimientos de padrón* (small fried green chilli peppers) to *boquerones fritos* (fried small white fish). *c/ Sant Alonso, 2.* ☎ *971/71-49-08. www.taberna. name. Main course 7–18€. AE, MC, V. Lunch & dinner Mon–Sat. Bus no. 2. Map p 65.*

Chic dining at Living.

★ **Living** SANTA CATALINA *ASIAN/ MEDITERRANEAN FUSION* This restaurant is one of the more chic and contemporary spots in this formerly rough neighbourhood. The menu is either a nightly tasting menu (four courses, including both a fish and meat course, for just 20.50€) or a daily three-course fixed price lunch (a steal at 11.50€). *c/ Cotoner, 47 (Santa Catalina).* ☎ *971/45-56-28. www.restaurante-living.com. Main course 7–18€. AE, MC, V. Lunch & dinner Mon–Sat. Bus no. 1. Map p 65.*

★ **kids Orient Express** SA LLOTJA *CREPES* This unusual restaurant is based on a train theme and it looks like a two-level *vagón comedor* (train dining car) with luggage racks and old train posters. The house speciality is crêpes, and there are about eight different kinds on the menu, both savoury and sweet, as well as more substantial dishes, such as beef stroganoff with mushrooms. *c/ de Sa Llotja, 6.* ☎ *971/71-11-83. www.todoesp.es. Main course 7–18€. AE, MC, V. Lunch & dinner Mon–Fri; dinner only Sat. Bus no. 1. Map p 65.*

★★★ **Simply Fosh** PLAÇA MAJOR & ENVIRONS *HAUTE INTERNATIONAL* The English chef Marc Fosh (see also Fosh Food, p 68) has now taken over this sleek restaurant tucked inside the equally stylish hotel Convent de la Missió (p 73). It's taken a huge leap forward with Fosh's inventively stripped-down, more casual menu, featuring fresh local market ingredients and accessible prices. *c/ de la Missió 7A, Hotel Convent de la Missió.* ☎ *971/22-17-47. Main course 15–28€. AE, DC, MC, V. Lunch & dinner Mon–Sat; July–Aug, lunch & dinner Mon–Fri. Bus no. 2. Map p 65.*

★★ **Taberna de la Bóveda** SA LLOTJA *TAPAS/SPANISH* A sister

Surtido de setas, Taverna El Burladero.

restaurant to La Bóveda (p 68) just a couple of streets away, this incarnation serves very similar tapas, but it has one advantage: a privileged, sunny terrace on Palma's waterfront promenade. The *pá amb oli* (rustic bread rubbed with tomatoes and olive oil and topped with green olives) is a meal in itself. *Pg. de Sagrera, 3.* ☎ *971/72-00-26. www. tabernadelaboveda.com. Main course 8–18€. MC, V. Lunch & dinner Mon–Sat. Bus no. 1. Map p 65.*

★★ **Taverna El Burladero** PLAÇA MAJOR & ENVIRONS *TAPAS/ WINE BAR* This good-looking, contemporary Spanish wine bar and restaurant would be a highlight if only for its extraordinary wine list and trendy library feel, but it does quality traditional tapas as well. The house speciality is oxtail, and I'm especially partial to the *surtido de setas* (a sumptuous plate of sautéed mixed mushrooms). *c/ Concepció, 3B.* ☎ *971/12-34-59. www.taberna elburladero.com. Main course 11–15€. AE, MC, V. Lunch & dinner Mon–Sat. Bus no. 2. Map p 65.*

Lodging Best Bets

Best **Aristocratic Palace Masquerading as a Hotel**
★★★ Palacio Ca Sa Galesa $$$$ c/ Mirador, 8 (see p 74); and ★★★ Dalt Murada $$$ c/ Almudaina 6A (see p 72)

Best **Seafront Hotel**
★★ Hotel Azul Playa $$$ Isla de rodes, 24 (see p 72); and Portixol Hotel & Restaurante $$$ c/ Sirena 27 (see p 75)

Best **Business Hotel**
★ AC Ciutat de Palma $$ Pl. Puente, 3 (see p 72)

Best **Value Upscale Hotel**
★★★ Santa Clara Urban Hotel & Spa $$$ c/ Sant Alonso, 16 (see p 75)

Best **On a Budget**
★ Hostal Brondo $ c/ C'an Brondo, 1 (see p 72)

Best **Interior Courtyard**
★ Missió de Sant Miquel $$$ Can Maçanet, 1a (see p 74); and ★★ Palau Sa Font $$$ c/ dels Apuntadors, 8 (see p 74)

Best **Chill-out Hotel**
★★ Portixol Hotel & Restaurante $$$ c/ Sirena 27 (see p 75)

Best **Swimming Pool**
★★★ Palacio Ca Sa Galesa $$$$ c/ Mirador, 8 (see p 74); and ★★ Portixol Hotel & Restaurante $$$ c/ Sirena 27 (see p 75)

Best **For Families**
★★★ Portixol Hotel & Restaurante $$$ c/ Sirena 27 (see p 75)

Best **Rooftop Deck**
★★ Hotel Tres $$$ c/ dels Apuntadors 3 (see p 74); and ★★★ Palacio Ca Sa Galesa $$$$ c/ Mirador, 8 (see p 74)

Best **Spa Facilities**
★★★ Santa Clara Urban Hotel & Spa $$$ c/ Sant Alonso, 16 (see p 75)

Best **Hotel Restaurant**
★ Hotel Convent de la Missió $$$$ c/ de la Missió, 7a (see p 73)

Friendliest Service
★★ Palau Sa Font $$$ c/ dels Apuntadors 8 (see p 74); and ★★★ Dalt Murada $$$ c/ Almudaina 6A (see p 72)

Best **Cheap Old World Charm**
★ Hotel Born $ c/ Sant Jaume, 3 (see p 73)

The friendly Dalt Murada.

Palma Lodging

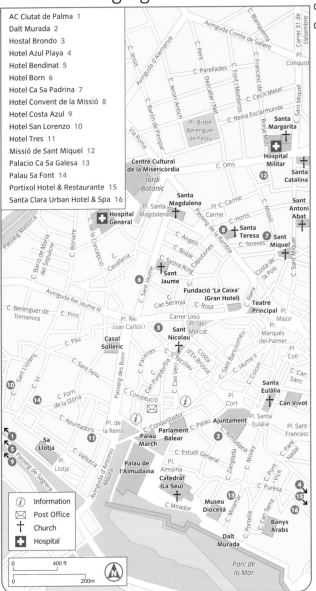

Palma Lodging **A to Z**

17th-century elegance at Dalt Murada.

★ **AC Ciutat de Palma** PASSEIG MARÍTIM   Near the waterfront, this contemporary business traveller's hotel is the best option for anyone looking for good service and modern amenities (including a free minibar), and wanting to avoid the warren of Old Palma streets. Rooms are sleek with a white-and-wenge wood décor and plasma TVs, and are comparatively good value. *Pl. Puente, 3.* ☎ *971/22-23-00. www.ac-hotels.com. 65 units. Doubles 120–169€ w/breakfast. AE, DC, MC, V. Bus no. 1. Map p 71.*

★★★ **Dalt Murada** OLD QUARTER   This elegant boutique hotel in a 17th-century mansion on a quiet alleyway is brimming with old-fashioned charm, spectacular antiques and artwork. Rooms have high ceilings and are incredibly spacious and elegant. In warm months, breakfast is served on the interior patio, surrounded by lemon trees. The massive top-floor suite, with a private terrace and views of the cathedral, is one of the most desirable rooms in the city (and relatively affordable). *c/ Almudaina 6A.* ☎ *971/42-53-00. www.daltmurada.com. 8 units. Doubles 159–199€ w/breakfast. AE, DC, MC, V. Bus no. 2. Map p 71.*

Hostal Brondo PLAÇA MAJOR & ENVIRONS   If you can put up with street noise, small rooms and perhaps sharing a bathroom, this English-owned place is one of the least expensive options in downtown Palma. The simply decorated rooms renovated in the old house are a step up from hostels. However, there's no air-conditioning, and some rooms (like the one in the basement) are to be avoided. Room 3, on the other hand, is quite likeable. *c/ C'an Brondo, 1.* ☎ *971/71-90-43. www.hostalbrondo.com. 20 units. Doubles 55–70€. AE, DC, MC, V. Bus no. 2. Map p 71.*

★★ **Hotel Azul Playa** CIUTAT JARDÍ   Facing the seafront and a short bus ride or healthy walk to the historic quarter, this modern, impeccably clean boutique hotel, painted a bold blue, is the perfect choice (and excellent value) for those who need to see and smell the surf. Rooms are sunny, smart and bright; if you can, opt for a sea view and terrace. *Isla de Rodes, 24, Ciutat Jardí.* ☎ *971/91-90-20. www.hotelazulplaya.com. 17 units. Doubles 90–198€ w/breakfast. AE, DC, MC, V. Bus no. 15. Map p 71.*

★★ **Hotel Bendinat** BADIA DE PALMA (PORTALS NOUS)   On a quiet cove with its own rocky beach (and just paces from a sandy one), this good value hotel is one of the best options in a Bay of Palma resort. It has small bungalows set amid gardens and a main Mediterranean-style villa. The updated 1950s' hotel, with a small pool overlooking the sea, has a low-key charm noticeably absent at most resort hotels. *c/ Andres Ferret Sobral, 1, Bendinat/ Portals Nous.* ☎ *971/67-57-25. www.hotelbendinat.es. 52 units. Doubles 98–154€. AE, DC, MC, V. Map p 71.*

★ **Hotel Born** PLAÇA MAJOR & ENVIRONS   This small old hotel, in a 16th-century palace, has plenty of charm and a central location. Rooms have high ceilings but aren't nearly as grand as the courtyard and sweeping spiral staircase. In fact, they're smallish and a bit plain, but having breakfast under the palm trees on a sunny morning compensates. Rooms on Floor 1 and facing the street can be uncomfortably noisy. *c/ Sant Jaume, 3.* ☎ *971/71-29-42. www.hotelborn.com. 20 units. Doubles 90–130€ w/breakfast. AE, DC, MC, V. Bus no. 2. Map p 71.*

Hotel Ca Sa Padrina PLAÇA MAJOR & ENVIRONS   Owned by Dalt Murada (p 72), this is a similar concept: a converted old house with antiques and paintings, only much less luxurious and spacious. This operates more like a guest-house, with no staff on hand; you communicate by closed-circuit camera, which can seem odd. Rooms are clean but several are small and there is no elevator or breakfast service. *c/ Tereses, 2.* ☎ *971/42-53-00. www.hotelcasapadrina.com. 15 units. Doubles 105€. AE, DC, MC, V. Bus no. 2. Map p 71.*

★ **Hotel Convent de la Missió** PLAÇA MAJOR & ENVIRONS   A self-consciously chic hotel located in a former 17th-century convent, this minimalist design hotel is pricey and exclusive, but the streets that surround it are rather dismal. Rooms are spacious, with gauzy curtains, stone arches, ceiling beams and modern bathrooms. Whether you find it fashionable or pretentious, the new addition of British chef Marc Fosh at the helm of the restaurant, Simply Fosh (p 69), shows that the owners are reaching beyond mere gloss. *c/ de la Missió, 7a.* ☎ *971/22-73-47. www.convent delamissio.com. 20 units. Doubles 230€. AE, DC, MC, V. Bus no. 2. Map p 71.*

★ **Hotel Costa Azul** PASSEIG MARÍTIM   With views of the Palma harbour and bay, as well as the cathedral, this large hotel, a long-time presence in Palma, is a straightforward choice: well-located and comfortable, with a sunny terrace and covered pool, and not bad on the wallet. Most rooms have sea views. *Avda. Gabriel Roca, 7.* ☎ *971/ 73-19-40. www.esperanza hoteles.com. 126 units. Doubles 94–131€ w/breakfast. Bus no. 1. AE, DC, MC, V. Map p 71.*

★ **Hotel San Lorenzo** SA LLOTJA   With just nine rooms in a 17th-century townhouse, this intimate place has a charming pool garden and

The rooftop pool at Hotel Tres.

Plunge pool at boutique hotel, Palau Sa Font.

terrace, with fetching views of the cathedral. However, the inn offers few services and little attention from staff. Rooms are cosy—with nice touches such as Mallorcan tiles in the bathrooms—but not luxurious. All are different, and so have a look online. The romantic junior suites, a hefty step up in price, have their own terraces and fireplaces. *c/ San Lorenzo, 14.* ☎ *971/72-82-00. www.hotelsanlorenzo.com. 9 units. Doubles 150–190€. AE, DC, MC, V. Bus no. 1. Map p 71.*

★★ **Hotel Tres** SA LLOTJA Marrying a 16th-century palace to a modern structure in the heart of Palma's restaurant and nightlife district, urbane Tres feels like a boutique hotel with the amenities of a larger property. The rooftop terrace, with a plunge pool, sundeck and superb views of La Seu, is a major selling point. Rooms are minimalist, with large bold photographs of the human body over the beds and cowhide benches. My favourites are the doubles that flow out onto a private terrace. *c/ dels*

Apuntadors 3. ☎ *971/71-73-33. www.hoteltres.com. 41 units. Doubles 235–255€ w/breakfast. AE, DC, MC, V. Bus no. 2. Map p 71.*

★★ **Missió de Sant Miquel** PLAÇA MAJOR & ENVIRONS This fairly new hotel is built around an impressive courtyard—a surprise to discover, since the hotel is hidden off a hard-to-find street not far from Plaça Major. Rooms are contemporary and sophisticated, but not self-conscious. The attractive onsite restaurant—where breakfast is served—is an unexpected bonus. *Can Maçanet, 1a.* ☎ *971 21-48-48. www.urbanrustichotels.com. 32 units. Doubles 180–267€ w/breakfast. AE, DC, MC, V. Bus no. 2. Map p 71.*

★★★ **Palacio Ca Sa Galesa** OLD QUARTER This sumptuous 15th-century mansion in the shadow of the cathedral is Palma's most distinguished hotel—although it seems more like staying at a royal palace. It's exquisitely decorated, with original art by Miró, Calder and Tàpies on the walls, luxurious original hardwood floors, dazzling antiques and leaded stained glass. To relax, there's a handsome reading salon, a quiet ivy-covered patio, an underground Roman-bath-style pool and sauna, and an expansive rooftop deck with views of the bay and cathedral. *c/ Mirador, 8.* ☎ *971/71-54-00. www.palaciocasagalesa.com. 12 units. Doubles 348€ w/breakfast. AE, DC, MC, V. Bus no. 2. Map p 71.*

★★ **Palau Sa Font** SA LLOTJA A cheery boutique hotel, carved out of a 16th-century manor house that's just a few streets from the epicentre of Palma's trendiest restaurant district, but removed enough to be quiet and very private. Rooms are modern and just short of austere, with just a few bursts of colour—although each is distin-guished by original art on the door. The rooftop plunge pool and quiet tower, with views over the city, are perfect places to unwind. Room 15 is the best double, while the junior suite has its own sunny terrace. *c/ dels Apuntadors 8.* ☎ *971/71-22-77. www.palausafont.com. 19 units. Doubles 155–203€ w/breakfast. AE, DC, MC, V. Bus no. 1. Map p 71.*

★★ kids **Portixol Hotel & Res-taurante** PORTIXOL   East of Palma along the waterfront, this laid-back place is a perfect solution for guests not exploring more of Mallorca. Built in 1956, the place has a Nordic and Mediterranean vibe and was one of the first design hotels in Palma. It gets plenty of repeat visitors who come to enjoy the marina and sea views and ven-ture into town occasionally. The restaurant, spa and fantastic old-school pool are enough to keep you from wandering. You can upgrade

to a room with a view of the Medi-terranean. *c/ Sirena 27.* ☎ *971/27-18-00. www.portixol.com. 24 units. Doubles 200–310€ w/breakfast. AE, DC, MC, V. Bus no. 15. Map p 71.*

★★★ **Santa Clara Urban Hotel & Spa** OLD QUARTER   This stylish mix of old and new is a welcome addition to the Palma hotel scene in the old Jewish quarter. One of Pal-ma's newest hotels (and currently also one of the best value), it is design-conscious, with exposed stone walls, high wood-beamed ceil-ings and bold modern furnishings in the attractive and spacious rooms. Most welcome is the small spa, with a sauna, Jacuzzi and full comple-ment of treatments and massages, as is the rooftop deck with views over the city. *c/ Sant Alonso, 16.* ☎ *971/72-92-31. www.santaclara hotel.es. 16 units. Doubles 160–180€ w/breakfast. AE, DC, MC, V. Bus no. 2. Map p 71.*

The expansive rooftop deck of Palacio Ca Sa Galesa.

Shopping Best Bets

Gourmet delights at Son Vivot.

Best **Gourmet Food Shop**
★★★ Son Vivot, *Pl. Porta Pintada, 1* (see p 80)

Best **Leather Goods**
★★ Loewe, *Avda. Jaume III, 1* (see p 78)

Best **Spot for** *Sobressada*
★★★ Colmado Santo Domingo, *c/ Santo Domingo, 1* (see p 80)

Best **Wacky Bookstore**
★★ El Baxar del Libro, *c/ Sant Crist, 4* (see p 78)

Best **Island Shoes**
★ Alpargateria La Concepció, *c/ Concepció 17 (bajos)* (see p 81); and ★★ Camper, *c/ Sant Miquel, 17* (see p 81)

Best **Food Market**
★★★ Mercat de l'Olivar, *Pl. Olivar, s/n* (see p 55)

Best **Pastries &** *Ensaïmades*
★★★ Forn des Teatre, *Pl. de Weyler, 9* (see p 80)

Best **Wine Shop**
★★★ Lo Di Vino, *Carmen, 19* (see p 80); and ★★★ Son Vivot, *Pl. Porta Pintada, 1* (see p 80)

Best **Chocolates**
★★ Confiteria Frasquet, *c/ Orfila 4* (see p 80)

Best **Sexy Underwear**
★★ Intimissimi, *Avda. Jaume III, 3* (see p 78)

Best **Blown Glass**
★★ Vidreres Gordiola, *c/ de la Victoria, 2* (see p 78)

Palma Shopping

Alpargateria La Concepció 1	La Casa del Olivo 14
Camper 2	La Favorita 15
Chocolat Factory 3	Lo Di Vino 16
Colmado Santo Domingo 4	Loewe 17
Confiteria Frasquet 5	Majórica 18
Custo Barcelona 6	Mallorca Gold 19
El Baxar del Libro 7	Modanostra 20
Farrutx 8	Passy 21
Fet a Mà 9	Persepolis 22
Forn des Teatre 10	Son Vivot 23
Forn Fondo 11	Vidreres Gordiola 24
Intimissimi 12	Zara 25
Jaime Mascaró 13	

(i) Information
✉ Post Office
🚋 Train Station
✝ Church
✚ Hospital

0   400 ft
0   200m

Palma Shopping **A to Z**

Antiques & Home Goods

★ Fet a Mà SANT MIQUEL A craft shop featuring artisan objects that are all handmade (the meaning of the shop's name), including glass, ceramics, pottery and olive-wood bowls. *c/ Sant Miquel 52.* ☎ *971/71-10-95. AE, DC, MC, V. Bus no. 2. Map p 77.*

★ La Casa del Olivo PASSEIG D'ES BORN/JAUME III Olive wood is very traditional in Mallorca, and at this olive-carvers' workshop in an alley off carrer Jaume II, you can pick up some beautifully crafted items, such as salad bowls. *c/ Pescateria Vella, 4.* ☎ *971/72-70-25. MC, V. Bus no. 2. Map p 77.*

★ Persepolis PASSEIG D'ES BORN/ JAUME III This handsome antiques shop has fine pieces, including religious art, Old Master paintings, and silver and enamel. *Avda. Jaume III, 23.* ☎ *971/72-45-39. www.persepolis-antiques.com. AE, DC, MC, V. Bus no. 2. Map p 77.*

★★ Vidreres Gordiola OLD QUARTER A family-owned glass-making shop that's been trading since 1719, with a selection of bowls,

You could spend hours at El Baxar del Libro.

glasses, vases and art glass, including chandeliers. There's also a branch at Avda. Jaume II (☎ 971/71-55-18) and a factory-museum outside Palma (Ctra. Palma~Manacor Km 19; ☎ 971/66-50-46). *c/ de la Victoria, 2.* ☎ *971/71-15-41. www.gordiola.com. AE, DC, MC, V. Bus no. 2. Map p 77.*

Bookstores

★ El Baxar del Libro OLD QUARTER This bookshop resembles a mad professor's office. The jumble of books and maps stacked haphazardly in every corner makes it a bit of a maze, but book lovers will be in heaven, sifting through old and rare books, documents and posters. *c/ Sant Crist, 4.* ☎ *971/71-11-55. No credit cards. Bus no. 2. Map p 77.*

Fashion & Clothing

★ Custo Barcelona PASSEIG D'ES BORN/JAUME III Trendy types love the wildly colourful and psychedelic t-shirts and skirts, as well as whimsical dresses and cool accessories from this shop that's become a global phenomenon. *Avda. Jaume III, 13.* ☎ *971/71-46-96. www.custo-barcelona.com. AE, MC, V. Bus no. 2. Map p 77.*

★★ Intimissimi PASSEIG D'ES BORN/JAUME III If you're in Palma for your honeymoon or a romantic getaway, this is the place for ultra-sexy women's lingerie and men's fashionable boxers from this Italian chain. *Avda. Jaume III, 3.* ☎ *971/71-92-16. www.intimissimi.com. AE, MC, V. Bus no. 2. Map p 77.*

★★ Loewe PASSEIG D'ES BORN/ JAUME III One of Spain's most elite purveyors of leather goods and fashion, Loewe (pronounced 'loh-ebby' in Spain) isn't cheap but is high quality.

Shopping Zones & Mallorcan Specialities

Palma's main shopping enclaves are well defined. Passeig d'es Born joins the arcaded Avinguda Jaume III, and both are lined with smart boutiques. The long, pedestrianised **carrer Sant Miquel**, leading north of the **Plaça Major,** is Palma's most popular retail thoroughfare. Mallorca is known for its shoes and leather goods, glassmaking, artificial pearls and indigenous pastries (everyone leaving Palma seems to have a large bakery box taking fluffy *ensaïmades* (p 23) back home).

Avda. Jaume III, 1. ☎ *971/71-52-75. AE, DC, MC, V. Bus no. 2. Map p 77.*

★★ **Modanostra** OLD QUARTER For unique women's fashions, this cool shop—where the owner sits with her sewing machine—has very pretty handmade skirts with bold prints and designs. If you have a few days, she can even custom-make items. *c/ Pont i Vic, 8.* ☎ *971/ 22-74-38. AE, MC, V. Bus no. 2. Map p 77.*

Zara PASSEIG D'ES BORN/JAUME III This Spanish mega-chain of clothing (and now home-furnishing) shop took off from Galicia. It stocks inexpensive, trendy items for young men, women and children. *Passeig d'es Born.* ☎ *971/71-98-28. AE,DC, MC, V. Bus no. 2. Map p 77.*

Food & Wine
★ **Chocolat Factory** PASSEIG D'ES BORN/JAUME III This colourful chocolate shop, part of a Barcelona-based chain, smells and looks enticing. The girls behind the counter wear aprons that say 'I give pleasure', which is one

Chocolat Factory.

Palma's Historic Shops

At least three dozen shops in Palma have been around, in their original incarnations, for more than a century—and several have been in business even longer. **Confiteria Frasquet,** a chocolate shop, opened its doors in 1697, and the bakery **Ca'n Miquel** (Also known as Forn Sa Pelleteria) (c/ de Sa Pelleteria, 8; ☎ 971/71-57-11) has existed, incredibly, since 1565. The popular café and 'milk bar' **Ca'n Joan de S'Aigó** has been serving hot chocolate since 1700 and the family-owned glassmaker, **Vidreres Gordiola,** first started blowing glass in 1719.

way to think about chocolate. *Pl. d'es Mercat, 9.* ☎ *971/22-94-93. www. chocolatfactory.com. AE, DC, MC, V. Bus no. 2. Map p 77.*

★★★ **Colmado Santo Domingo** SANT MIQUEL   A Palma institution, this atmospheric shop overflows with *sobressada* (raw pork sausage) and other meats hanging in thick bunches from the ceiling and walls. *c/ Santo Domingo, 1.* ☎ *971/71-48-87. www.colmadosantodomingo. com. MC, V. Bus no. 2. Map p 77.*

★★ **Confiteria Frasquet** PASSEIG D'ES BORN/JAUME III   A traditional Palma chocolate shop, which has been serving up sweets, such as *turrónes* (almond nougat) since 1697. The dark chocolate creations are to die for. *c/ Orfila 4.* ☎ *971/72-13-54. MC, V. Bus no. 2. Map p 77.*

★★★ **Forn des Teatre** PASSEIG D'ES BORN/JAUME III   Subject of many a postcard, this Modernista landmark produces what many argue is the island's best *ensaïmades* (a matter of intense debate). Apparently, King Juan Carlos buys his here. *Pl. de Weyler, 9.* ☎ *971/71-52-54. AE, DC, MC, V. Bus no. 2. Map p 77.*

★★★ **Forn Fondo** PASSEIG D'ES BORN/JAUME III   Another Palma classic since 1745, this bakery and confectionery has an attractive

Modernista shopfront and a clientele of regulars who come for the amazing cakes and pies, *ensaïmades*, as well as savoury delectables such as *empanadas* (stuffed meat pies), raviolis, quiches and pasta salads. *c/ Unió, 15.* ☎ *971/71-16-34. AE, DC, MC, V. Bus no. 2. Map p 77.*

★★★ **La Favorita** SANT MIQUEL This charming gourmet shop calls itself a *mantequería y charcutería* (roughly a dispenser of dairy items and charcuterie). On its green shelves are all kinds of *fuet* (a Catalan sausage), *sobressada* and unusual cheeses. *c/ Sant Miquel, 38A.* ☎ *971/71-37-40. MC, V. Bus no. 2. Map p 77.*

★★★ **Lo Di Vino** SANT MIQUEL This addictive, homely place is primarily a wine bar, although it's also one of the city's best wine shops. If you come to buy a bottle, I defy you not to do a tasting. There's a country kitchen and library room, ideal for lingering and learning about wine. It has a good Spanish selection and a knowledgeable owner, Juanjo. *c/ Carmen, 19.* ☎ *971/72-62-56. www.lodivino.com. AE, DC, MC, V. Bus no. 2. Map p 77.*

★★★ **Son Vivot** SANT MIQUEL Stuffed with *sobressada*, olive oil and hundreds of other local gourmet food products (several of which you can taste), as well as an excellent selection of Mallorcan and Spanish wines (including several in gift boxes), this fantastic shop looks much older than it is. *Pl. Porta Pintada, 1.* ☎ *971/72-07-48. www.son-vivot.com. AE, DC, MC, V. Bus no. 2. Map p 77.*

Jewellery

Majórica PASSEIG D'ES BORN/ JAUME III The largest (and generally most expensive) of Mallorca's artificial pearl manufacturers, with a large selection of colours and styles. There's another shop in Palma at Plaça Mercat, 9. *Avda. Jaume III, 11.* ☎ *971/72-52-68. AE, DC, MC, V. Bus no. 2. Map p 77.*

★ Mallorca Gold OLD QUARTER A friendly, traditional jewellery shop just across from Santa Eulàlia church, with a good selection of fashionable necklaces, bracelets and earrings, including stylish designs of locally made artificial pearls. *Pl. de Santa Eulàlia, s/n.* ☎ *971/13-80-34. MC, V. Bus no. 2. Map p 77.*

Shoes

★ Alpargateria La Concepció OLD QUARTER This shoe shop has been around for more than 60 years and specialises in *alpargatas* (rope-soled espadrilles), which are the classic summer shoe in the Balearic Islands. You can also buy *abarcas*, which feature a patch of leather over the toes and a strap around the ankle: these Menorcan peasant shoes have become fashionable across Spanish society. *c/ Concepció, 17 (bajos).* ☎ *971/71-07-09. MC, V. Bus no. 2. Map p 77.*

★★ Camper SANT MIQUEL These are the uniquely funky shoes that put casual Mallorcan shoes on hipsters across Spain, Europe and North America. The shops are as whimsically designed as the shoes, for men,

women, boys and girls. There are four shops in Palma. *c/ Sant Miquel, 17.* ☎ *971/22-85-88. AE, MC, V. Bus no. 2. Map p 77.*

★★ Farrutx PASSEIG D'ES BORN/ JAUME III Women's and men's sandals, shoes and clothing, can be found at this old Mallorcan manufacturer. For women, there are espadrilles, ballerina slippers and some serious *Sex & the City*-style pumps, as well as sleek leather jackets. *Passeig d'es Born, 16.* ☎ *971/71-53-08. AE, MC, V. Bus no. 2. Map p 77.*

★★ Jaime Mascaró PASSEIG D'ES BORN/JAUME III Both classic and modern shoes for women are produced by Jaime and Ursula Mascaró, a family-owned business in Menorca since 1918. Lindsay Lohan and Claudia Schiffer are among the celebs spotted here. *Avda. Jaume III.* ☎ *971/72-98-42. AE, DEC, MC, V. Bus no. 2. Map p 77.*

★ Passy PASSEIG D'ES BORN/ JAUME III A shoe shop with a fine selection of women's stylish shoes, boots and handbags—I've bought my wife several items here and each has been a hit. *Avda. Jaume III, 6.* ☎ *971/71-33-38. MC, V. Bus no. 2. Map p 77.*

Colourfully dressed mannequin in Mallorca Gold.

Nightlife & Performing Arts
Best Bets

Best **Theatre Space**
★★★ Teatre Principal, *Pl. Weyler, 16 (see p 86)*

Best **Live Jazz Club**
★★ Jazz Voyeur Club, *c/ dels Apuntadors, 5 (see p 86)*

Best **Timeless Bar**
★★ Café La Lonja, *c/ de Llotja de Mar, 2 (see p 84)*

Best **Recording Studio-cum-Rock Bar**
★ Exit Rock Bar, *c/ Sant Magi, 60 (see p 85)*

Best **DJ & Music**
★★★ Garito Café, *Dársena de Ca'n Barbarà, s/n (see p 85)*

Best **Gay Scene**
★ Black Cat, *Avda. Joan Miró, 75 (see p 85)*

Best **Film Set Cocktail Lounge**
★★ Abaco, *c/ Sant Joan, 1 (see p 84)*

Best **Place to See Beautiful People in Their Natural Habitat**
★ Puro Hotel Lounge, *c/ Monte Negro 12 (see p 85)*; and ★★ Puro Beach Club, *Pagell, 1 Cala Estancia (see p 63)*; and ★★ King Kamehameha, *Pg. Maritim, 29 (see p 85)*

Most **Seductive Bar**
★★ Idem Café, *Sant Magi 15*

Mural at Exit Rock Bar.

Palma Nightlife & Performing Arts

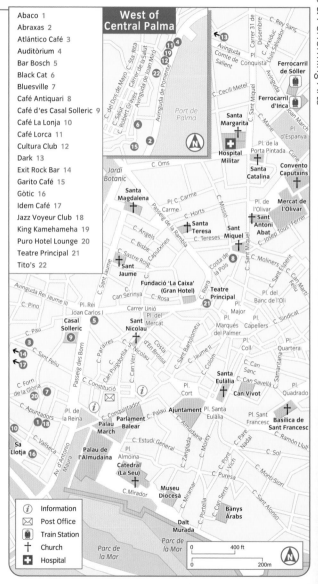

Abaco 1
Abraxas 2
Atlántico Café 3
Auditòrium 4
Bar Bosch 5
Black Cat 6
Bluesville 7
Café Antiquari 8
Café d'es Casal Solleric 9
Café La Lonja 10
Café Lorca 11
Cultura Club 12
Dark 13
Exit Rock Bar 14
Garito Café 15
Gòtic 16
Idem Café 17
Jazz Voyeur Club 18
King Kamehameha 19
Puro Hotel Lounge 20
Teatre Principal 21
Tito's 22

West of Central Palma

Port de Palma

Information
Post Office
Train Station
Church
Hospital

0 — 400 ft
0 — 200m

Palma Nightlife & Performing Arts **A to Z**

Bars, Pubs & Cocktail Lounges

★★ Abaco SA LLOTJA   A wildly Baroque cocktail lounge in the courtyard of a historic manor house, stuffed with bowls of fruit, fresh flowers and dripping candelabra, Abaco looks like the sybaritic set for a Peter Greenaway film. You have to see the place, but a cocktail will set you back 16€ and so I wouldn't plan to spend your whole evening here. The outdoor patio is almost more hip than the main room. *c/ Sant Joan, 1.* ☎ *971/71-49-39. Bus no. 1. Map p 83.*

Atlántico Café SA LLOTJA   This intimate bar is flooded with memorabilia and graffiti on the walls and a soundtrack of classic rock. *c/ Sant Feliu, 12.* ☎ *619/10-87-08. Bus no. 1. Map p 83.*

★ Bar Bosch PLAÇA MAJOR & ENVIRONS   An enduringly popular tapas joint, the outdoor terrace café is a classic place to start the evening with a couple of beers and a *lla-gosta* (grilled sandwich). *Pl. Rei Joan Carles I.* ☎ *971/72-11-31. Bus no. 2. Map p 83.*

★ Café Antiquari SANT MIQUEL   On a side street off carrer Sant Miquel, this laid-back, atmospheric bar is quite new but has the patina of age, with antiques on the walls and hanging from the rafters. A good stop early in the evening or later on; if the two salons or downstairs room get too smoky, head for one of the tables spilling out onto the alleyway. *c/ Arabi, 5.* ☎ *971/71-96-87. www.cafe-antiquari.com. Bus no. 2. Map p 83.*

Café d'es Casal Solleric PASSEIG D'ES BORN   If you're looking for a place to meet up with friends, this agreeable bar, which is ideal for people-watching, fills the bill. It's adjacent to the wonderful courtyard of Casal Solleric (p 53, ❸), the art space carved out of an attractive old mansion. *Pg. des Born d'Es Molinar 27.* ☎ *971/72-61-22. Bus no. 2. Map p 83.*

★★ Café La Lonja SA LLOTJA   This old-fashioned and popular café has a marble-topped bar, turnstile door and old mirrors; the perfect spot for a caipirinha or *pomada* (gin

Laid-back Café Antiquari.

with lemonade). Drinks are generous and inexpensive and the place is a good mix of locals and visitors. *c/ de Llotja de Mar, 2.* ☎ *971/72-27-99. Bus no. 1. Map p 83.*

★ **Exit Rock Bar** SANTA CATALINA   You can't miss this place—its exterior is an eye-catching mural of classic rock 'n roll visages such as Janis Joplin, the Beatles and Jim Morrison. The small bar, a favourite of local rockers, is ideal for some tunes and a well-prepared cocktail, but even better is the recording studio upstairs, which stages live rock performances that patrons are welcome to attend. *c/ Sant Magi, 60.* ☎ *971/28-77-21. www.exitrockbar. com. Bus no. 1. Map p 83.*

Gòtic SA LLOTJA   A compact and genial café-bar with a terrace in the square overlooking Sa Llotja, the 15th-century landmark (p 57, ②). Start or end the evening here with a gin and tonic or a beer. *Pl. Sa Llotja, 2.* ☎ *971/72-12-55. Bus no. 1. Map p 83.*

★★ **Idem Café** SANTA CATALINA   With crushed red velvet, candles and chandeliers, there's a bordello feel to this bar in Santa Catalina, the happening restaurant district west of central Palma. It has a small outdoor terrace but the serious drinking and seducing goes on in the two rooms past the front bar. *Sant Magi, 15 Santa Catalina.* ☎ *971/28-08-54. Bus no. 1. Map p 83.*

★ **Puro Hotel Lounge** SA LLOTJA   This chic, Swedish-owned boutique hotel is a bit self-conscious for my tastes, but the hip cocktail lounge with fur on the ceiling and DJs from Thursday to Saturday is a good spot if you're on the hunt for Palma's beautiful people. *c/ Monte Negro 12.* ☎ *971/42-54-50. Bus no. 2. Map p 83.*

Clubs

★ **Abraxas** PASSEIG MARÍTIM   Previously known as the Palma branch of Pacha, the legendary nightclub in Ibiza, this huge dance club may have changed names but the wildness is still the same and uninhibited revellers pack the two dance floors. It occasional holds gay nights. *Avda. Gabriel Roca (Pg Marítim), 42.* ☎ *971/45-59-08. www. abraxasmallorca.com. Cover charge 10–20€. Bus no. 1. Map p 83.*

★★★ **Garito Café** PASSEIG MARÍTIM   This trendy club has a terrace and lounge space, but the emphasis is definitely on the music, with an array of international DJs spinning everything from Brazilian jazz to hip-hop and house. *Dársena de Ca'n Barbarà, s/n.* ☎ *971/73-69-12. www.garitocafe.com. Cover charge 5–10€. Bus no. 1. Map p 83.*

★★ **King Kamehameha** PASSEIG MARÍTIM   One of Palma's hippest nightspots, with a fashionable international clientele, electronica pulsating in the club and a chilled vibe out on the terrace overlooking the bay. *Pg. Maritim, 29.* ☎ *971/93-92-00. www.king-kamehameha.com. Cover charge 15–20€. Bus no. 1. Map p 83.*

Tito's PASSEIG MARÍTIM   Open at weekends only, this stalwart of the Palma nightlife scene has been, incredibly, around since the 1920s. It's a monster club with something for everyone (except those who prefer a quiet evening), including five bars, two dance floors, and exotic fancy dress theme nights in summer. *Pg. Maritim 33.* ☎ *971/73-00-17. www.titosmallorca.com. Cover charge 10–25€. Bus no. 1. Map p 83.*

Gay & Lesbian

★ **Black Cat** PASSEIG MARÍTIM   Palma's biggest gay club and something of a local institution, it plays host to all sorts of wild parties and exotic shows and is open nightly until 5am. *Avda. Joan Miró, 75. No phone. Cover charge 5–20€. Bus no. 1. Map p 83.*

Café Lorca WESTERN PALMA Near Castell de Bellver, in the neighbourhood where many of the gay establishments are located, this laid-back café by day becomes a dance bar at night. *c/ Federico Garcia Lorca, 21. ☎ 971/45-19-30. www.cafelorca. com. Bus no. 3. Map p 83.*

Dark NORTHERN PALMA Not for the timid, this newly opened gay bar features cabins, beds, a dark room and a maze. On weekends it's open until 10:30am the next day—just in case you get lost in that maze. *c/ Ticià, 22. No phone. www.darkpalma. com. Map p 83.*

Live Music
★ **Bluesville** SA LLOTJA A smoky, rocking bar with live performances and cheap beer, this blues dive plays host to local and visiting bands playing blues, funk, rock and reggae every night. *c/ de Ma d'es Moro, 3. ☎ 692/68-42-87. www.bluesvillebar. com. No cover charge. Bus no. 2. Map p 83.*

★ **Cultura Club** PASSEIG MARÍTIM This is an indie rock club featuring live shows of rock and pop, with the emphasis on alternative, on Friday and Saturday nights, open until the small hours. *Pg. Marítim, 26. No phone. www.myspace.com/cultura club. No cover charge. Bus no. 1. Map p 83.*

★★ **Jazz Voyeur Club** SA LLOTJA An intimate, dark and smoky jazz club, inhabiting a section of a 16th-century manor house in the heart of Sa Llotja, with nightly happy hours

and late-night jazz that ranges from Brazilian and blues to soul and bebop. *c/ dels Apuntadors, 5. ☎ 971/90-52-92. www.jazzvoyeur. com. Cover charge 5–10€. Bus no. 2. Map p 83.*

Theatre, Symphony & Dance
Auditòrium PASSEIG MARÍTIM A crisply modern theatre on the waterfront that looks from the outside like an apartment or office building, but inside hosts major concerts, from classical and city opera to occasional pop performances. *Pg. Maritim, 18. ☎ 971/73-47-35. www.auditoriumpalma.es. Tickets 20–70€. Bus no. 1. Map p 83.*

★★★ **Teatre Principal** PLAÇA MAJOR & ENVIRONS A handsome mid-19th-century theatre that was restored in 2007, this is the city's top spot for theatre, music and dance productions, with excellent sound and good sight lines. *Pl. Weyler, 16. ☎ 971/71-33-46. www.teatre principal.com. Tickets 20–50€. Bus no. 1. Map p 83.* ●

Teatre Principal.

Northwest Coast of Mallorca

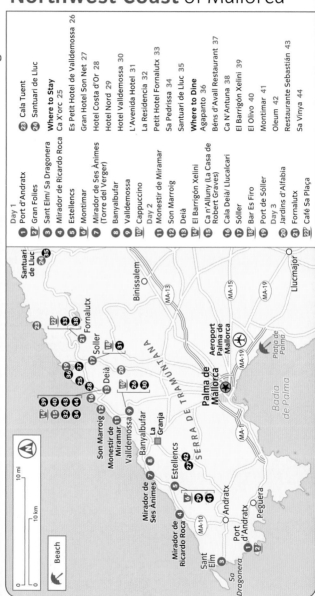

Previous page: Take off in a Mallorcan sail boat.

Mallorca's northwest coast is worlds removed from the island's popular image of high-rise hotels and sun worshippers. What it lacks in beaches, it more than makes up for with picturesque mountain villages, the forested Serra de Tramuntana range and dramatic high cliffs slicing into the sea. START: MA-1 (coastal road) from Palma to Andratx (28 km/17 miles). Trip length: 3 days.

Travel Tip

Public transportation along the Mallorcan coast is complicated, time-consuming and limited; thus, the tours in this chapter are envisioned as driving tours. Although you can return each day to Palma to spend the night, it's considerably more enjoyable to stay at one or more hotels along the coast. For hotels in Palma, see Chapter 3. For hotels in other areas, see the relevant lodging section at the end of each regional tour.

Dip your toes in the clear waters of Port d'Andratx.

Day One

1 ★ kids Port d'Andratx. Previously a sleepy fishing village, the sheltered natural harbour of Andratx has gone genteel, with yachts bobbing in the marina and elegantly dressed visitors and summer homeowners sipping cocktails in waterfront cafés. Surrounded by cliffs, it's an attractive place, with the air of privilege blowing in from the Mediterranean. Head to **Cala Llamp,** just south of the harbour, to dip your toes in clear waters (but no sand). ⏱ *45 min.*

2 ★ Gran Folies. This restaurant/ beach club with an infinity pool overlooking the water makes an enjoyable stop before getting back in the car. You can pick up breakfast or coffee and a snack out on the terrace. *Cala Llamp s/n.* ☎ *971/67-10-94. www.granfolies.net. $$.*

5km (3 miles) inland from Port d'Andratx.

3 ★ kids Sant Elm/ Sa Dragonera. The tiny village and mini-resort of Sant Elm is worth visiting for its small beach, seafood restaurants and dramatic views of Illa de Sa Dragonera, a 4km (2½-mile) long mass of rock just offshore, said to resemble a dragon rising out of the sea. The island is classified as a nature park, and those who do venture over via ferry go for a scenic hike along the trails around the island and to **Cap de Tramuntana** (information on walks: Tourist Office in Sant Elm: Avda. de Jaume I, 28; ☎ 971/23-92-05). Sa Dragonera is also a popular diving spot—for more information, see Diving & Snorkelling, p 132. ⏱ *2 hr. Ferry: 15 min; March–Nov; 10€ roundtrip.*

Retrace your steps to Andratx and then travel 14 km (9 miles) northeast along MA-10.

4 ★★ kids Mirador de Ricardo Roca. Perched atop cliffs along the coastal road are several *miradors* (viewpoints), many of which are ancient towers, once used to protect the island from pirates. This first mirador has a small tower and is situated next to a restaurant, **Café Es Grau** (Ctra Andratx-Estellencs/MA-10 km. 98; ☎ 971/61-85-27), with its own superb panoramic coastal views. 🕘 *30 min. Free admission.*

6km (4 miles) northeast along MA-10.

5 ★ Estellencs. This mountain village of old stone houses and steep cobbled streets set among citrus groves cascades down the hill to a rocky cove, **Cala d'Estellencs.** Stop for lunch at one of the restaurants off the main road through town, with pretty views extending to the sea. 🕘 *20 min.*

About 5km (3 miles) northeast of Estellencs along MA-10.

6 ★ Montimar. This easy-going restaurant with home-cooked Mallorcan specialities has views over town and makes a delightful pitstop along the coast, especially for its midday fixed price menu, a bargain at 15€. *Pl. de la Constitució, 7, Estellencs.* ☎ *971/61-85-76. $$.*

7 ★★★ kids Mirador de Ses Ànimes (Torre del Verger). This is perhaps the finest viewpoint of the entire coast. The 16th-century tower clings to the very edge of the cliff. If vertigo's not an issue, climb up a narrow ladder for coastal views. 🕘 *15 min. Free admission. Open access. Early morning and late afternoon are best for photos, avoiding the haze of midday.*

Another 3km (1.8 miles) on MA-10 takes you to the next mountain village.

8 ★ Banyalbufar. Derived from Arabic, the town's name means 'little vineyard by the sea'. Surrounded by steep agricultural terraces called *marjades*, farmed since Moorish times along the mountain slopes, this is one of the most photogenic villages on the northwest coast. Banyalbufar is acclaimed for its traditional *malvasia* (white) wines, on the rebound after centuries of dormancy, as well as others made from additional indigenous varietals. Visit **Cooperative Malvasia de Banyalbufar,** a small winery and bodega in town, just off the main road, producing *malvasia* and other wines. Try the aromatic *Cornet Blanc.* 🕘 *45 min. MA-10, km 86.* ☎ *971/14-85-05. www.malvasia debanyalbufar.com. Free admission. Wed–Sun 11am–2pm & 4–8pm.*

16km (10 miles) northeast on MA-10.

9 ★★★ Valldemossa. Tucked into a valley along the northwest coast, Valldemossa is one of Mallorca's most celebrated, historic towns, best known for the Reial Cartoixa monastery. The Polish composer Frédéric Chopin and his lover, writer George Sand, spent one miserable winter (1838–39) in the monastery, later immortalised in Sand's book, *A Winter in Mallorca.* Sand disparaged locals as 'barbarians' and dismissed Mallorca as 'Monkey Island'.

Marjades on the mountain slopes at Banyalbufar.

Valldemossa

The **9A ★★ Reial Cartoixa de Valldemossa,** which graces the town with its distinctive green-tiled bell tower, dates to the 14th century, but what you see today are neoclassical 17th- and 18th-century buildings. In addition to monk cells (incredibly, only 13 brothers lived here at a time), there are rooms dedicated to Chopin and Sand (cell no. 4 features Chopin's Pleyel piano), and the monks' pharmacy and library. Included in the visit is the chapel and **9B Palau del Rei Sanç,** a medieval royal palace built around a cloister. Venture downhill toward the parish church **9C Església de Sant Bartolomeu.** Nearby, down a side street (c/ de la Rectoria, 5) is the small **9D Casa Natal de Santa Catalina Thomàs,** the birthplace of the 16th-century nun later beatified as Mallorca's only saint (the house has been transformed into a small chapel dedicated

Valldemossa.

to her memory). ⏱ *2 hr. Reial Cartoixa.* ☎ *971/61-21-06. www. valldemossa.com. Admission 8.50€ adults, 4€ seniors & students, free children under 10. Mar–Oct Mon–Sat 9:30am–6pm & Sun 10am–1pm, Nov–Feb Mon–Sat 9:30am–6pm & Sun 10am–1pm. Casa Natal de Santa Catalina Thomàs: Free admission. Daily 9am–3pm.*

10 ★ **Cappuccino.** In the heart of town, just steps from Sa Cartoixa and with a delightful terrace, this is a pleasant stop for a coffee or a full lunch: I recommend the baguette sandwiches and salads. *Praça Ramón Llull, 5, Valldemossa.* ☎ *971/61-60-59. $$.*

Day Two
5km (3 miles) northeast of Valldemossa on MA-10.

11 Monestir de Miramar. Although George Sand may not have been enamoured of Mallorca, the Habsburg Archduke Ludwig Salvator (1847–1915), an Austrian aristocrat and conservationist, certainly was, and his love affair with the island meant he bought as many properties on the northwest coast as he could. Miramar, a *possessió* or manor house acquired by Salvator, is built on the site of a 13th-century monastery founded by the Mallorcan mystic Ramón Llull (1232–1315). It's a pretty coastal site, with the

Pillars from the old cloisters at Miramar.

arch-and-pillar remains of the cloisters, a small chapel and the main house. ⏱ *30 min.* ☎ *971/61-60-73. www.sonmarroig.com. Admission 4€ adults, free children under 12. Tues–Sat, 9:30am–6pm.*

2km (1¼ miles) east on the road to Deià.

12 ★ **Son Marroig.** Just 2km (1 mile) east on the road to Deià is the best known of the Archduke's properties, Son Marroig, a mansion perched on the cliff, with period furnishings, a collection of the Archduke's books and gardens. By far its best feature is the view of the wooded, jagged coast, including down to the famous rock promontory **Sa Foradada,** which juts out into the sea and through which wind and waves have pierced a large hole (walkers with good footwear can reach it in less than an hour). ⏱ *1 hr.* ☎ *971/63-91-58. www.sonmarroig.com. Admission 3€, free children under 12. Tues–Sat 9:30am–6pm.*

5km (3 miles) northeast on MA-10.

13 ★★★ kids **Deià.** Perhaps the most picturesque village in Mallorca is this tiny gem, perched on a hillside and all honey-coloured stone houses, tiled roofs and green shuttered windows. To one side is the Mediterranean, while the steep Puig des Teix of the Tramuntana mountains forms a backdrop on the other. Deià's beauty and serenity have long attracted expat artists, prominent among them Robert Graves, the author of *I, Claudius*, who made his home here in 1929 and spent most of the rest of his life, until his death in 1985, in Deià. Graves is buried in the endearingly modest cemetery next to the parish church on the top of the hill. His gravestone is a very simple 'Robert

Graves, Poeta, 1895–1985. E.P.D.' (*en paz descanse*, or 'rest in peace') 🕐 *1 hr.*

Detail from the cemetery at Deià, resting place of poet and author Robert Graves.

14 ★★ **El Barrigón Xelini.**
The outdoor covered terrace is the most coveted spot for a good-value lunch of salads, tapas and *montaditos* (small sandwiches). *c/ Archiduque Luis Salvador, 19, Deià.* ☎ *971/63-91-39. $$.*

1km (½ mile) past Deià on MA-10, just before the turnoff to Cala Deià.

15 ★★ **Ca n'Alluny (La Casa de Robert Graves.** The former home of the English poet Robert Graves has been transformed into a museum about his life in Deià. The house remains exactly as Graves left it (and as he himself found it upon return after a decade of exile during the Spanish Civil War), and you can imagine him sitting writing at his desk, ready to hop onto his old bicycle, which is still propped up against a wall. 🕐 *1 hr. Ctra. Deià-Sóller, km 1.* ☎ *971/63-61-85. www.lacasade robertgraves.com. Admission 5€ adults, 2.50€ children under 12. Mon–Fri 10am–4:20pm & Sat 10am–2:20pm.*

3km (1.8 miles) down a twisting road off MA-10.

16 ★ **kids Cala Deià/ Llucalcari.** Just beyond the Graves house (the walk down from town is actually shorter), is the small, rocky cove and beach of Cala Deià—much admired by Graves. Just east, accessible by a footpath, is Llucalcari, a tiny hamlet of just a handful of

homes and a laid-back hotel tucked into the cliff. 🕐 *1 hr. See p 97.*

12km (7 miles) east along MA-10.

17 ★★ **Sóller.** Prosperous Sóller sits in a fertile valley full of citrus groves, and the profitable produce trade is what paid for the railroad. The wooden cars of the 1912 narrow-gauge train (*Ferrocarril*) from Palma arrive several times daily (see p 168) at the vintage railroad station. The imposing 16th-century parish church, **Sant Baromeu,** is a curious combination of Gothic interior and a remodelled Modernista façade—the work of a Gaudí disciple, Joan Rubió i Bellver. Next to the church is the distinctive **Banco de Sóller,** with its sculpted Modernista

Sun bathing at Cala Deià.

Relax at a café in the main square in Sóller.

wrought-iron balconies. The main square, **Plaça de Constitució,** is an amenable place to hang out and wait for the antique tram (*tranvia*) that travels through town on its way down to the port. Also worth a look is the **Jardí Botànic de Sóller,** botanical gardens full of native Balearic and Mediterranean plants and flowers. Sóller's **tourist information office** inhabits an old railway car on Plaça d'Espanya, 15 (☎ 971/ 63-80-08). ⏲ *2 hr. Jardí Botànic de Sóller: Cta. Palma-Sóller, km. 30.5.* ☎ *971/63-40-14. www.jardibotanic desoller.org. Admission 5€ adults, free for children under 12, Tues–Sat 10am–6pm & Sun 10am–2pm.*

18 **Bar Es Firo.** This agreeable little old-fashioned café, a long-time favourite of locals, is the place on the main square to have a coffee or cocktail and watch Sóller and the trams go by. *Plaça de Constitució, 10. No phone. $.*

5km (3 miles) north of Sóller on MA-11.

19 ★ **kids** **Port de Sóller.** The *tranvia de Sóller*, a vintage tram, connects Sóller to a natural harbour, departing from outside the *Estació de Tren* (station). The track, laid in 1913, is lined by orange and lemon trees. The beaches along the horseshoe-shaped harbour aren't as good as those farther along the north coast, but the **Passeig es Través** promenade alongside sailing and fishing boats makes for a pleasant afternoon walk towards the lighthouse, **Faro de sa Creu.** ⏲ *2 hr. Tranvia.* ☎ *971/75-46-31. www.trendesoller.com. 4€ each way from Sóller to Port de Sóller. 7am– 8:50pm every 30 min. in summer; on the hour in winter.*

Day Three
South of Sóller on MA-11, or take the longer, scenic old road, full of hairpin turns (cyclists: the turnoff is left just before the tunnel entrance); the gardens are on the other side of Coll de Sóller, next to the tunnel entrance.

⑳ ★★ kids Jardins d'Alfabia.
These terraced gardens and country estate, an oasis among the Serra de Tramuntana mountains, make a delightful inland detour. An estate that once belonged to a Moorish viceroy in the 12th century (at the entrance to the rambling, 17th-century seigniorial mansion is a Moorish coffered ceiling, with inscriptions in Arabic that date from A.D.1170), waters still flow in fountains and ripple through irrigation canals. Sample freshly squeezed Sóller orange juice at the bar under towering palm trees providing shade. Parents may find it a great place for the children to unwind. 🕐 1 hr. Ctra Palma-Sóller, km. 17. ☎ 971/61-31-23. www.jardinesdealfabia.com. Admission 4.50€ (check online for downloadable discount voucher). Nov–Mar Mon–Fri 9:30am–5:30pm Sat 9:30am–1pm, Apr–Oct Mon–Sat 9:30am–6:30pm, closed December.

Back in Sóller, follow signs to Fornalutx along MA-10 for 3km (1.8 miles). Walkers can take an enjoyable and easy trek from Sóller.

㉑ ★★ Fornalutx. The name of this village may not be easy to pronounce (Fohrn-ah-looch), but the immaculate ensemble of medieval stone houses and cobbled streets is a treasure, full of bougainvillea, cacti

Take a detour to the Jardins d'Alfabia.

and palm trees. It's a captivating place to spend a tranquil afternoon, and with several appealing boutique hotels and restaurants also makes an excellent base for exploring the region. 🕐 2 hr.

㉒ Café Sa Plaça. Occupying the little main square in Fornalutx, you can while away the afternoon here sipping a coffee or orange juice or enjoying an ice cream. Pl. d'Espanya, 3. ☎ 971/631-19-21. $.

Valldemossa's Chopin Festival

Frédéric Chopin's brief, ill-fated stay in Mallorca from 1838–39 is commemorated annually by the Chopin Festival, hosted in the cloister of Reial Cartoixa monastery (p 91, ㉒A) in Valldemossa on four consecutive Sundays in August. The festival—one of the cultural highlights of the summer—dates back to 1930, and programmes typically include mostly Chopin compositions played by both celebrated and up-and-coming pianists and other musicians (www.festivalchopin.com; reservations (beginning in July) ☎ 971/61-23-51).

Take MA-10 13km (8 miles) towards Pollença, past the Mirador de Ses Barques, with a detour towards the coast to Sa Calobra/Cala Tuent.

23 ★ kids **Cala Tuent.** The famed, twisting road of white-knuckle, hairpin turns is aptly called **Sa Calobra** (The Snake). It's a demanding drive and can be a nightmare when crowded with summer tourist buses. The reward at the bottom is Cala Tuent, a pretty beach with clear turquoise waters reached by a fork in the road, and beyond the overly commercial port, the beach at a river gorge, **Torrent de Pareis.** 🕑 *2 hr.*

30 km (19 miles) east on MA-10.

24 ★★ **Santuari de Lluc.** A revered place of pilgrimage and the spiritual centre of Mallorca, the monastery of Lluc owes its existence to mystical appearances and legends dating to the 13th century and a sanctuary that grew up around a statue of a small, carved, dark-skinned Madonna (*La Moreneta*), said to have been found in the woods by a local shepherd boy, Lluc. Today the highlight of the monastic complex is the Baroque **Basilica de la Mare de Deu de Lluc.** The Virgin of Lluc is tucked away in a chapel behind the main altar. A monastery museum features archaeology and folklore displays, and the Escolania de Lluc boys' choir, known for their blue cassocks (and thus called *Els Blauets*), performs during Sunday Mass when in town. 🕑 *2 hr.*
☎ *971/87-15-25; www.lluc.net. Free admission. Daily 8am–8pm. Museum: admission 4€; daily 10:30am–1pm & 2:30–5pm.*

Where to **Stay**

★★ **Ca X'orc** SÓLLER ENVIRONS Two adjoining, 200-year-old *fincas* (farms), hidden among olive groves and the foothills of the mountains outside Sóller, have been converted into an emphatically Mediterranean country hotel, which is both sophisticated and rustic. Rooms achieve a clever balance between traditional Mallorcan and exotic Moroccan flair. The grounds are spectacular, with an infinity pool, hot tub and terraces with distant mountain and coastal views. *Carretera de Deia, km 56.1, Sóller.* ☎ *971/63-82-80. www.cas xorc.com. 12 units. Doubles 195–315€ w/breakfast. Closed Nov to mid-Mar. AE, DC, MC, V. Map p 88.*

kids **Es Petit Hotel de Valldemossa** VALLDEMOSSA   On a quiet street in the village, this cosy hotel has a pleasant living room and bar and an outdoor garden. The rooms are simple, with splashes of colour and tiled floors. The most rewarding features are the village location and i.e. great views of the valley, so opt for a room with a terrace. *c/ Uetam, 1, Valldemossa.* ☎ *971/61-24-79. www.espetithotel-valldemossa.com. 12 units. Doubles 125–170€ w/ breakfast. AE, DC, MC, V. Map p 88.*

★★★ kids **Gran Hotel Son Net** PUIGPUNYENT   One of the island's grandest rural hotels, this 17th-century estate, a pink Renaissance palace, has surprising design elements. There's a deep green and pale stone bar, an impressive modern art collection and an audacious restaurant space, Oleum (p 101). Rooms are huge, the bathrooms uniquely so. The large swimming pool, with stunning views of the valley and private cabanas, looks like something straight out of Hollywood.

c/ de Castillo Son Net, s/n. ☎ 971/14-70-00. www.sonnet.es. 31 units. Doubles 340–590€ w/breakfast. AE, DC, MC, V. Map p 88.

★★ **kids Hotel Costa d'Or** LLUCALCARI   In a tiny village just around a bend from Deià, this hotel has enjoyed a recent makeover and is stylish yet low-key—just the way its many fans like it. With a gorgeous setting above the Mediterranean coastline, a pool and plenty of activities, including a walking path with a route down to Cala Deià, cycling (and bike rental), sun terraces and a good restaurant, it's a winning formula. *c/ Luc Alcari, s/n, Llucalcari.* ☎ *971/63-90-25. www.epoquehotels. com. 41 units. Doubles 160–240€ w/ breakfast. MC, V. Map p 88.*

★ **kids Hotel Nord** ESTELLENCS   A charming small country hotel— and excellent value—with eight stylishly decorated rooms with white bedspreads and flowing canopies, tile floors, wood beams, stone walls and antique pieces. The old stone building features an interior courtyard, sun terrace and lounge with a wood-burning fireplace. *Plaça d'es Triquet, 4, Estellencs.* ☎ *971/14-90-06. www.hotelruralnord.com. 8 units. Doubles 88–130€ w/breakfast. AE, DC, MC, V. Map p 88.*

★★ **Hotel Valldemossa** VALLDEMOSSA   This small Relais & Chateaux property just down the hill from the famous Carthusian monastery is a serene, unfussy retreat. Two connected 19th-century stone houses sit amid olive and orange groves, with views of the monastery and surrounding terraced valley. Rooms feature elegant antiques, and many have private terraces. A surprise is the small indoor pool and spa, where the walls are painted with murals that mirror views from the hotel. *Ctra Vieja de Valldemossa, s/n, Valldemossa.* ☎ *971/61-26-26. www.valldemossahotel.com. 12 units. Doubles 180–330€ w/ breakfast. AE, DC, MC, V. Map p 88.*

★★ **L'Avenida Hotel** SÓLLER This swanky boutique hotel, in a century-old mansion in the heart of town, notches up the luxury quotient in Sóller. Hip and urbane,

Gran Hotel Son Net.

unlike most hotels on the coast, it features design-oriented rooms with funky wallpaper, chandeliers and wenge hardwood floors. The elegant courtyard pool is surrounded by palm trees, while the chic bistro restaurant has poolside dining. *Gran Via 9, Sóller.* ☎ *971/63-40-75. www.avenida-hotel.com. 8 units. Doubles 225–245€ w/breakfast. Closed Nov to Feb. AE, DC, MC, V. Map p 88.*

★★★ La Residencia DEIÀ   One of the most famous hotels on Mallorca, this exclusive luxury hotel, in an ivy-covered 16th-century manor house overlooking Deià and ensconced in 12 hectares (29 acres) of gardens and orchards, draws the most elite travellers to the northwest coast, including Richard Branson (a former owner) and, once upon a time, Princess Diana. In addition to the handsome rooms, there's a pool, a luxurious spa and tennis courts. Strict minimum stays in high season. *c/ Son Canals, s/n, Deià.* ☎ *971/63-90-11. www.hotellaresidencia.com. 60 units. Doubles 510–730€ w/breakfast. AE, DC, MC, V. Map p 88.*

★ Petit Hotel Fornalutx FORNALUTX   In a former convent down a side street, this small hotel has plenty going for it. Contemporary pieces (such as the work of Mallorcan artists, for sale) complement the old townhouse. Your best bet is one of the top-floor rooms with a small terrace, or splurge for the romantic suite that's designed like a small chapel. The rear of the house—where you'll find a slender infinity pool, breakfast terrace and a hot tub—overlooks the mountains and orange groves. *c/ Alba, 22, Fornalutx.* ☎ *971/63-19-97. www.fornalutxpetithotel.com. 8 units. Doubles 141–152€ w/breakfast. AE, DC, MC, V. Map p 88.*

★★★ kids Sa Pedrissa DEIÀ   One of my top places to stay, this charming, historic and family-owned 'agrotourism' boutique hotel just outside Deià has commanding views of the coast from its perch on a hill. Rooms are snug and understated rather than fancy, overshadowed by the pool extending over the cliff and breakfast terrace, where the views (and the breakfast) simply could not be better. The entire family works at the hotel, with one son helming the restaurant kitchen. For privacy, check out one of the suites (rooms 4 and 5) removed from the main house and set among lovely

View from the pool at Petit Hotel Fornalutx.

Agrotourism boutique hotel Sa Pedrissa.

gardens. *Ctra de Valldemossa, s/n, Deià.* ☎ *971/63-91-11. www.sa pedrissa.com. 8 units. Doubles 120–327€ w/breakfast. AE, DC, MC, V. Map p 88.*

★ **kids Santuari de Lluc** LLUC This place is a favourite of the faithful and hiking fanatics who come to stay in the austere but inexpensive former monks' cells, surrounded by mountains and treks along the northwest coast. Some rooms are smaller and darker than others, but there are also singles, rooms for two, three, four or six people, as well as apartments. *Monestir de Lluc, Lluc.* ☎ *971/87-15-25. www. lluc.net/eng/ahostatg.html. 129 units. Doubles 25€. MC, V. Map p 88.*

Where to **Dine**

★ **Agapanto** PORT DE SÓLLER *INTERNATIONAL/MEDITERRANEAN* Port de Sóller's coolest restaurant, with ambient music, creative cocktails and a fantastic terrace overlooking the harbour, Agapanto is the perfect place to enjoy an early dinner as the sun sets. *Camino del Faro, 2, Port de Sóller.* ☎ *971/63-38-60. Main course 30–45€. AE, DC, MC, V. Lunch & dinner Tues–Sun. Map p 88.*

★★★ **Béns d'Avall Restaurant** SÓLLER ENVIRONS *HAUTE MALLORCAN/MEDITERRANEAN* Renowned for its views and creative cuisine, this stalwart of the northwest coast has been luring patrons off the beaten track for a couple of decades now. Benet Vicens is one of the island's top chefs and the tasting menus—there is even one for vegetarians—are comparatively good value. Get here early in the

Seafood dish at Montimar.

evening for sunset. *Urb. Costa Deià/Ctra. Sóller-Deià, near Sóller.* ☎ *971/63-23-81. www.benetvicens. com. Main course 30–45€. MC, V. Lunch & dinner Tues–Sun. Closed Nov–Mar. Map p 88.*

★ kids **Ca N'Antuna** FORNALUTX *TRADITIONAL MALLORCAN* Plain and brightly lit, this relaxed restaurant is perfect for homemade dishes such as *arroz brut* (a thick stew with rabbit, pork and chicken). Don't expect anything fancy, but do expect a well-prepared and very affordable meal. *c/ Arbona Colom, 8, Fornalutx.* ☎ *971/63-30-68. Main course 7–12€. MC, V. Lunch & dinner Tues–Sun. Map p 88.*

★★ **Ca X'orc** SÓLLER ENVIRONS *MALLORCAN/MEDITERRANEAN* The restaurant of this secluded boutique hotel (p 96) is worth locating even if you're not a guest. Dine in the antique olive press or out on the terrace, with distant views of the mountains. In the evening it's your

chance to try out the six-course tasting menu (65€). The wine list is excellent, but remember that non-guests have to negotiate those hairpin turns after dinner. *Carretera de Deia, km 56.1, Sóller.* ☎ *971/63-82-80. www.casxorc.com. Main course 21–25€. AE, DC, MC, V. Lunch & dinner daily. Closed Nov to mid-Mar. Map p 88.*

★★ kids **El Barrigón Xelini** DEIÀ *TAPAS/MEDITERRANEAN* With a cellar-like 130-year-old main room, handsome bar and sunny terrace just across the road from town, this casual, fun venue serves very good *montaditos* (tapas-like sandwiches), salads, dozens of tapas as well as homemade pastas and lamb dishes. *c/ Archiduque Luis Salvador, 19, Deià.* ☎ *971/63-91-39. www.xelini. com. Main course 7–18€. MC, V. Lunch & dinner Tues–Sun. Closed mid-Nov to Dec. Map p 88.*

★★ **El Olivo** DEIÀ *MEDITERRANEAN/ INTERNATIONAL* Stylish and romantic, this upscale restaurant—in a 16th-century olive press at the exclusive hotel La Residencia (p 98)—has long set the standard along the northwest coast. Although it's pricey, it still might be worth the splurge for a memorably seductive meal, especially if you dine outdoors under torches. *c/ Son Canals, s/n, Deià.* ☎ *971/63-90-11. Main course 36–42€. www.hotellaresidencia. com. AE, DC, MC, V. Lunch & dinner daily Apr–Oct. Map p 88.*

★ kids **Montimar** ESTELLENCS *MALLORCAN* A surprisingly sprawling, homespun restaurant with a covered terrace and views overlooking town. It serves an excellent-value midday fixed-price menu for 15€, and the homemade flan is delectable. *Pl. de la Constitució, 7, Estellencs.* ☎ *971/61-85-76. Main course 8–17€. MC, V. Lunch & dinner Tues–Sun. Map p 88.*

Oleum at the Gran Hotel Son Net.

★★★ Oleum PUIGPUNYENT
MALLORCAN/MEDITERRANEAN
The contemporary restaurant of
Gran Hotel Son Net (p 96), set in a
soaring old olive press with high-
backed red-velvet booths, is easily
one of the island's best-looking restaurants. House specialities include
oven-baked fish for two and suckling
pig. Wine aficionados will find one of
Mallorca's most extensive cellars,
including many hard-to-find collect-
ibles. *c/ Castillo de Sonnet s/n, Puigpunyent.* ☎ *971/14-70-00. Main
course 28–33€. AE, DC, MC, V. Lunch
& dinner Mon–Sat, brunch & dinner
Sun. Map p 88.*

★★★ Restaurante Sebastián
DEIÀ *MEDITERRANEAN* This
romantic, relaxed gourmet restaurant—with burning candelabra,
exposed stone walls and large pic-
ture windows—is my favourite in

Deià, serving exquisitely prepared
fresh fish and meat dishes. Everything is refined, subtle and fairly
priced. *c/ Felipe Bauza, s/n, Deià.*
☎ *971/63-94-17. www.restaurante
sebastian.com. Main course 7–18€.
AE, DC, MC, V. Dinner Thurs–Tues.
Closed Dec to Feb. Map p 88.*

★★ kids Sa Vinya DEIÀ *MEDITER-
RANEAN* Tucked back from the
main road in a garden terrace, this
immediately welcoming restaurant
is perfect for a sunny, casual lunch.
The tables under a thick canopy of
orange trees and the night stars are
also ideal for a romantic dinner of
fresh fish or grilled rabbit. *c/ Sa
Vinya Vella, 3, Deià.* ☎ *971/63-95-
00. Main course 9–23€. AE, DC, MC,
V. Lunch & dinner Tues–Sun. Closed
mid-Nov to Dec. Map p 88.*

North & East Coasts of Mallorca

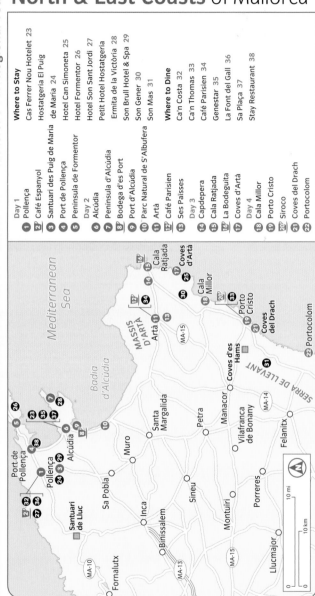

Day 1

① Pollença
㉗ Café Espanyol
③ Santuari des Puig de Maria
④ Port de Pollença
⑤ Peninsula de Formentor

Day 2

⑥ Alcúdia
⑦ Peninsula d'Alcúdia
㊲ Bodega d'es Port
⑨ Port d'Alcúdia
⑩ Parc Natural de S'Albufera
⑪ Artà

㉜ Café Parisien
⑬ Ses Païsses

Day 3

⑭ Capdepera
⑮ Cala Ratjada
㉞ La Bodeguita
⑰ Coves d'Artà

Day 4

⑱ Cala Millor
⑲ Porto Cristo
㉚ Siroco
㉑ Coves del Drach
㉒ Portocolom

Where to Stay

Cas Ferrer Nou Hotelet 23
Hostatgeria El Puig
  de Maria 24
Hotel Can Simoneta 25
Hotel Formentor 26
Hotel Son Sant Jordi 27
Petit Hotel Hostatgeria
Ermita de la Victòria 28
Son Brull Hotel & Spa 29
Son Gener 30
Son Mas 31

Where to Dine

Ca'n Costa 32
Ca'n Thomas 33
Café Parisien 34
Genestar 35
La Font del Gall 36
Sa Plaça 37
Stay Restaurant 38

Dramatic bays and capes make up the north coast, while the east coast comprises quiet coves and remarkable caves. History helps define the region: the Romans settled Pollentia, and walled medieval villages dot the shores. START: **From Palma, take MA-13 to Inca and then MA-220 north to Pollença. From Lluc, take MA-20 for 20 km (12 miles) to Pollença. Trip length: 4 days.**

Vía Crucis, Pollença.

artist. 🕐 *3 hr. Fundació Martí Vicenç; c/ Calvari, 10.* ☎ *971/53-28-67. www.martivicens.org. Free admission. Mon–Fri 10:30am–6pm, Sat 10:30am–3pm, Sun 11am–1pm.*

2 ★ Café Espanyol. Also known as Ca'n Moixet, this small bar is perfect for a coffee and pastry or sandwich on the wide terrace spilling onto the old town's principal square; in evenings the interior becomes a locals' watering hole. *Plaça Major, 2, Pollença.* ☎ *971/53-42-14. $.*

Day One

1 ★★ kids Pollença. Lively and family-friendly, this British favourite resort, just 7km (4 miles) inland from the sea, has hosted everyone from Winston Churchill to Agatha Christie. It's a small, genteel city, the old town full of stylish boutiques and café terraces spilling onto the Plaça Major. Founded in 1230, the city was the property of the Knights of St. John until the 19th century. Pollença is famed for its **Vía Crucis** (Way of the Cross), a long, gentle climb of 365 stone steps lined with cypress trees that leads to **El Calvari** and a small *oratori* (chapel). The 180-degree views from the top gaze out over Pollença all the way to the sea. Halfway up is **Fundació Martí Vicenç**, a small and interesting museum dedicated to the multi-faceted talents of Martí Vicenç (1926–95), a local craftsman and

2km (1¼ miles) south of Pollença, just east off MA-2200.

3 ★★ Santuari des Puig de Maria. The views from this hilltop are glorious, although it does require a steep hour's trek up (the 1½km (1-mile) drive up is only for the most agile and confident drivers, and there's no real car park, and so best to leave your car in Pollença and walk). The views take in the cape of Formentor (p 104, **5**) and the impressive sweeps of both Pollença and Alcúdia bays. At the top (330m (1,100 ft)) of a winding, 17th-century stone footpath is a hermitage where hikers can spend the night (Hostatgeria El Puig de Maria, see p 109), and a 15th-century Gothic chapel and refectory, part of an abandoned monastery. Grab a drink or ice cream at the small café on the premises and enjoy the views. 🕐 *3 hr.*

Windsurfing at Port de Pollença.

7km (4 miles) northeast of
Pollença along MA-2200.

4 ★ kids Port de Pollença.
Although hugely popular in summer,
this amenable beach isn't crass like
some of the resorts to the south.
Instead, the sheltered bay and
sandy beach lined by a long promenade (Passeig Anglada Camarasa)
and palm trees are wonderful for
families. ⏱ *2 hr.*

7km (4 miles) northeast along
MA-2210.

**5 ★★★ kids Península de For-
mentor.** The craggy promontory at
the northeastern tip of the island is
legendary. The lunar-like, eerily
beautiful landscape of cold stone
and windswept cliffs juts 13km (8
miles) out and plunges into the surf
below. On the south side is the tranquil **Platja de Formentor** (p 29),
a lovely, pine-shaded beach with
panoramic views of the bay. Just
beyond the beach is **Hotel Formentor** (p 110), a hideaway of the glitte-
rati over the decades, including
Charlie Chaplin, Grace Kelly, Audrey

Hepburn and F. Scott Fitzgerald.
Another 12km (7 miles) out is the
Far de Formentor (lighthouse),
popular with birdwatchers who
come to view local falcons and
other species. A worthwhile detour
is to **Cala Figuera,** a small cove
with crystal-clear water. ⏱ *2 hr.*

Península de Formentor.

Day Two
8km (5 miles) south of Port de Pollença on MA-2220.

6 ★★ kids **Alcúdia.** A delightful small town, Alcúdia is encircled by what appear to be medieval walls (in fact they are largely modern imitations). The settlement was first inhabited by the Phoenicians in the 8th century B.C., before the Romans installed their strategic Mediterranean capital here behind heavy fortifications c. 70 B.C. The Gothic **Església de Sant Jaume** forms the bastion of the southern wall. Mallorca's finest Roman ruins, from that original Pol·lèntia settlement (despite the proximity to Alcúdia, Pollença somehow ended up with the name), lie just across the ring road. The **Teatre Romà** (Roman Amphitheatre) about 1km (½ mile) away is carved out of rock and makes use of the terrain's natural slope. Back in town is the **Museu Monogràfic,** a small museum of items unearthed at the ruins. Within the town walls, the principal building of interest is the 18th-century **Ajuntament** (Town Hall), on c/ Major. 🕐 *3 hr. Pol·lèntia ruins: Avda. Princeps d'Espanya s/n.* ☎ *971/89-71-02. www.pollentia.net. Museu Monogràfic: c/ Sant Jaume, 30,* ☎ *971/54-70-04. Admission 3€ adults, 2€ seniors & students (ticket valid for all three Roman sites & Museu Monogràfic); free children under 16. May–Sep Tues–Sun 9:30am–8:20pm, Oct–Apr Tues–Fri 10am–4pm, Sat–Sun 10am–2pm.*

7km (4 miles) east along carrer de Mal Pas & carrer Vell de la Victoria.

7 ★ **Península d'Alcúdia.** A scenic drive out along the promontory (or a 5-hour hike for the very energetic, for more information see Hiking & Nature Walks, p 134) takes you to **Ermita de la Victòria,** a 17th-century

Ermita de la Victòria.

chapel with a surprisingly comfortable inn (Petit Hostatgeria) upstairs (see p 110). Farther out on **Cap des Pinar** are a couple of engaging beaches and small coves. Walking trails and an unpaved road lead to **Fundació Yannick y Ben Jakober,** a curious neo-Moorish mansion and art museum that houses the owners' subterranean and impressively lit (if somewhat peculiar) collection of 16th- to 19th-century children's portraits and contemporary art and sculpture. 🕐 *2 hr. Sa Bassa Blanca.* ☎ *971/54-98-80. www.fundacionjakober.org. Admission 9€ adults, one exhibit, 12€ complete visit; free for children under 10. Tues 9:30am–12:30pm & 2:30–5:30pm, Wed–Sat, guided visit by previous appointment.*

Just south of Alcúdia on MA-12.

8 **Bodega d'es Port.** This traditional bodega, or tavern, overlooking the beach promenade and bay, makes a refreshing late lunch stop for classic Spanish tapas or more substantial Mallorcan dishes. *c/ Teodor Canet, 8, Port d'Alcúdia.* ☎ *971/54-96-33. $$.*

9 kids Port d'Alcúdia. Once a fishing harbour, this commercial port is built-up with a string of high-rise hotels, apartment blocks, discos and shops all targeting the summer tourists, although the development isn't as unseemly or overwhelming as the resorts near Palma. The main focus, the long curve of sandy beach, is a major holiday draw for families. ⏱ *2 hr.*

2km (1¼ miles) south of Platja d'Alcúdia along MA-12, with parking and the entrance on the right.

10 ★ kids Parc Natural de S'Albufera. This reclaimed 1,700-hectare (4,200-acre) tract was declared a wetlands nature preserve in the 1980s. Frequented by naturalists and especially birdwatchers, it's home to more than 270 bird species, including grey herons, egrets and grebes, and 400 plant species. It's a diverting escape, especially if the beach crowds in summer become too much. ⏱ *1 hr. MA-12 (south of Port d'Alcúdia).* ☎ *971/89-22-50. Free admission. Apr–Sept 9am–6pm, Oct–Mar 9am–5pm.*

28km (18 miles) southeast along MA-12.

A steep climb to the Santuari de Sant Salvador, Artà.

11 ★ Artà. A relaxed and historic hill town, this former Moorish stronghold has more in common with Mallorca's interior than the coast. Artà is known principally for its fortified (but reconstructed) 14th-century hilltop church, **Santuari de Sant Salvador**—more castle than church, and long a place of pilgrimage—and the **Vía Crucis** (Way of the Cross) steps that lead up to it. At the top are exceptional views of the town, surrounding countryside and coast. ⏱ *1 hr. Open access. Free admission.*

12 ★ Café Parisien. Ideal for an afternoon coffee, this French bistro has a few tables on the street and a charming garden out the back. *c/ Ciutat, 18, Artà.* ☎ *971/83-54-40. $$.*

13 ★ Ses Païsses. This rocky set of ruins on the outskirts of Artà is one of the island's most important prehistoric settlements. A Talayotic village (1300–800 B.C.), the thick walls and a watchtower hint at its defensive purposes. Although it's difficult to piece together, the shroud of mystery that envelops the ancient peoples who built these megalithic sites simply adds to their appeal for some. ⏱ *30 min. Camí Corballa, s/n.* ☎ *619/07-00-10. Admission 2€. Apr–Oct Mon–Sat 10am–1pm & 2:30–6:30pm, Nov–Mar 9am–12:30pm & 2–5pm.*

9km (5½ miles) east of Artà along MA-15.

Day Three
14 ★ Capdepera. This small hilltop village near the coast is crowned by a 14th-century castle, **Castell de Capdepera,** surrounded by crenellated battlements that once served to protect King Jaume II's villa against marauding pirates. Behind the walls is the tiny, austere chapel

Capdepera.

Nostra Senyora de l'Esperança.
🕐 45 min. Sitjar, 5. ☎ 971/81-87-46.
*Admission 2€. Apr–Oct daily 9am–
8pm, Nov–Mar, daily 10am–5pm.*

2km (1¼ miles) east of Capdepera
on MA-15.

⓯ ★ kids **Cala Ratjada.** The sandy
beaches and waterfront promenade
make Cala Ratjada one of the most
popular resorts along the northern
section of the east coast. The somewhat secluded small cove **Cala Gat** is
protected by a pine-studded hill, but
the best beaches are immediately
north and south. Beach lovers should
head south of the lighthouse on Cap
de Capdepera to **Cala Moltó** and
Cala Agulla, and to the north to the
often near-private coves (inaccessible
by car), **Cala Torta** and **Cala Mitjana.** 🕐 2 hr.

⓯' **La Bodeguita.** With tables
on the terrace under an awning, this
bar-restaurant right on the beach
has a varied menu and is a dependable place to duck out of the sun
and grab a drink or anything from
breakfast croissants to fresh prawns
and pizza. *Pg. America, 14, Cala Rat-
jada.* ☎ 971/81-90-62. $$.

From Capdepera, south along
MA-4040 before a turnoff east
(1km (½ mile) north of Canyamel).

⓱ ★★★ kids **Coves d'Artà.** The
east coast of Mallorca is famously
dotted with deep caves penetrating
the cliffs, and these 300-million-year-
old caves are less commercial and
crowded than Coves del Drach
(㉑), farther south. Dramatically lit,
with bizarre and oddly shaped stalac-
tite and stalagmite formations that
have given rise to nicknames such as
'Purgatory' and 'Inferno' chambers,
the caves are said to have inspired
Jules Verne to write *Journey to the
Centre of the Earth.* 🕐 1 hr (may
have to wait for tour). Ctra. de ses

Cala Gat.

Porto Cristo.

Coves. s/n. ☎ 971/84-12-93. www.
cuevasdearta.com. Admission 10€
adults & students, free for children
under 6. Daily May–Oct 10am–6pm,
Nov–Apr 10am–5pm.

Day Four

15km (9 miles) southwest on
MA-4040.

⓲ kids Cala Millor. A sprawling,
congested resort, this is the kind of
place to which the east coast of Mallorca owes its reputation. Although
massively built up, it also possesses
a dazzlingly long beach. In summer
even this massive expanse of sands
is packed. Still, the water is clear
and gentle, making it a hit with families. ⏱ 1 hr. See p 17.

10km (6 miles) south on MA-4023.

⓳ kids Porto Cristo. A one-time
fishing village, this unassuming town
with a natural harbour and small but
clean beach is appealing precisely
because it's lacking in the customary
resort glitz. Along the coast south of
town, it's worth visiting the prized
beaches of **Cala Romàntica** and

and **Cala Anguila** (accessible by car)
and **Cala Varques** (accessible by
foot only). ⏱ 1 hr.

⓴ ★ Siroco. Take a seat on the
terrace overlooking the port and
enjoy a lunchtime beer, grilled fish
or a rice dish. c/ del Veri, 2. ☎ 971/
82-24-44. $$.

Just off PMV-4014, immediately
south of Porto Cristo.

㉑ ★★ kids Coves del Drach.
The 'Caves of the Dragon' draw
crowds for a reason: they're spec-
tacular, especially the large subter-
ranean lake (whether you enjoy
seeing classical musicians playing in
a small boat as they paddle across
may be another matter). Children,
though, love the opportunity to
cruise the lake, which they can do
after their visit. Queues in the height
of summer can be infernal (and,
oddly, no photos are permitted).
⏱ 1½ hr (may have to wait for tour).
Ctra de ses Coves, s/n, Porto Cristo.
☎ 971/82-07-53. www.cuevasdel
drach.com. Admission 10.50€ adults
& students, free children under 7.
Daily Apr–Oct 10am–5pm, Nov–Mar
10:45am–4:30pm (set times for
entrance).

19km (12 miles) south on
MA-4014.

㉒ Portocolom. Built around a
large natural harbour, this low-key
resort is especially appealing to
walkers, who set out along the 8km
(5-mile) series of trails linking a
number of small coves along the
coast. The two best beaches are
Cala d'en Marçal and **Cala
S'Arenal.** ⏱ 45 min.

Where to **Stay**

Cas Ferrer Nou Hotelet, Alcúdia.

★ Cas Ferrer Nou Hotelet

ALCÚDIA   Within Alcúdia's medieval-looking walls, this small and chic boutique hotel in a historic townhouse is unexpectedly delightful. It features an interior courtyard, exposed old stone, and a rooftop terrace with big views. Although it somewhat self-consciously calls itself a 'design hotel', it's made cheery by a touch of whimsy and colour. *c/ Pou Nou, 1, Alcúdia.* ☎ *971/89-75-42. www.nouhotelet. com. 6 units. Doubles 110–160€ w/ breakfast. AE, DC, MC, V. Map p 102.*

★ kids Hostatgeria El Puig de Maria POLLENÇA   Perched on top

of a hill, you can stay in the former monk's quarters of an historic hermitage that's now a refuge. The rooms are therefore spartan, but the jaw-dropping views and

tranquillity—especially for active travellers who are walking for part of their holiday—make this a relaxing and incredibly cheap place to stay. There's full meal service but this is really a place for backpackers, because there's no choice but to pack your belongings in and out— meaning up and down the hill! *Cta Sant Jordi, 29, Pollença.* ☎ *971/18-41-32. hostatgeriapuig@yahoo.es. 12 units. Doubles 17–22€. MC, V. Map p 102.*

★★★ Hotel Can Simoneta CAN-

YAMEL   Perched right at the edge of a cliff, with astounding panoramic Mediterranean views, this rural luxury hotel is one of the finest properties on the east coast. In an old stone manor house, surrounded by gardens and a 15th-century

Hotel Can Simoneta, Canyamel.

Hotel Son Sant Jordi, Pollença.

estate, it ensures privacy. With an indulgent pool looking to the sea, clifftop hot tubs, stairs down to the beach, lounge areas with fireplaces, and an elegant restaurant, most guests have little reason to leave. Rooms are warmly minimalist but not overly large. I especially like the ones with their own terrace in the separate 19th-century building peering over the edge of the cliff. *Ctra. Artà a Canyamel, km. 8, Canyamel.* ☎ *971/81-61-10. www. cansimoneta.com. 17 units. Doubles 185–320€ w/breakfast. AE, DC, MC, V. Map p 102.*

★★ **Hotel Formentor** FORMENTOR   The most legendary hotel in the Balearics, with an intriguing history (instrumental in precluding development on this pristine promontory), the Formentor has served as a glamorous retreat for hundreds of stars, business magnates and politicians since the 1930s. It recently underwent a full-scale renovation to bring it back to its former glory. The 1,200-hectare (2,900-acre) estate and gardens, near-private beach and old-school elegance still draw both the curious and the regulars. *Platja de Formentor, 3, Formentor.* ☎ *971/89-91-00. www.barcelo formentor.com. 132 units. Doubles*

300–480€ w/breakfast. AE, DC, MC, V. Closed Jan–Mar. Map p 102.

★★ **kids** **Hotel Son Sant Jordi** POLLENÇA   In the heart of Pollença, this friendly, family-owned boutique hotel has just a handful of rooms but services and comforts that belie its small size. In an old stone house on its own small square, this warm and invitingly decorated inn has a lush interior garden with a pool and decent café-restaurant downstairs. *c/ Sant Jordi, 29, Alcúdia.* ☎ *971/53-03-89. www. hotelsantjordi.com. 8 units. Doubles 86–186€ w/breakfast. AE, DC, MC, V. Map p 102.*

★ **kids** **Petit Hotel Hostatgeria Ermita de la Victòria** PENÍNSULA D'ALCÚDIA   This inn—occupying the upstairs of a church dating back to 1400, way out on the Alcúdia peninsula overlooking the bay—has a big name for such a simple, out-of-the-way place. For beauty and isolation, it would be hard to do better. Rooms are restful and unexpectedly attractive, with thick stone walls, and there's a good restaurant on the premises (closed Mondays). This is a sound option for walkers and those who want to get away from it all. *Ctra. Cap des Pinar, Península d'Alcúdia.* ☎ *971/54-99-12. www.lavictoriahotel.com. 12 units. Doubles 68€ w/breakfast. AE, DC, MC, V. Map p 102.*

★★★ **Son Brull Hotel & Spa** POLLENÇA ENVIRONS   One of the most impressively stylised places on Mallorca, this converted one-time Jesuit monastery and 18th-century rural estate at the foot of Puig Maria is incredibly chic and exclusive, but also manages to be a relaxed country hotel. Rooms are contemporary and up-to-the-minute, the public spaces even more so (especially the Restaurant 365, set in an old olive press). With a magnificent outdoor pool and terraces, full spa, gourmet restaurant and activities from hiking to biking and golf and tennis, Son Brull is a sophisticated retreat. *Ctra. Palma-Pollença (MA-2200), km. 50, Pollença.* ☎ *971/53-53-53. www. sonbrull.com. 23 units. Doubles 262–465€ w/breakfast. AE, DC, MC, V. Closed Dec–Jan. Map p 102.*

★★ **Son Gener** SON SERVERA ENVIRONS Nipping at the heels of Son Mas (below) and Hotel Can Simoneta (p 109), this stately 18th-century stone farmhouse—the owners also operate the swank Convent de la Missió in Palma (p 73)—has an outdoor pool, full spa with long indoor pool ensconced in exposed stone, and elegant, large understated rooms with individual terraces. Like Son Mas, this architecture and design-driven property is extremely tasteful and sophisticated. New rooms are in a modern annexe and yoga seminars and packages are available. *Cta. Vella Son Servera – Artà, km 3, Son*

Son Mas, near Porto Cristo.

Servera. ☎ *971/18-36-12. www. songener.com. 15 units. Doubles 280€ w/breakfast. AE, DC, MC, V. Map p 102.*

★★★ **Son Mas** PORTO CRISTO ENVIRONS An exquisite 300-year-old *possessió* (farm) that's been ingeniously updated and converted, this is simply one of the finest hotels anywhere. With vaulted ceilings and unpolished marble on floors and baths, it bears the mark of its owner-architect but has a warmth and elegance that make it inviting. Rooms in both the main house and former stables (several of which have private terraces with unparalleled country views) are gigantic, but the incredible 200,000-hectare (500,000-acre) property—with an immense and secluded infinity pool and miles of walking paths, is just as much the star. With an indoor pool and small spa, this is the place for total peace and relaxation. *Ctra. Porto Cristo – Porto Colom, Porto Cristo.* ☎ *971/55-87-55. www. sonmas.com. 16 units. Doubles 244–276€ w/breakfast. AE, DC, MC, V. Map p 102.*

Son Brull Hotel & Spa, near Pollença.

Where to **Dine**

Ca'n Costa, Pollença.

★★ **Ca'n Costa** POLLENÇA *MOD-ERN MEDITERRANEAN* This stylish and petite restaurant, under new management, is a stone's throw from the Calvari steps and inhabits the large, 19th-century home of a well-known poet. The varied menu includes rosemary-skewered monk-fish with marinated red peppers and tiger prawns, roast cod fillet on a bed of saffron-scented mussels and special vegetarian and gluten-free dishes. *c/ Costa i Llobrera, 11 (Pollença).* ☎ *971/53-12-76. www.restaurantcancosta.com. Main course 11–22€. Dinner Mon–Sat. Closed mid-Nov to Mar. AE, MC, V. Map p 102.*

kids C'an Thomas PORTO CRISTO *MALLORCAN/TAPAS* This is one of those low-key and traditional restaurants that, when you want something easy and inexpensive, fits the bill very nicely. Not far from the port, it offers homemade pastas (including huge raviolis with a choice of three

sauces), tapas and daily specials. It's tiny and feels reminiscent of eating in your auntie's kitchen; a comfortable fit for families. *c/ de la Mar, 33, Porto Cristo. No phone. Main course 9–16€. Lunch & dinner daily. MC, V. Map p 102.*

★ **kids Café Parisien** ARTÀ *FRENCH BISTRO* On Artà's restaurant row, if that's not a misnomer, this congenial, high-ceilinged bistro and very agreeable outdoor patio has a diverse menu of well-prepared, good-value dishes ranging from wild mushroom risotto to duck and imaginative salads, soups and homemade pastas. *c/ Ciutat, 18 (Artà).* ☎ *971/83-54-40. Main course 11–19€. Lunch & dinner daily. MC, V. Map p 102.*

★★★ **Genestar** ALCÚDIA *MEDITER-RANEAN* This remarkable restaurant, virtually a one-man show, is one of the best-value gourmet meals to be had in Mallorca. Every night sees a brand new five-course tasting menu and the chef-owner Juanjo does it all. Everything is exquisite, masterfully prepared, plentiful, innovative and based on local fresh ingredients. The chic and architectural interior is an unexpected delight but nothing is more unexpected than the very low price. It costs just 25€ for all five courses (not including beverages, but even the wines are a great deal) at dinner, and only 18€ at lunch (Mon–Fri). It's a steal. *Plaça Porta de Mallorca, 1 baixos, Alcúdia.* ☎ *971/54-91-57. www.genestarestaurant.com. Fixed-price menu 18–25€. Lunch & dinner Thurs–Sat & Mon–Tues, dinner only Sun. AE, MC, V. Map p 102.*

★ **La Font del Gall** POLLENÇA *INTERNATIONAL* An English-Scottish couple owns this appealing restaurant, with a Scotsman in the

Stay Restaurant, Port de Pollença.

kitchen, serving a variety of well-prepared Mediterranean dishes. The fixed-price meal at lunch and dinner (14€ for two courses, 18€ for three courses) is an excellent deal, and a la carte items include delicious roast lamb loin. In summer, the tables on the terrace along a shaded street in the heart of the old town are the place to be. *c/ Montesion, 4 (Pollença).* ☎ *971/53-03-96. www.lafont delgall.com. Main course 11–18€. Dinner Sun–Fri & lunch Sun, July–Aug dinner daily & lunch Sun. Closed Nov. MC, V. Map p 102.*

kids Sa Plaça ALCÚDIA *SPANISH/ MALLORCAN* Come to this attractive restaurant right on the main square within the old city walls, with tables on the terrace and a sophisticated interior, for lunch or dinner. The lunch menu is inexpensive and a very good deal at just 9€. Choices are numerous, from *bacalao* (salted cod) to paella and tapas, and there's a children's menu too. *Plaça Constitució,*

1, Alcúdia. ☎ *971/54-91-57. Main course 10–19€. Lunch & dinner Thurs– Sat & Mon–Tues. AE, MC, V. Map p 102.*

★★ kids Stay Restaurant PORT DE POLLENÇA *SEAFOOD/MEDITER-RANEAN* A contemporary glass box perched out on a pier, with views of Pollença bay and the hills in the distance, this is the place to soak up the sun and devour some fresh seafood. The covered terrace is just about the most ideal place to relax (youngsters will probably enjoy sitting perched out over the water) and the food, including the daily 32€ set menu (including wine) is very well done. As well as fish, there are Mediterranean vegetables, pastas, fresh salads and other gastronomic delights to get stuck into. *Port de Pollença.* ☎ *971/86-40-13. www.stayrestaurant.com. Main course 11–41€. Breakfast, lunch & dinner daily. AE, DC, MC, V. Map p 102.*

Southern & Interior Mallorca

Day 1
1 Binissalem
2 Inca
3 Sineu
4 Sa Plaça Petra
5 Petra

Day 2
6 Felanitx
7 Cala d'Or

Day 3
8 Parc Natural de Mondragó
9 Cala Figuera
10 Colònia de Sant Jordi
11 Gelateria Colonial
12 Platja d'es Trenc
13 Illa de Cabrera

Day 4

Where to Stay
Blau Porto Petro Beach Resort & Spa 14
Hotel León de Sineu 15
La Hospedería Santuari de Cura 16
Petit Hotel Hostatgeria Sant Salvador 17
Son Penya Petit Hotel 18
Son Pons 19
Torrent Fals 20

Where to Dine
Bacchus (Read's Hotel) 21
Céller C'an Ripoll 22
Céller Es Grop 23
Hostal Restaurante Playa 24
Port Petit 25

The island's largely flat interior called, simply, **Es Pla** (literally 'The Plain') is its traditional heartland, home to historic villages, agricultural landscapes and vineyards. The southern coast mostly consists of fishing villages and a long strand of undeveloped sand. START: **Palma to Binissalem (27km (17 miles)) along MA-13A (the more scenic old road). Trip length: 4 days.**

Day One

1 ★ Binissalem. Just north of Palma is the epicentre of the Mallorcan wine industry, which is newly ascendant but in fact ancient. Wine aficionados are excited to discover that many Mallorcan wines, both white and red, are based on indigenous varietals cultivated only here. For more information on visiting wineries and tasting local wines, see Gourmet Mallorca (p 30). The town of Binissalem is distinguished by a number of notable 18th-century, white-stone manor houses. **Casa-Museu Llorenç Villalonga** functions as a museum allowing a look at a historic, elite country house. ⏱ *2 hr. Casa-Museu Llorenç Villalonga: c/ de Bonaire, 25.* ☎ *971/88-60-14. www.cmvillalonga.org. Free admission. Mon–Sat 10am–2pm, Thurs–Fri 4pm–8pm.*

7km (4 miles) northeast of Binissalem along MA-13A.

2 Inca. This rather unlovely city, home to Mallorca's leather industry, is known for two things: outlet shopping and restaurants. Factory outlets offer first-rate leather goods and shoes. Two of the best-known Spanish shoe brands are Mallorcan, and they both started in Inca: Camper and Farrutx (each of which has a factory outlet here). Main shopping destinations are Avda. Jaume II, Avda. del General Luque and Polígono Industrial. A dozen or so rustic eateries, such as Celler C'an Ripoll (p 122) are housed in the cavernous old winemaking cellars that once dominated Inca. ⏱ *1½ hr.*

Binissalem is the epicentre of the Mallorcan wine industry.

13km (8 miles) southeast of Inca along MA-3240.

3 ★★ Sineu. Smack in the middle of the island, this handsome, historic small town is where King Jaume II built a royal palace in 1309 (today the site is the **Convent de la Concepció,** on c/ Major). A distinguished late-Gothic parish church, **Església de Santa Maria,** dates from the early 16th century and dominates a small square. Also worth seeking out is the **Creu dels Morts** (Cross of the Dead), a 16th-century waymarker stone cross on carrer Creu, one block northeast of Sa Plaça. On Wednesdays until 2pm, Sineu hosts an interesting traditional market, which features not only produce from around the island but also livestock. ⏱ *1 hr.*

11km (7 miles) southeast of Sineu along MA-3300.

Miquel Oliver's Winery.

4 Sa Plaça Petra. Petra's main square is ringed by cafés whose terraces are particularly popular with cyclists seeking mid-ride sustenance. Do as they do and grab some coffee, pastries and orange slices, or something more substantial, such as paella or cuttlefish stew. *Pl. Ramón Llull, 4, Petra.* ☎ *971/56-16-46.* $$.

5 Petra. A modest rural town with a large reputation, at least among

Església de Sant Miquel, Felanitx.

religious historians, Petra was the birthplace of a Franciscan monk, **Juniper Serra** (1713–84), who went on to found the Catholic missions in California and Baja California—effectively founding the settlements that would give rise to San Diego, Los Angeles and San Francisco—and was later beatified by Pope John Paul II. Next to Serra's house is a monument and museum to his life, missions and followers: **Museu i Casa Pairal de Fra Juniper Serra.** Serra's birthplace is at no. 4 and is worth a look for its humble, cramped interior. Also in Petra is a small and smart winery, **Vinyes i Bodegues Miquel Oliver.** The owner is usually on hand to talk you through his wines, including a surprising dry white Muscat. ⏱ *1 hr. Museu i Casa Pairal de Fra Juniper Serra: c/ des Barracar Alt, 6.* ☎ *971/56-11-66. Mon–Sat 9am–6pm; donation suggested. Vinyes i Bodegues Miquel Oliver: c/ Font, 26.* ☎ *971/ 56-11-17. www.miqueloliver.com. Free admission. Mon–Fri 10am– 1:45pm & 3:30–6pm, July–Aug Mon– Fri 10am–3pm.*

Day Two
14km (9 miles) southwest of Manacor along MA-14.

6 ★★ kids Felanitx. This town's 13th-century church, **Església de**

Sant Miquel, with its handsome honey-coloured Renaissance façade, sits high atop a steep set of stairs. A church wall collapsed here in 1844, killing more than 400 people taking part in an Easter procession. Looming over the town is the **Santuari de Sant Salvador,** a chapel perched on top of **Puig Sant Salvador,** the highest peak of the Serra de Llevant (5km (3 miles) southeast of Felanitx). The 1348 sanctuary remains an important place of pilgrimage, although it also draws hordes of hardcore cyclists who test their conditioning as they climb the switchbacks of the 509m (1,700 ft) hilltop (for more information on cycling, see Cycling p 132). At the windy summit they are rewarded with spectacular panoramic views all the way to the coast. Strong, determined walkers can set out from the ruins of **Castell de Santuari,** 7km (4 miles) southeast of Felanitx (off MA-14), and walk along a relatively clear path to the sanctuary. You can even spend the

Cala Mondragó.

night up here, at the quiet and inexpensive hermitage hotel. ⏱ *2 hr.*

⑦ **kids** **Cala d'Or.** It's easy to disparage this mega-resort, but the fact is that it has some appealing beaches and coves, with pristine azure waters, if you can look past the massive development. **Cala Gran** is perhaps the nicest of the coves, while **Port Petit** is a

Siurells: The Art of the Clay Whistle

A children's toy and item of popular folk art, the *siurell,* or clay whistle, has become a symbol of Mallorca—aided surely by the surrealist painter and sculptor Joan Miró, who was fascinated and even said to be influenced by them. Made on Mallorca at least since the Moors inhabited the island, the whitewashed whistles are dabbed with distinctive green and red (or occasionally blue and yellow) brushstrokes. Their origin is unclear (some believe they date to the Bronze Age), although they may have been used to ward off evil spirits or summon the winds for the harvest. Traditionally they depict the devil or a peasant figure, though they have been adapted to include other images including shepherds, winged donkeys and even full nativity scenes. They are mostly produced in Es Pla, the Mallorcan interior, around Inca and especially the town of Marratxí.

Cala Figuera.

fashionable marina gleaming with ostentatious yachts. 🕐 *1 hr.*

19km (12 miles) south on Ctra. Palma-Porto Petro.

⑧ ★★ kids Parc Natural de Mondragó. An oasis of unspoiled nature, designated an 'Area of Special Protection for Birds' and a world apart in spirit from the large coastal developments to the north, this 800-hectare (2,000-acre) nature park is an idyllic retreat for walkers and birdwatchers (look for migratory birds and white cranes, shags and Audouin's gulls). Trails through the park's pine forest lead to wetlands and the coves of **Cala Mondragó** and **S'Amarador,** both with curved sandy beaches sheltered by pine trees. Trail maps are available at the visitor centre. 🕐 *2 hr. Ctra. de Cala Mondragó s/n.* ☎ *971/18-10-22. Free admission. Daily 9am–4pm.*

Day Three
7km (4 miles) south along MA-6102.

⑨ ★ Cala Figuera. A small, natural harbour of considerable beauty, this peaceful spot is still home to small fishing boats along the pine-studded coastline. There's no beach to speak of, although **Cala Santanyi,** about 4km (2½ miles) to the west, is a good bet. If you don't mind a 2km (1 mile) walk (from Cala Llombards), head to **Caló des Moro** (see p 126), a protected and uncrowded cove beach with limpid waters. 🕐 *2 hr.*

18km (11 miles) west along MA-6102 & MA-6100.

⑩ ★ kids Colònia de Sant Jordi. Although a family-oriented coastal resort with a surprisingly substantial town at its core, Colònia de Sant Jordi is known mostly for the distinctively untamed natural beauty of its environs, something that has endeared it to generations of Palma residents. There are a few very enjoyable beaches in town, particularly to the south and west, and you can also set off by ferry in season for the small island nature park of **Illa de Cabrera** (see below). 🕐 *2 hr.*

⑪ ★ kids Gelatería Colonial. Families come from miles around for this treasured ice cream shop in downtown Sant Jordi. There's also a restaurant with outdoor seating, serving Mallorcan dishes, fresh fish and garden vegetables. *c/ de l'Enginier Gabriel Roca, 9, Colònia de Sant Jordi.* ☎ *971/65-52-26. $.*

Head north out of town towards Campos; turn left on a country lane, where 'Es Trenc' is signposted.

⑫ ★★ kids Platja d'es Trenc. The longest undeveloped beach on Mallorca, this 4km (2½-mile) stretch of sand is one of the island's wildest coasts, punctuated by dunes. Spurred on by local environmental concerns, the government has stepped in to rule out most development. It's a long, 30-minute walk from Colònia de Sant Jordi, but you can drive to a car park among the dunes. ◷ *2 hr. See p 127.*

Day Four
Take a boat from Colònia de Sant Jordi (summer only).

⑬ ★ kids Illa de Cabrera. A small, uninhabited archipelago off the coast of Colònia de Sant Jordi, 'Goat Island' is a rocky and largely barren place, comprising 18 tiny islands protected as a nature park since 1991. Cabrera, the largest island, is home to a 14th-century castle, a lighthouse and a fragile

The wild coastline of Platja d'es Trenc.

ecosystem of scrubby plants, crystalline waters and indigenous wildlife including Balearic lizards and rare Eleonora's falcons. There are numerous walking trails (including the steep trek uphill to the castle), although some require permission. Hour-long boat trips (part of all-day, organised excursions, limited to 200 people per day, 300 in August) depart from Colònia de Sant Jordi daily in summer; it's wise to reserve places in advance. Food and drinks are sold on board, or bring your own. ◷ *6 hr.* ☎ *971/64-90-34. www.excursionsacabrera.com. 35€ adults, 15€ children 15 & under.*

Historic Cabrera

Although today the tiny archipelago is uninhabited by humans and home mostly to lizards and birds, Cabrera has seen its share of historic incidents. Some writers, including Pliny, claimed that Cabrera was the birthplace of none other than Hannibal. Pirates hid out here during raids on Mallorca in the Middle Ages and, during the Napoleonic Wars, Spanish forces dumped nearly 10,000 French prisoners of war on Cabrera in 1809 and left them to die (about half did).

Where to **Stay**

★★ kids **Blau Porto Petro Beach Resort & Spa** PORTO PETRO   A self-contained resort complex, this sprawling and well-managed hotel wends its way around a protected part of the southern coast. It has virtually anything anyone looking to stay put could want: smartly decorated rooms, a full spa with indoor pool, 10 tennis courts, three outdoor pools, a private beach cove, a children's club and three gourmet restaurants. It's big enough that you'll probably need to get around on a golf cart, but private and friendly enough that it doesn't seem impersonal. *c/ des Far, 16, Porto Petro.* ☎ *971/64-82-82. www.blauhotels. com. 319 units. Doubles 200–305€ w/breakfast. AE, DC, MC, V. Map p 114.*

Hotel León de Sineu SINEU A 15th-century building right in town, with a vaulted-ceiling restaurant, backyard pool and gardens and comfy, old-world-style rooms, this is a sensible option if you want to try staying in one of Es Pla's most attractive and historic towns. *c/ dels Bous, 129, Sineu.* ☎ *971/52-02-11. www.hotel-leondesineu.com 15 units. Doubles 100–150€ w/breakfast. MC, V. Map p 114.*

La Hospederia Santuari de Cura PUIG DE RANDA   For something a little different—monastic, austere and on top of a mountain—this hermitage at an important religious sanctuary might just tick those boxes. It's all about the location and views from the mountaintop, and the spirituality of the place, because rooms are somewhat on the simple side. *Santuari de Cura, Randa.* ☎ *971/12-02-60. www. santuaridecura.org. 35 units. Doubles 65€. AE, DC, MC, V. Map p 114.*

Blau Porto Petro Beach Resort & Spa.

La Hospederia Santuari de Cura, Randa.

Petit Hotel Hostatgeria Sant Salvador FELANITX One of the best options for bargain hunters looking for a unique place to stay—preferably with a view—is the series of old mountaintop hermitages converted into simple inns. The modern, clean rooms at this quiet little hotel atop the 509m (1,700 ft) Puig Sant Salvador are unspectacular—something you definitely can't say about the vistas you'll wake up to, overlooking the whole of southeast Mallorca. The Can Calco restaurant, with vaulted ceilings, will save you from having to head down the mountain for dinner. *Santuari de Sant Salvador, Felanitx.* ☎ *971/51-52-60. www.santsalvadorhotel.com. 35 units. Doubles 65€. MC, V. Map p 114.*

★★ Son Penya Petit Hotel SAN LLORENÇ This stylish country boutique hotel is near enough to the coast to function perfectly well for beach lovers as well as those exploring Mallorca's interior. On a large and peaceful property, the traditional stone house features ample terraces, a designer pool, gardens and olive trees and romantically decorated rooms in which white and stone dominate. *c/ de Son Berga s/n, Sant Llorenç des Cardassa.* ☎ *971/82-66-40. www.esturodesonpenya.com. 12 units. Doubles 98–189€ w/breakfast. AE, DC, MC, V. Map p 114.*

★ kids Son Pons BÚGER This pleasant-looking country estate just a bit off the beaten track is perfect for people looking for a stylish rural experience without some of the fuss and high prices of designer *fincas*. Rooms in the 16th-century house are thoughtfully decorated, spacious and shockingly good value. *Ctra. Búger - Sa Pobla s/n, Búger.* ☎ *971/87-71-42. www.sonpons.com. 10 units. Doubles 55–85€ w/breakfast. AE, DC, MC, V. Map p 114.*

★★ Torrent Fals SANTA MARÍA DEL CAMÍ Incredibly, this restful 10-hectare (25-acre) property with a rustic old stone farmhouse has remained in the same family since the 15th century. With a past in wine production, today it's a comfortable rural hotel and a better deal than many offering chic country ambience. Amenities include an expansive infinity pool, a great wine cellar, gardens and pine forests just made for private strolls. Rooms feature handsome antiques and neutral palettes. *Ctra. Santa Maria - Sencelles, s/n, Sineu.* ☎ *971/52-02-11. www.torrentfals.com. 7 units. Doubles 135–155€ w/breakfast. AE, DC, MC, V. Map p 114.*

Where to **Dine**

Céllar C'an Ripoll, Inca.

★★★ Bacchus (Read's Hotel)

SANTA MARÍA DEL CAMÍ *CONTEM-PORARY INTERNATIONAL*   Although the British chef Marc Fosh, who earned a Michelin star in the kitchen here, has moved on, this restaurant is still one of the most distinguished on the island, serving haute cuisine in an elegant 16th-century dining room. For a splurge opt for the seven-course tasting menu (which isn't absurdly priced at 89€). *Crta. Vieja Santa Maria-Alaró, Santa Maria del Cami.* ☎ *971/14-02-61. www.readshotel.com. Main course 16–45€. Lunch & dinner Tues–Sun. AE, DC, MC, V. Map p 114.*

★★ kids Céller C'an Ripoll INCA

MALLORCAN   One of Inca's classic restaurants, this cavernous former wine cellar from 1761 has soaring ceilings and stone arches, massive wine vats and a gregarious, rustic ambience. The food is hearty, even wintry: *tumbet* (baked aubergine, potato and vegetables) and lamb are among the specialities. The midday lunch menu is very reasonable.

c/ Jaume Armengol, 4, Inca. ☎ *971/50-00-24. www.canripoll.com. Main course 10–19€. Lunch & dinner Mon–Sat. MC, V. Map p 114.*

★ kids Céller Es Grop SINEU

MALLORCAN   Set in an antique cellar, with a backdrop of vast wine barrels, this atmospheric family-owned eaterie in the heart of Sineu serves filling traditional Mallorcan fare, including grilled fish and delicious fried dishes, such as the *frito mallorquí* (fried lamb, offal with potatoes, onions and peppers). *c/ Major, 18, Sineu.* ☎ *971/52-01-87. Main course 10–15€. Lunch & dinner Tues–Sun. MC, V. Map p 114.*

kids Hostal Restaurante Playa

COLÒNIA DE SANT JORDI *SEAFOOD/SPANISH*   A small inn and restaurant that's been in the same family since 1934, this endearingly simple place overlooks the ocean, and so pick a table on the terrace. The menu is simple but focuses on grilled fish and shellfish from the waters near Cabrera. *c/ Major, 25, Colònia de Sant Jordi.* ☎ *971/65-52-56. www.restauranteplaya.com. Main course 12–25€. Lunch & dinner Tues–Sun, lunch only Mon. MC, V. Map p 114.*

★★ Port Petit CALA D'OR SEA-FOOD/MALLORCAN

This upscale restaurant, with a spectacular terrace overlooking the sleek yachts parked in the Cala d'Or marina, is excellent for fresh grilled fish and creative twists on Mediterranean dishes. The lunchtime bistro menu is a great deal at 21.50€, and the three different tasting menus are also well thought-out and attractively priced (35–60€). *Avda. Cala Llonga, Marina de Cala d'Or, Cala d'Or.* ☎ *971/64-30-39. www.portpetit.com. Main course 19–39€. Lunch & dinner Tues–Sun. AE, DC, MC, V. Map p 114.* ●

5 The Great **Outdoors**

The Great Outdoors

Mallorca's **Beaches**

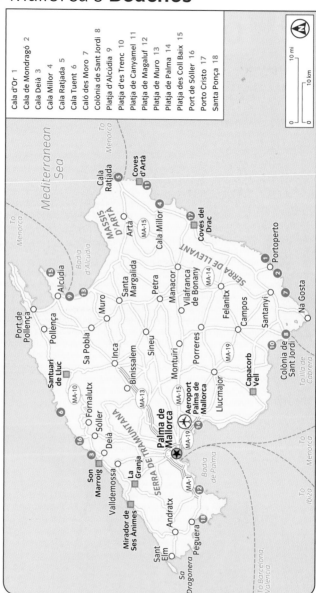

Cala d'Or 1
Cala de Mondragó 2
Cala Deià 3
Cala Millor 4
Cala Ratjada 5
Cala Tuent 6
Caló des Moro 7
Colònia de Sant Jordi 8
Platja d'Alcúdia 9
Platja d'es Trenc 10
Platja de Canyamel 11
Platja de Magaluf 12
Platja de Muro 13
Platja de Palma 14
Platja des Coll Baix 15
Port de Sóller 16
Porto Cristo 17
Santa Ponça 18

Previous page: Trekking Puig Santa Maria on the northeast coast of Mallorca.

Mallorca's international reputation rests largely on its **pristine beaches** and clear Mediterranean swimming waters. The vast coastline—more than 200 beaches—includes everything from long and serene family-oriented beaches with every facility and service, to crowded sands elbow-to-elbow with party-mad holiday-makers, and unspoiled secluded coves accessible only by foot or boat. *Note:* This is not a tour.

Cala Gran.

kids **Cala d'Or** SANTANYÍ/SOUTHEAST COAST   A large resort comprising five beach coves. **Cala Gran,** the largest and most developed, is probably also the best bet, with fine-grain white sand, calm waters and pine woods. It's well protected by cliffs, and there's a park for children. *15km (9 miles) from Portocolom along MA-4013.*

★★ kids **Cala de Mondragó** SANTANYÍ/SOUTHEAST COAST Within the 800-hectare (2,000-acre) Mondragó nature park are 2 pretty coves, **Cala de Mondragó,** a blue flag beach, and **s'Amarador,** with gently sloping curved beaches of fine white sand sheltered by pine

woods and beautiful rock formations**.** Both are perfect for swimming. *5½km (3 miles) from Santanyi along MA-6100.*

★★ kids **Cala Deià** DEIÀ/NORTHWEST COAST   This small, rocky cove with limited sand but very clear water is excellent for swimming. There's a restaurant and bar, as well as a beautiful footpath that climbs to Llucalcari. *1km (½ mile) east of Deià, off MA-10 (and a 2km (1¼-mile) road to beach parking).*

★ kids **Cala Millor** SON SERVERA/ EAST COAST   The 2km (1¼-mile) long, blue-flag beach of fine white sand at this mega-resort, one of the busiest in summer, has gentle,

Clamber around the rocky cove at Cala Deià.

transparent waters and a promenade that runs its entire length. There are bike rentals and pedal boats for rent, as well as a windsurfing school. *3km (1.8 miles) from Son Servera along MA-4023.*

★★ kids **Cala Ratjada** CAPDEPERA/EAST COAST   A popular resort along the northern section of the east coast, Cala Ratjada has several sandy beaches and a waterfront promenade. Of the coves, the most attractive is **Cala Gat,** a small and quiet cove protected by a pine-studded hill. The best beaches are north or south, such as **Cala Agulla,** a pristine (blue-flag) stretch of very fine white sand on a calm bay. To the north, **Cala Torta** is unspoiled and remote, with fine white sand, transparent water. Its laid-back open-air bar also serves food and is the best beach bar in Mallorca. Swimming can be dangerous, although it's excellent for diving (see Diving & Snorkelling, p 132). You can also walk from Cala Mesquida along a mountain trail (45 minutes) or from Cala Mitjana (15

minutes). *2km (1¼ miles) from Capdepera along MA-15. Drive 9km (6 miles) from Artà, take the road at the fork on the right and continue for 1.3km (¾ mile) until reaching the beach.*

★ kids **Cala Tuent** ESCORCA/ NORTHWEST COAST   This beautiful, pebbly, semicircular beach at

Cala Torta, a remote beach with white sands.

the foot of a mountain has sparkling turquoise waters but can be windy. The tiny cove at the river gorge, **Torrent de Pareis,** is spectacular and good for swimming, but it's often crowded. Note that it's not the easiest of drives as you have to brave the famously twisty road— 13km (8 miles) of hairpin turns called 'The Snake'. *40km (25 miles) east of Sóller along MA-10; take the well signposted turn-off from PM-2141 and a fork after 11km (7 miles) in the direction of Sa Calobra.*

★★ Caló des Moro Santanyí/ SOUTHEAST COAST   A tiny, protected and secluded beach cove, just 20m (66 ft) long, this prized, beautiful spot is sandwiched between cliffs covered in pines and bushes, with a few large boulders right at the edge of the sands. The sand is pearly white, the waters limpid. The beach is accessible only by a 2km (1¼-mile) walk from Cala Llombards. *6km (3½ miles) from Santanyí (between Cala s'Almunia and Cala Llombards).*

★★ Colònia de Sant Jordi SES SALINES/SOUTH COAST   There are several good beaches in this family-oriented resort town as well as others to the south and west, including **Es Marquès,** with white sand, surrounded by pine trees and dunes, and sun loungers and parasols for hire; **Es Port,** with a promenade lined by palm trees, next to the port in Colònia de Sant Jordi; **Es Dolç,** a beautiful and unspoiled beach, reached by walking along the promenade from Es Port; and unspoiled and uncrowded **Es Carbó** (1½km (about 1 mile) away. For all these beaches, park at the resort of Colònia de Sant Jordi and walk southeast around the coast, which may be difficult with small children. *14km (9 miles) south of Campos along MA-6040 and then MA-6100.*

★★ kids Platja d'Alcúdia
BADIA D'ALCÚDIA/NORTH COAST This long (2km/1¼-mile) family-friendly, blue-flag beach features fine white sand and clear, shallow water. Services include numerous restaurants, open-air bars, sports facilities, sun loungers, umbrellas and pedal boats for hire, as well as water skis, jet skis and paragliding. *1.6km (1 mile) south of Port d'Alcúdia on MA-12.*

★★ kids Platja d'es Trenc
SOUTH COAST   The longest undeveloped beach on Mallorca, this 4km (2½-mile), narrow stretch of white, fine-grained sand has very clean, clear, shallow water, a gentle slope and sand dunes bordering the beach. The beach is popular on weekends with residents of Palma and good for children, but parents should note that there's a nudist area to the west. *6½km (4 miles) west of Colònia de Sant Jordi along MA-6040 and then a signposted country, 30-minute walk from Colònia de Sant Jordi. Car park 6€.*

★ kids Platja de Canyamel CAP-DEPERA/EAST COAST   Just across the bay from the Artà caves, this long sweep of golden-sand and blue-flag beach can be crowded, although not as busy as the large resorts farther south. The beach is lined with pine trees, and you'll find restaurants, showers, sun loungers, and pedal boats and parasols for hire. *7km (4 miles) south of Cala Ratjada along MA-4042.*

Platja de Magaluf BADIA DE PALMA/WEST COAST   Massively popular, this blue-flag beach has fine sand and clear water, palm trees for shade and a chic promenade. Magaluf draws hordes of young people for water skiing, jet skis and sailing boat trips, but also

Platja de Palma.

for the noisy pubs, restaurants and discos along the waterfront. *7km (4 miles) south of Calvià along MA-1015.*

★★ kids **Platja de Muro** PORT D'ALCÚDIA/NORTH COAST A long, pleasant sweep of fine-grained, golden sand and a favourite of families, this beach is one of the best swimming spots on the island. The blue-flag beach, between Port d'Alcúdia and C'an Picafort, is sheltered by the bay and shaded by pine trees. Facilities include sun loungers, parasols and a wide selection of bars and restaurants. *2km (1¼ miles) north of C'an Picafort along MA-3431.*

★ kids **Platja de Palma** BADIA DE PALMA/SOUTH COAST For many, Platja de Palma—one of the island's longest stretches of sand at 4½km (2¾ miles) long—is synonymous with Mallorca. It actually comprises several crowded beaches and run-on resorts, including **Ca'n Pastilla** (popular with windsurfers), small **Cala Estància** (an inlet and favourite of families, with calm waters) and its extension southeast, **S'Arenal** (including the beaches **Sometimes** and **Ses Maravelles**), where the young, tanned and minimally clothed come to party. Sands are fine grained and slopes are gentle. *14km (9 miles) east of Palma along MA-19. Bus no. 25.*

★★ **Platja des Coll Baix** ALCÚDIA PENINSULA/NORTH COAST One of the north's most secluded beaches, backed by high cliffs. The beach is a mix of coarse-grained sand and pebbles, but the water is perfectly translucent. From Alcúdia, head out towards Cap des Pinar along Camí de Sa Muntanya, which becomes an unpaved road. The last section is a 15-minute (1km (½-mile) walk downhill along a trail to the beach. *9km (6 miles) east of Alcúdia.*

★ kids **Port de Sóller** BADIA DE SÓLLER/NORTHWEST COAST Along the Badia de Sóller are two

What Do the Flags Mean?

Green flags signal no danger; yellow advise precaution; and red mean no swimming. 'Blue-flag' beaches are singled out for exceptional environmental conditions and cleanliness. For hours, swimming conditions and transport, visit www.mallorcabeachguide.com.

Cala Romàntica near Porto Cristo.

beaches. The city beach, simply called **Port,** alongside the harbour promenade is lined with seafront restaurants; only the first section is decent sand, the rest being very narrow and rocky. The other, preferable, beach is **Platja d'en Repic,** which has a pedestrian-only promenade. The beach is mostly sand but it has a deep slope into the water. There are sun loungers, pedalos and parasols for hire, as well as boat trips from the beach. Vintage trams connect the town of Sóller to the Port, and so the journey can be fun for all the family. *4km (2½ miles) north of Sóller along MA-11. See also p 94,* **19**.

★★ **kids Porto Cristo** MANACOR/ WEST COAST   This former fishing village has a small, clean and protected blue-flag beach with good swimming, and sun loungers, pedal boats and parasols for hire. Prettier beaches lie just to the south: **Cala**

Romàntica and **Cala Anguila** are both accessible by car, with fine golden sand and clear turquoise water on an inlet, but **Cala Varques** is reachable by foot only. *Porto Cristo, 12km (7 miles) east of Manacor on MA-4020); coves to south, 3–12km (2–7 miles) south of Portocristo along MA-4014.*

★ **kids Santa Ponça** WEST COAST   This broad, sandy beach west of Palma, popular with families and especially British visitors, is shaded by pine trees. The clear water is shallow and propitious for most kinds of water sports, including diving (see Diving & Snorkelling, p 132). Although a large resort with many shops, restaurants and bars, its development is relatively tame. Facilities include sun loungers, umbrellas and pedal boats. *16km (10 miles) west of Palma along MA-20.*

The Active **Outdoors**

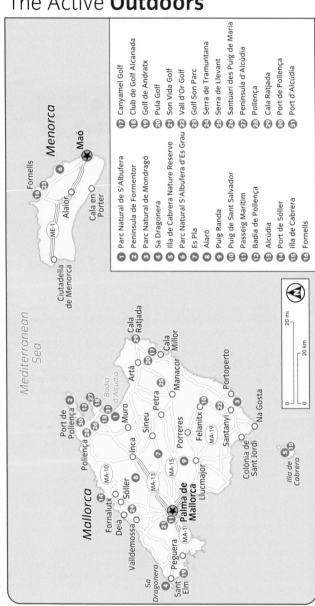

1. Parc Natural de S'Albufera
2. Peninsula de Formentor
3. Parc Natural de Mondragó
4. Sa Dragonera
5. Illa de Cabrera Nature Reserve
6. Parc Natural S'Albufera d'Es Grau
7. Es Pla
8. Alaró
9. Puig Randa
10. Puig de Sant Salvador
11. Passeig Marítim
12. Badia de Pollença
13. Alcúdia
14. Port de Sóller
15. Illa de Cabrera
16. Fornells
17. Canyamel Golf
18. Club de Golf Alcanada
19. Golf de Andratx
20. Pula Golf
21. Son Vida Golf
22. Vall d'Or Golf
23. Golf Son Parc
24. Serra de Tramuntana
25. Serra de Llevant
26. Santuari des Puig de Maria
27. Peninsula d'Alcúdia
28. Pollença
29. Cala Ratjada
30. Port de Pollença
31. Port d'Alcúdia

Beautiful and sunny Mallorca is prized by outdoor enthusiasts. The island's varied terrain is ideal for year-round active pursuits, including hiking and nature walks among the northwest coast, cycling on flat plains and mountainous ascents, and sailing and windsurfing. Golfers will find some of the most scenic and well-designed courses in the Mediterranean.

Birdwatching

Birdwatchers come to Mallorca and Menorca to view not only resident birds, but also migrating birds en route from Africa; the Balearics are rare among Mediterranean islands in that they have natural wetlands that attract migrant birds.

Top spots for birdwatchers include: **①** **★★ Parc Natural de S'Albufera** (p 106, **⑩**), the wetlands on Mallorca's northeast coast with more than 200 species, two-thirds of the island's permanent resident birds; **②** **Peninsula de Formentor** (p 104, **⑤**); **③** **Parc Natural de Mondragó** (p 118, **⑧**); **④** **Sa Dragonera** (p 89, **③**); **⑤** **Illa de Cabrera Nature Reserve** (p 119, **⑬**); and **⑥** **Parc Natural S'Albufera d'Es Grau** (p 117, **①**) on Menorca. Dedicated twitchers should check out the online forum **Birding in Spain** (www.birdinginspain.com/birding-in-mallorca.html) for additional information on trips to the Balearic Islands.

Boating & Sailing

The Balearics are highly prized by boating and sailing aficionados, with plenty of gentle, safe harbours and nearly four dozen marinas on Mallorca and Menorca. Several quiet, unspoiled beach coves are only accessible by boat. Visitors can rent a variety of watercraft for hours, days or weeks as well as find sailing schools in Palma and Port de Pollença. A number of beach resorts along the north and east coasts feature glass-bottomed cruise boats—a great option for families.

Find charter, rental and nautical-school information at **Balears Nautic** (http://en.balearsnautic.com), www.infomallorca.net and www.baleares.com. Reputable companies specialising in luxury charters with a skipper include **Blue Sky Cruising** (Paseo Mallorca 2, Palma de Mallorca; ☎ 687/89-84-82; UK: ☎ 0870-855-0007); and **Mallorca Sea School and Charters** (Local 37, Puerto Portals, Calvia; ☎ 971/67-93-42), with a fleet of boats and yachts.

Top birdwatching spot Parc Natural de S'Albufera.

Explore the quiet, unspoilt coves by boat.

Cycling

As many as 50,000 people a year come to cycle Mallorca's roads and tracks. The flat ★★ **Es Pla** (interior) is perfect for gentle rides, while thousands of pro and amateur road cyclists flood the back roads late winter and early spring (decked out in their pro kits) to cycle the mountainous northwest coast and a handful of steep peaks in the interior: ★★ **Alaró**, ★★ **Puig Randa**, and ★★★ **Puig de Sant Salvador** just outside Felanitx. The tourism office puts out a *Ciclotourismo* brochure and map, with details of 10 different cycling routes ranging from 19½km (12 miles) to 86km (53 miles) and including difficulty levels, elevations, and a list of hotels specialising in cyclotourism (many have special facilities). For additional information on routes and cycling tours, see: www.illesbalears.es/ing/balearicislands/cycling-tourism (the *Ciclotourismo* brochure can be printed out there as well). You'll find additional cycling routes and information at www.baleares.com.

For laid-back cycling around the Bay of Palma, the waterfront ★★ **Passeig Marítim** in Palma is a hugely popular spot. Bike rentals and tours of Palma are available through **PalmaOnBike.com** (Av. Gabriel Roca, 15, Palma; ☎ 971/91-89-88; www.palmaonbike.com). See also box, Biking Palma, p 57.

Bike rentals are also available through **Tramuntana Tours** (Passeig de Traves, 12, Port de Sóller, Mallorca; ☎ 971/63-24-23; www.tramuntanatours.com) and **Rent a Bike Vivas** (c/ Santa Teresa, 20, Sóller, Mallorca; ☎ 971/63-02-34; www.rentabikevivas.com), both of which rent racing, touring and mountain bikes. **Velo Sport Mallorca** (Apartado 82, Primera Vuelta 108, Son Prohens/Felanitx, Mallorca; ☎ 626/27-29-09 www.velosportmallorca.com) rents high-end road bikes (carbon Scotts and Cérvelos with Dura-Ace components). Rentals range from about 8€ to 20€ per day. Bike transport is allowed on the Ferrocarril Inca—Manacor train only.

Menorca is largely flat and has very narrow secondary roads, many of which are lined by ancient *paredes secas* (stone walls). Distances are short, perfect easygoing rides.

Diving & Snorkelling

Diving along the coasts of Mallorca isn't quite the spectacular experience one might expect, although there is plenty on offer in **Badia de Pollença** (p 103,), **Alcúdia** (p 105,) and **Port de Sóller** (p 94,), (the east coast resorts are generally less good). Best diving spots on Mallorca are the two island formations off the northwest and southern coasts: **Illa de Cabrera** (p 119,) and **Sa Dragonera** (p 89,). For diving from Sa Dragonera, try

Scuba Activa (Pl. Monseñor Sebastian Grau, 7, Sant Elm; ☎ 971/23-91-02; www.scuba-activa.com).

More rewarding still is Menorca, with its clear waters and high visibility along the north and west coasts, where you can dive shipwrecks. One of the best spots is ★★★ **Fornells** (p 148, ❸). A number of diving schools and equipment providers are listed at www.baleares.com and www.infomallorca.net. On Menorca, contact **Diving Center Fornells** (Avda. La Font, 12, Fornells; ☎ 971/34-85-65; www.divingfornells.com).

Golf

There are excellent courses in the Balearics to complement the perfect golfing weather; you can play 365 days a year. Mallorca has about two dozen golf courses, most in the interior around the Bay of Palma and along the east coast, but there's only one on Menorca. Greens fees range from 55€ to 150€. Pick up the *Mallorca Golf* brochure published by the Illes Balears tourism office. **Golf Mallorca** is a specialist travel company focusing on golfing holidays and has links to all the major courses, including greens fees and special holiday packages (www.golfmallorca.com).

Some of the top courses include:

⓱ ★★★ **Canyamel Golf** Beautiful and demanding 18 holes, par 73, 5,740m (6,277 yards). *Avda. des Cap Vermell, s/n, Capdepera.* ☎ 971/84-13-13. www.canyamelgolf.com.

⓲ ★ **Club de Golf Alcanada** Designed by Robert Trent Jones, Jr. 18 holes, par 72, 6,499m (7,107 yards). *Ctra. del Faro, s/n, Port d'Alcúdia.* ☎ 971/54-95-60. www.golf-alcanada.com.

⓳ ★★★ **Golf de Andratx** ANDRATX Hilly and scenic, designed by Scottish architects. 18 holes, par 72, 6,085m (6,655 yards). *Urbanización Camp de Mar, Andratx.* ☎ 971/23-62-80. www.golfdeandratx.com.

⓴ ★★★ **Pula Golf** Redesigned by the Spanish golfer José María Olazábal. 18 holes, par 72, 6,006m (6,568 yards). *Ctra. Son Servera a Capdepera, km. 3, Son Servera.* ☎ 971/81-70-34. www.pulagolf.com.

Cycling around Serra de Tramuntana.

Active Outdoors: Best Bets

The following spots are my top choices for outdoors enthusiasts in the Balearic Islands.

Most Scenic Golf: ★★★ Canyamel Golf, Capdepera/East Coast (p 133); and ★★★ Golf de Andratx, Andratx/Northwest Coast (p 133)

Best Diving: ★★ Sa Dragonera, Northwest Coast (p 89); and ★★★ Fornells, North Coast (Menorca) (p 148)

Best Windsurfing: ★★★ Fornells, North Coast (Menorca) (p 148)

Best for Birders: ★★ Parc Natural S'Albufera, North Coast (p 106)

Best for Gentle Cycling: ★★ Es Pla (around Sineu and Petra), Interior (p 132); and ★★ Passeig Marítim, Palma (p 132)

Best Hiking: ★★★ Ruta de Pedra, Northwest Coast (p 135); and ★★★ Puig Major, Serra de Tramuntana, Northwest Coast (p 135)

Best for Hardcore Road Cyclists: ★★★ Puig de Sant Salvador, Es Pla (p 132)

㉑ ★★ **Son Vida Golf** The oldest course on Mallorca. 18 holes, par 72, 5,824m (6,369 yards). *Urbanización Son Vida, Palma.* ☎ *971/79-12-10. www.sonvidagolf.com.*

Golfing along the northeast coast.

㉒ ★ **Vall d'Or Golf** 18 holes, par 71, 5,740m (6.277 yards). *Ctra. Cala d'Or a Portocolom, km. 7.7, S'Horta.* ☎ *971/83-70-01. www. valldorgolf.com.*

In Menorca, ㉓ **Golf Son Parc** (18 holes, par 69, 5,169m (5,653 yards); Urbanización Son Parc s/n, Es Mercadal; ☎ 971/18-88-75; www.golfsonparc.com) is the single course along the north coast.

Hiking & Nature Walks

Walking and hiking is a favourite pursuit on both islands, but especially on Mallorca, with the stunning beauty of its rugged and varied terrain. Spring and autumn are by far the best seasons, because summer can get unforgivably hot and winter quite cold, especially in the mountains facing the northerly Tramuntana winds.

The premier destinations for hikers are the ㉔ ★★★ **Serra de Tramuntana,** along the northwest and north coast, with several peaks reaching more than 1,000m (3,330 ft) high (1,450m (4,830 ft) in the case of Puig Major), and the lower ㉕ **Serra de Llevant** mountains to the east.

Routes are very well signposted. There is a string of hostels and refuges along many routes, offering good-value accommodations for hikers (look for the brochure *Refugis, albergs i santuaris/ Hostels, shelters and shrines*).

The Consell de Mallorca Department of Tourism office publishes several good multilingual brochures: *Ruta de Pedra en Sec* (the Dry Stone Route), a gruelling 5- to 7-day hike all the way along the northwest coast, from Port d'Andratx to Pollença; *Rutes per Mallorca* (Mallorca Itineraries), detailing 6 hikes in all regions of the island; *Caminar per l'Altra Mallorca* (Walking in the Other Mallorca), covering 12-day hikes, principally along the northwest coast, with a couple along the east coast; *Caminar per La Serra de Tramuntana* (Walking in the Tramuntana Mountains),

highlighting eight-day hikes through the beautiful mountain range along the northwest and north coasts; *Caminar per Mallorca* (Walking in Mallorca), detailing a dozen fantastic and scenic day hikes across the island, including several of historic and cultural interest (such as the trek to the Castell de Santueri outside Felanitx); and *Senderismo* (Walking), a booklet of 17 short gentle walks around the island (as short as 1km (½ mile) or 15 minutes). Also visit www. infomallorca.net for additional information and pdf downloads of several of these brochures, including *Walking in Mallorca* and *Mallorca Itineraries*, and www.illesbalears.es, with an additional four short hikes, including Deià to the Cala Deià and Port d'Andratx to Sant Elm.

Two additional enjoyable day hikes not included in those brochures are: ㉖ ★★ **Santuari des Puig de Maria** (1 hour; see p 103, ❸) and ㉗ ★★ **Península d'Alcúdia** (5–6 hours; see p 105, ❼).

Hiking to Cala Torta on the east coast.

For guided treks and walking holidays, contact: Richard Strutt at **Mallorcan Walking Tours** (Port de Pollença; ☎ 609/70-08-26; www.mallorcanwalkingtours.puerto pollensa.com), who offers 57 guided day hikes and several week-long trekking itineraries in spring and autumn for groups of four or more.

Tramuntana Tours (c/ de la Luna, 72, Sóller; ☎ 971/63-24-23; www.tramuntanatours.com) organises gentle strolls and day treks along remote paths, such as the walk to Torrent de Pareis near Cala Tuent.

On Menorca, for 7-night holidays with five guided walks, check out **Menorca Walking Holidays** (☎ 0800/0724832; www.menorca walkingholidays.com).

Horseback Riding

Horseback riding is offered in popular tourist resorts, such as ㉘ **Pollença** (p 103, ❶) and ㉙ **Cala Ratjada** (p 107, ⓯) on Mallorca.

Windsurfing at Pollença Bay.

Local tourist information offices have information on riding at local ranches and stables. Additional information (including a list of clubs) is available through the **Federació Hípica de Les Illes Balears** (Cl. Metge Camps, Es Mercadal, Menorca; ☎ 971/15-42-25; www.hipicabaleares.com in Spanish only). Other riding clubs and stables can be found at: www.mallorcaonline.com/malhomu.htm.

Hot-Air Ballooning

One-hour flights over the coastline cost about 150€ per person. Offering hot-air balloon rides across the island are: **Mallorca Balloons** (Calla Millor; ☎ 971/81-81-82) and **Illes Balears Ballooning** (Cala Ratjada; ☎ 607/64-76-47; www.ibballooning.net).

Sea Kayaking

Sea kayaking is a sport that seems destined to take off on both Mallorca and Menorca. For now, it's mostly offered in the north, at ㉚ **Port de Pollença** (p 104, ❹) and ㉛ **Port d'Alcúdia** (p 106, ❾). Try **Kayak Mallorca** (La Gola/Passeig de Londres, Port de Pollença; ☎ 648/11-16-18; www.kayak mallorca.com) for lessons and rentals, as well as **Tramuntana Tours** (Passeig de Traves, 12, Port de Sóller; ☎ 971/63-24-23; www.tramuntanatours.com).

Windsurfing

The windsurfing destination par excellence is ★★★ **Fornells** (p 148, ❸), on the north coast of Menorca. The ample, protected bay, waveless waters and northerly winds are perfect for windsurfing. Wind Fornells (Ctra. Mercadal-Fornells, s/n; ☎ 971/18-81-50; www.wind fornells.com) has offered windsurfing and sailing lessons since 1986. ●

Maó & the Southeast Coast

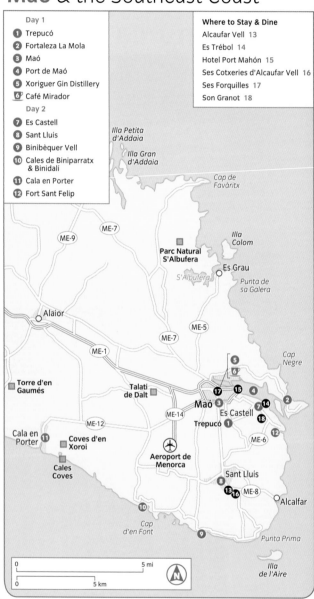

Day 1
1. Trepucó
2. Fortaleza La Mola
3. Maó
4. Port de Maó
5. Xoriguer Gin Distillery
6. Café Mirador

Day 2
7. Es Castell
8. Sant Lluís
9. Binibèquer Vell
10. Cales de Biniparratx & Binidalí
11. Cala en Porter
12. Fort Sant Felip

Where to Stay & Dine
Alcaufar Vell 13
Es Trébol 14
Hotel Port Mahón 15
Ses Cotxeries d'Alcaufar Vell 16
Ses Forquilles 17
Son Granot 18

Illa Petita d'Addaia

Illa Gran d'Addaia

Cap de Faváritx

ME-9

ME-7

Illa Colom

Parc Natural S'Albufera

Es Grau

S'Albufera

Punta de sa Galera

Alaior

ME-7

ME-5

ME-1

Cap Negre

Torre d'en Gaumés

Talati de Dalt

Maó

Es Castell

ME-14

Trepucó

Cala en Porter

Coves d'en Xoroi

ME-12

ME-6

Cales Coves

Aeroport de Menorca

Sant Lluís

ME-8

Alcalfar

Cap d'en Font

Punta Prima

0   5 mi

0   5 km

Illa de l'Aire

Previous page: Cala Pregonda at dusk.

Just 45 km (27 miles) from end to end, Menorca is largely flat and unusually peaceful. Its capital, Maó, sits on one of the deepest natural harbours in the world. Southeast of Maó are small resorts, a handful of orderly towns with a French or British colonial feel, fishing villages and some relaxed beaches. START: **Trepucó**, 1½ km (1 mile) south of Maó. Trip length: 2 days.

Day One

Drive 6km (3¾ miles) east of the Menorca Aeroport along ME-12 and then Avda. de la Mediterrània to Camí de Trepucó.

1 ★ kids **Trepucó.** One of Menorca's many prehistoric Talayotic monuments, this ancient settlement of 5,000 sq m was once entirely walled. What remain are the island's largest T-shaped taula and two cone-shaped talayots (see box, Prehistoric Menorca, p 150). The site suffered significant damage during the second Punic War (218–201 B.C.). ⏲ *30 min. c/ Gràcia–Trepucó, Maó. ☎ 902/ 92-90-15. www.menorcamonumental. org. Admission 1.80€ adults, 1.10€ seniors and students, free children under 8. Nov–mid-Apr, free admission (open access). Mid-Apr–Sep Tues– Sun 9am–9pm & Sun–Mon 9am–3pm, Oct Tues–Sun 9am–3pm.*

North and then east of Maó; head north in the direction of ME-7 toward Es Grau and then left toward Cala Llonga on ME-3 and follow signs to Fortaleza La Mola.

2 ★★★ kids **Fortaleza La Mola.** This huge architectural marvel was completed in 1875 and built by the Spanish to protect the Maó port against resumed British or French incursions in the Mediterranean. Yet by that point the fort was already obsolete in its weaponry. The architectural jewel is the *galleria amb espitlleres*, a long series of perfectly aligned arches (perfections in stone that might be more expected in a cathedral or convent than a garrison) leading to 45 cells. Although you can

visit on your own, I recommend the guided visit, which really helps bring La Mola's distinguishing characteristics to life. ⏲ *2 hr. Ctra. de la Mola, Maó. ☎ 971/36-40-40. www. fortalesalamola.com. Admission 7€, free children under 12. Jun–Sep daily 10am–8pm, May & Oct daily 10am– 6pm, Nov–Apr, Tues–Sun 10am–2pm.*

3 ★★ **Maó.** The business and administrative capital of Menorca, Maó (**Mahón** in Spanish) remains above all a port city. Whole sections of this small, pleasant town call to mind 18th-century coastal English cities such as Plymouth in Devon, although the town itself isn't as old or picturesque as its rival on the other side of the island, Ciutadella (p 153). ⏲ *3 hr.*

Arches inside the Fortaleza La Mola.

Maó

	Information
	Post Office
	Bus Station
	Ferry Terminal

Built in 1829, and the oldest opera house in Spain, the **3A** ★★ **Teatre Principal** is one of the finest small opera houses you'll see. **3B** **Plaça d'Espanya** rises from the remains of a Renaissance-era city wall, and is marked by a fish market, 18th-century Església del Carme and the town market within its cloisters. In **3C** **Plaça de Constitució** are the 17th-century *Ajuntament* (Town Hall) and Gothic Església de Santa María, with its austere interior and massive pipe organ. Turn left on carrer Sant Roc to see **3D** **Portal de Sant Roc,** the town's only surviving medieval gateway. Carrer Isabel II leads to

Teatre Principal, Maó.

3E ★ **Museu de Menorca,** the island's largest museum—exhibiting archaeological artefacts as well as 18th- and 19th-century paintings and engravings—in the monks' quarters and cloisters of a former Franciscan monastery. Next door, behind the Baroque façade of **3F** ★ **Sant Francesc** is the Churrigueresque Chapel of the Immaculate Conception.

Museu: Pl. des Monestir. 971/35-09-55. *Admission 2.40€, 1.30€ reduced; free admission Sat 6–8pm & Sun 10am–2pm. Apr–Oct Tues–Sat 10am–2pm & 6–8pm Sun 10am–2pm, Nov–Mar Mon–Fri 9:30am–2pm Sat–Sun 10am–2pm. Sant Francesc: free admission. Daily 10am–2pm & 5–7pm.*

Xoriguer Gin.

6 **Café Mirador.** A small café, usually with jazz or classical music playing and terrific views from the terrace perched above the harbour. It's popular with locals and good for a coffee or beer and some simple tapas. *Plaça d'Espanya, 2, Maó.* ☎ *971/35-21-07. $.*

Day Two
2km (1¼ miles) southeast of Maó along ME-4.

7 **Es Castell.** Founded in 1771 as Georgetown, Es Castell is very much an English-looking village with Georgian-style houses. It is, perhaps, best known for **Cales Fons,** an engaging harbourside cluster of restaurant terraces alongside a boardwalk. 🕐 *30 min.*

6 km (3¾ miles) south of Maó along ME-8.

8 ★ **Sant Lluís.** Like Es Castell, this attractive colonial town is constructed on a grid. Sant Lluis is French in origin, was founded in 1750 by a French commander and

Xoriguer Gin.

Port de Maó.

4 ★★ **kids** **Port de Maó.** Probably the best way to experience the 6km (4-mile) long port is by glass-bottomed boat. Sail past the small islets in the port for views of the city and fortresses that once protected it. Most tours last about an hour and cost 10€ per person. Three companies operate frequent departures in summer from their harbourside ticket kiosks, including La Pirata Azul. 🕐 *1hr.* ☎ *646/11-47-67. www.* *pirataazul.com. Admission 10€.* *Daily: check board for details.*

5 **Xoriguer Gin Distillery.** On the quayside is one of the most visible examples of the city's British legacy: gin, brought to Menorca by sailors. The distillery has been in continuous operation since the 19th century and doles out free samples of its omnipresent (at least in Menorca) gin and other herbaceous liqueurs. *Costa des Muret, s/n.* ☎ *971/36-21-97. Free admission.* *Jun–Sep Mon–Fri 8am–7pm & Sat* *9am–1pm, Oct–May Mon–Fri 9am–* *1pm & 4–7pm.*

Cales Fons, Es Castell.

used as the French headquarters during the Seven Years' War (1756–63). An interesting nearby diversion is **Binifadet Winery,** a compact but distinguished winery that's part of a

The white-washed Binibèquer Vell.

select breed of Menorcan winemakers. The stylish modern winery produces an outstanding chardonnay. ⏱ *1 hr. Binifadet: Ses Barraques, s/n.* ☎ *971/15-07-15. www.binifadet. com. Free admission. Mon–Sat 10am–2pm & 4pm–8pm.*

5km (3 miles) south of Sant Lluis along ME-5.

9 ★★ kids **Binibèquer Vell.** The coastline southeast from Sant Lluis was one of the first developed for tourism on Menorca, and although there are some tranquil and enticing cove beaches, the most interesting stop is this fishing village, with the houses and medina-like alleyways painted with so many coats of thick white paint they look Moroccan. Although it appears ancient and even carries 'old' (*vell*) as part of its name, it was built from scratch in the 1970s to recreate the image of a Mediterranean fishing village. ⏱ *30 min.*

4km (2½ miles) west along the coastal road.

⑩ ★ **Cales de Biniparratx & Binidalí.** These sheltered coves are ideal for a dip into the calm sea and their small size keeps them mercifully quiet, even in high season. ⏱ *1 hr. See also p 164.*

16km (10 miles) west.

⑪ kids **Cala en Porter.** Often derided for its *urbanització* (condo development) sprawl—massive, ugly and loud by Menorcan standards—Cala en Porter can actually be a pleasant cove, although summertime crowds in pubs may push you on to more isolated spots. Other than the beach, the big attraction in these parts is **Cova d'en Xoroi,** a bar/disco carved out of a cave in the sheer cliff face overlooking the Mediterranean, with unparalleled sea views (and ambient lounge with a DJ). ⏱ *2 hr. Cova d'en Xoroi: May through August.* ☎ *971/37-72-36. www.covadenxoroi.com. Cover 20€ after 11pm.*

15km (9 miles) east on ME-12.

⑫ ★★ kids **Fort Sant Felip.** Just beyond the quaint fishing village of Sant Esteve are two other fortresses built to defend the entrance to the port of Maó: Sant Felip and Fort Marlborough. Sant Felip was ordered by King Carlos V in 1550, although the Spanish themselves destroyed the stronghold in 1782 after British occupation ended. A local group stages theatrical night visits to the subterranean galleries with costumed actors and recreations of the experience of troops under siege, down to the bad smells and scary-sounding gunshots. ⏱ *2½ hr. Cala de Sant Esteve, Es Castell.* ☎ *971/36-21-00. www.museomilitarmenorca.com. 20€ adults, 15€ seniors, 10€ children under 12. Mid-Jun–mid-Sep Sat–Sun (visits in English and Spanish), 9:30pm (lasting 2½ hours). Group visits Mon–Thurs, 7pm.*

British Presence in Menorca

Tiny Menorca, settled by the Romans in 123 B.C., was elevated to modern strategic importance in the Mediterranean during the 18th century, coveted for its deep, 6km (almost 4-mile) long natural port. During the War of Spanish Succession in 1708, British forces seized the island and port for the Royal Navy. Menorca was formally ceded to England in 1713 at the Treaty of Utrecht, although the island would change hands five more times between Britain, Spain and France during the next century. Under General Richard Kane's governorship, the British moved the administrative capital from Ciutadella to Maó in 1722 and left a large presence along the southeast coast, with Georgian-style architecture and the importation of gin (which led to distilleries that continue to this day, such as Xoriguer (p 141, ⑤). In 1802, Britain finally ceded the island back to Spain under terms of the Treaty of Amiens.

Where to **Stay & Dine**

Alcaufar Vell, Sant Lluís.

★★★ Alcaufar Vell SANT LLUÍS

This grand, late 18th-century stone manor house—in the same family since the 14th century—has been converted into a truly elegant country hotel. The owners have done a superb job conserving ancient period details, including elements of a 14th-century Moorish defence tower, thick walls and vaulted ceilings. Rooms in the main house and adjoining stables are all different but elegant and full of character, with a warm, minimalist aesthetic and huge bathrooms. The top-floor suite in the tower has outstanding views across Menorca (as far as Monte El Toro, p 148, ⑤), and the restaurant, Ses Cotxeries d'Alcaufar Vell (see below), is one of the finest on the island. *Cta. Cala Alcalfar km. 8, Sant Lluís.* ☎ *971/ 15-18-74. www.alcaufarvell.com. 21 units. Doubles 130–240€ w/breakfast. AE, MC, V. Map p 138.*

★ Es Trébol CALES FONS SEA-

FOOD This relaxed seafood restaurant sits right at the edge of the harbour promenade in pretty Cales

Fons, with tables on the terrace little more than arm's reach from fishing boats bobbing in the bay. The focus, logically, is on the freshest seafood available, including lobster. The grilled fish, including monkfish and hake, is expertly prepared. *c/ Cales Fons, 43, Es Castell.* ☎ *971/36-70-97. www.restaurantrebol.com. Main course 16–35€. AE, DC, MC, V. Apr–Oct, lunch & dinner daily. Map p 138.*

★ kids Hotel Port Mahón

MAÓ   The large Georgian-style mansion overlooks the Maó port and has facilities smaller boutique hotels might lack, including two restaurants, a piano bar, a pool and a solarium. Rooms are crisply modern and comfortable. Although part of a small Spanish chain of hotels, this midsized hotel has genuine character. *c/ Fort de l'Eau, 13. Maó.* ☎ *971/ 36-26-00. www.sethotels.com. 82 units. Doubles 110–180€ w/breakfast. AE, DC, MC, V. Map p 138.*

★★★ Ses Cotxeries d'Alcaufar

Vell SANT LLUÍS *MENORCAN/ MEDI-TERRANEAN*   Under the vaulted ceilings of the old carriage house at this historic manor house and boutique hotel, Alcaufar Vell (see above), is one of my favourite restaurants on the island. Dishes are creative and elaborate, with some daring offerings such as ostrich carpaccio and grilled pork cheek stuffed with prawns and leeks. The lunch menu, three courses for 20€, is exceptional value for the quality and the wine list includes some intriguing, hard-to-find Spanish producers. *Cta. Cala Alcalfar km. 8, Sant Lluís.* ☎ *971/15-18-74. www.alcaufarvell.com. Main course 10–23€. AE, MC, V. Lunch & dinner Tues–Sat, lunch only Sun. Map p 138.*

★★ Ses Forquilles MAÓ *HAUTE*

MEDITERRANEAN   Touting itself as

a 'gastronomic space', this central restaurant is one of Maó's best. It features adventurous tasting menus, an excellently priced three-course lunch menu (16.50€) and a chalkboard of tapas. Downstairs, in the casual bar, most patrons eat lunch on barstools, while upstairs is the dining room with deep red walls. Tasting menus range from six to nine courses and focus on fresh local ingredients. *Rovellada de Dalt, 20.* ☎ *971/35-27-11. www. sesforquilles.com. Tasting menus 27–50€. AE, DC, MC, V. Lunch & dinner Mon–Sat. Map p 138.*

Son Granot., Es Castell.

★★ **Son Granot** ES CASTELL   A richly red Georgian mansion on a hill, dating from 1712 and surveying the countryside and coastline, this boutique hotel is an excellent base for exploring the southeast coast and Maó. The swish interior has been completely remodelled, with smart rooms and canopy beds. There's a large pool, the Son Granot restaurant (see below) and horses and a host of other farm animals nearby on the property, giving it a delightfully rustic feel. The charming owners take their roles as hosts and custodians of Menorcan history and culture seriously. *Avda. de Menorca, s/n (off ME-2), Es Castell.* ☎ *971/35-55-55. www.songranot.com. 8 units. Doubles 110–292€ w/breakfast. MC, V. Map p 138.*

★★ **Son Granot** ES CASTELL *MENORCAN/SPANISH*   The restaurant in the attractive rural boutique hotel of Son Granot (see above) is just minutes from Maó. The venue is a highly enjoyable place for elevated home cooking with local products and vegetables from the owner's garden. Specialities include stuffed squid and veal. Especially lovely is the candlelit terrace, with its knockout views over the peaceful countryside. *Avda. de Menorca, s/n (off ME-2), Es Castell.* ☎ *971/35-55-55. www.songranot. com. Main course 12–24€. MC, V. Dinner daily. Map p 138.*

Seafood Risotto, Ses Cotxeries d'Alcaufar Vell.

North Coast & Interior of Menorca

Day 1

1. Parc Natural S'Albufera d'Es Grau
2. Cap de Favaritx
3. Fornells
4. Cala Pregonda

Day 2

5. Monte El Toro
6. JM Café
7. Alaior
8. Torralba d'En Salort
9. Talati de Dalt

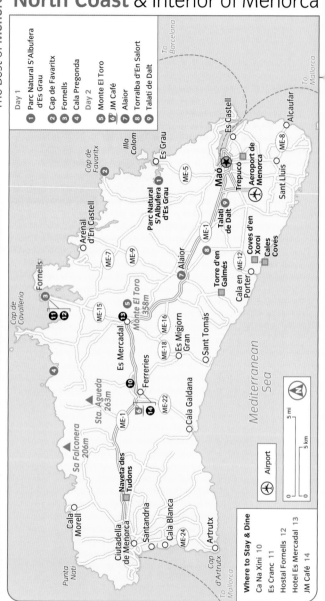

Where to Stay & Dine

Ca Na Xini 10
Es Cranc 11
Hostal Fornells 12
Hotel Es Mercadal 13
JM Café 14

The landscape of Menorca's wild and rocky north coast, with its reddish earth, is a dramatic departure from the white-sand coves, pine forests and limestone of the south coast. The interior is the island's heartland, with small market towns, the highest vantage point and prehistoric monuments. START: **Talatí de Dalt, 5km (3 miles) west of Maó off ME-1. Trip length: 2 days.**

Day One
Take ME-7 north from Maó; access road 2½km (1½ miles) off ME-7 to Fornells.

1 ★ kids Parc Natural S'Albufera d'Es Grau. This protected 700-sq-km nature park of sand dunes, wetlands and a large lagoon is rich with birdlife. Birdwatchers who coincide with migrating birds in spring and autumn will be delighted, and are likely to spot egrets, herons and booted eagles, as will walkers who set out among the clearly marked and gentle trails. ⏱ *1 hr. Ctra. Maó a Es Grau, km 3½.* ☎ *971/ 35-63-02. Free admission. Apr–Sept 9am–6pm, Oct–Mar, 9am–5pm.*

7km (4 miles) north on Ctra. del Far de Favaritx (Cf-1).

2 ★ kids Cap de Favaritx. A windswept cape crowned by a lighthouse, this spot is busy with Menorcans who venture out on select days to experience the dramatic wind (Sa Tramuntana) for which the north coast is famed. A road sign at

Lighthouse, Cap de Favaritx.

the fork right claims *Privado* (private) but that's just for an estate located out this way; the rest is public land. Keep driving out to the lonely lighthouse for rewarding, if barren, views. ⏱ *30 min.*

Camí d'en Kane

An alternative to the busy main highway (ME-1), this scenic old road runs 45km (27 miles) from one end of Menorca to the other—from the capital Maó to Ciutadella. Ordered to be built by the island's first British governor, General Richard Kane (appointed in 1713), it's lined with farms and estates and is a more relaxing way to travel from the capital to Es Mercadal, in roughly the middle of Menorca—although the route complicates seeing some of the sights along the north coast and in the interior.

26km (16 miles) northwest along ME-7 (9km (6 miles) north of Es Mercadal on ME-15).

3 ★★★ **kids** **Fornells.** A tranquil, whitewashed fishing village perched on a sheltered inlet, Fornells is impossibly attractive, with a harbour of sailboats, lined by tall palm trees and restaurant terraces. It's a popular summer destination, especially with gourmet diners who come to feast on one of the island's specialities, *caldereta de llagosta* (a rich and pricey lobster stew). The bay is also popular with windsurfers and scuba divers (see Diving & Snorkelling, p 132). Along the coast is **Fornells Tower,** a defence tower built by the British in the early 19th century, in a truncated cone shape, to defend the nearby Castell de Sant Antoni. ⏲ *2 hr. Defence tower: Sa Punta de sa Torre, s/n.* ☎ *902/92-90-15. Admission free. Easter–mid-Apr Tues–Sun 9:30am–3pm, mid-Apr–Sept Tues–Sat 9:30am–8:30pm Sun–Mon 9:30am–3pm, Oct Tues–Sun 9:30am–3pm, closed Nov–Easter.*

Peaceful harbour, Fornells.

15km (9 miles) west on ME-15 and Cf-3 and a 20-minute hike from car park.

4 ★★★ **kids** **Cala Pregonda.** My vote for the most spectacular beach on Menorca, and among my top choices anywhere, is this dreamy cove of deep red-brown sands with a collection of rock formations rising out of the bay. It's a 20-minute hike through grasslands and dunes to get here, but well worth the effort. ⏲ *2 hr.*

Day Two

9km (6 miles) south along ME-15.

5 ★ **kids** **Monte El Toro.** Menorca's highest peak may not be all that high at 357m (1171 ft), but it provides outstanding panoramic views of the entire island, from coast to coast, and the chance to look over Fornells and the reddish earth of beaches along the north coast, as well as over the rolling farmland to the south and west. El Toro has been a place of pilgrimage since, at least, the 13th century. ⏲ *45 min.*

Red-toned sands of Cala Pregonda.

★ **JM Café.** Just west of Es Mer-cadal, and attached to the shop and factory outlet of one of Menorca's top shoe designers, Jaime Mascaró, this little café is an ideal place for a good-value fixed-price lunch (12.75€) or coffee and pastry. The town of Ferreries is the cradle of the Menorca shoe industry, which gave rise to rustic *abarca* sandals before stylish stilettos. *ME-1, Poligono Industrial, Ferreries.* ☎ *971/37-38-37. $.*

18km (11 miles) east of Ferreries on ME-1.

7 **Alaior.** Menorca's third-largest city, this traditional market town clustered on a hill is renowned for its major contribution to the Menor-can diet: cheese. Two large cheese factories in the modern section of town, **La Payesa** and **Coinga,** pro-duce distinctive, creamy and intense Mahón cheese (*queso de Mahón*), with (similar to wine) their own *demoninació de origen* (Denomination of Origin) and shops open to the public. In the old town, the most distinctive feature is the imposing 17th-century **Església de Santa Eulàlia,** the parish church with an impressive, ornate Baroque

façade. Cheese lovers may also want to head west to Ferreries, where they'll find a good cheese and wine producer, **Hort Sant Patrici,** with free tours. ⏱ *30 min. La Payesa: c/ d'es Banyer, 64.* ☎ *971/37-10-72. www.lapayesa.es. Coinga: c/ Es Mercadal, 8.* ☎ *971/37-12-27. www.coinga.com. Hort Sant Patrici: Camí de Sant Patrici s/n.* ☎ *971/37-37-02. www.santpatrici. com.*

3km (2 miles) southeast of Alaior on the road to Cala en Porter.

8 ★★ **Torralba d'En Salort.** This is a large prehistoric settlement and place of worship dating from c. 1000 B.C., comprising two talay-ots, a magnificently carved and con-served taula, a rare 'hypostyle' hall (a flat ceiling supported by columns) with intact roof, and ruins of dwell-ings. A small bronze bull—an animal that may have been of significant rit-ualistic importance to prehistoric peoples and is now exhibited in Maó's Museu de Menorca (p 140, **3E**)—was found here. ⏱ *30 min. No phone. Admission 3.50€ adults, 2€ seniors & students, free children under 12. Daily Jun–Sep 10am–8pm (closed 1st Sat each month), Oct–May Mon–Sat 10am–1pm & 3–6pm.*

Impressive megalithic site Talatí de Dalt.

11km (7 miles) east, just off ME-1.

❾ ★★ kids Talatí de Dalt. One of Menorca's finest megalithic sites, this spectacular settlement, with a 3m (10-ft) high stone taula, dates to the end of the Bronze Age, around 1300 B.C. The site includes a cone-shaped talayot and three subterranean chambers, but the most distinctive feature is a column propping up the base of the taula (in all probability the stone merely fell and remained balanced). ⏱ *30 min. Admission 4€ adults, 3€ students and seniors, free children under 8. Apr–Oct daily 10am–7pm, Nov–Apr open access and free admission.*

Prehistoric Menorca

For a tiny island, Menorca is rich with megalithic monuments. The prehistoric cultures that inhabited Menorca are generally divided into two eras: the **pre-Talayotic** (prior to 1400 B.C.) and the **Talayotic** (1400–123 B.C.). Pre-Talayotic peoples lived in stone huts and created communal burial chambers or ossuaries called *navetas*, shaped like up-ended ships. The Talayotic era brought small urban settlements, with clear dwelling zones and monuments incorporated in public religious rituals. Talayots are cone-shaped mounds (thought to be watchtowers). Taulas (or 'tables') are massive T-shaped structures (as high as 4m (13 ft)), with a vertical pillar topped by a horizontal slab, most likely for religious worship and, maybe, offerings. Despite the stony abundance of archaeological finds, surprisingly little is known about the ancient cultures. You can see the top sites of **Trepucó** (p 139, ❶), **Talatí de Dalt** (see above) and **Naveta des Tudons** (p 153, ❶), en route from Maó to Ciutadella along ME-1.

Where to **Stay & Dine**

★★★ **Ca Na Xini** FERRERIES Connected to Hort Sant Patrici (p 149, ⑦), makers of artisan cheeses and wines, this handsome *finca* (farmhouse estate) with a *palacete* (manor house) dating from 1919, is both stylish and modern inside, with white-and-chrome rooms on two floors. The gardens and pool are fine places to relax. *Cami de Sant Patrici s/n, Ferreries. ☎ 971/37-37-02. www.canaxini. com. 8 units. Doubles 140–290€ w/ breakfast. AE, DC, MC, V. Map p 146.*

★★★ **Es Cranc** FORNELLS *SEAFOOD* One of the premier dining destinations on Menorca, this renowned, family-owned but down-to-earth restaurant in the centre of whitewashed Fornells serves maybe the finest fresh seafood—and specifically, *caldereta de llagosta*—on the island. Although the signature dish is a whopping 73€, you can opt for the lowly but much more affordable and still delicious fish soup or *caldereta de peix* (fish stew). *c/ Escoles, 31, Fornells. ☎ 971/ 37-64-42. Main course 15–73€. AE, DC, MC, V. Lunch & dinner mid-Mar– Oct Thurs–Tues. Map p 146.*

kids **Hostal Fornells** FORNELLS The smartest small hotel in pleasant Fornells, this friendly little locale in the centre of town has abundant personality and a pool. Most of the clean but simple rooms have balconies and views of Fornells bay, even if they're not particularly spacious. *c/ Major, 7, Fornells. ☎ 971/ 37-66-76. www.hostalfornells.com. 17 units. Doubles 35–110€ w/breakfast. MC, V. Map p 146.*

★ **Hotel Es Mercadal** ES MERCADAL This small, appealing hotel—in a 19th-century townhouse on the main street of an unassuming market town in the middle of Menorca—is excellent value. The rooms aren't large but they're very smart, well-equipped and colourfully decorated. For budget-conscious travellers who can live without a view of the beach, this is something of a find. *c/ Nou, 49, Es Mercadal. ☎ 971/15-44-39. www.hoteles mercadal.com. 6 units. Doubles 75– 139€ w/breakfast. MC, V. Map p 146.*

★ **JM Café** FERRERIES *MEDITERRANEAN* This breakfast- and lunch-only café serves up a superb three-course lunch menu (12.75€), including a glass of wine. *ME-1, Poligono Industrial, Ferreries. ☎ 971/ 37-38-37. Menu 12.75€. AE, DC, MC, V. Breakfast & lunch daily. Map p 146.*

An appealing budget option—Hotel Es Mercadal.

Ciutadella & the Southwest Coast

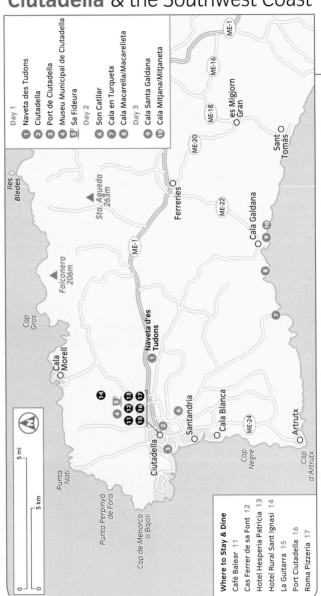

Day 1
1. Naveta des Tudons
2. Ciutadella
3. Port de Ciutadella
4. Museu Municipal de Ciutadella
5. Sa Fideura

Day 2
6. Son Catlar
7. Cala en Turqueta
8. Cala Macarella/Macarelleta

Day 3
9. Cala Santa Galdana
10. Cala Mitjana/Mitjaneta

Where to Stay & Dine

Café Balear 11
Cas Ferrer de sa Font 12
Hotel Hesperia Patricia 13
Hotel Rural Sant Ignasi 14
La Guitarra 15
Port Ciutadella 16
Roma Pizzeria 17

Ciutadella is the most beguiling city in the Balearics. Until the 18th century it was the capital of Menorca and is distinguished by a delightful port and an old town of limestone manor houses and churches. To the south and east are some of the Balearics' most spectacular beaches. START: **Naveta des Tudons, 5km (3 miles) east of Ciutadella just off ME-1. Trip length: 3 days.**

Day One

1 ★★ **Naveta des Tudons.** This impressively preserved, pre-Talayotic (early Bronze Age) rectangular stone structure, called a *naveta* (see box, Prehistoric Menorca, p 150), served as a burial chamber. The stones were fitted together without mortar and personal effects discovered inside reveal mass burials. ◷ *30 min. ME-1, km 40. No phone. Admission 1.80€ adults, 1.10€ seniors & students. Nov–mid-Apr free admission (open access). Mid-Apr–Sep, Tues–Sat 10am–9pm & Sun–Mon 9am–3pm, Oct Tues–Sun 9am–3pm.*

Naveta des Tudons.

2 ★★★ **Ciutadella.** This supremely elegant city was the capital of Menorca until 1722 (see box, British Presence in Menorca, p 143). The seductive old town is a compact labyrinth of cobblestoned streets. The largely pedestrian-only old town is a delight to stroll around, and proud locals of all ages are very fond of taking to the streets in early evening to soak in the Spanish Renaissance architecture and lively atmosphere.

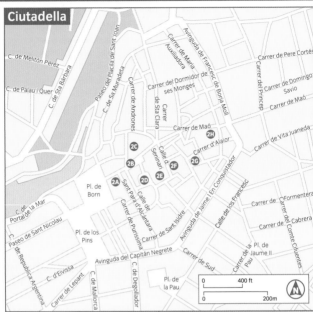

Ciutadella

Just outside the gate is the **2A** ★★★ **Praça d'es Born,** a ceremonial square dominated by the grand Moorish-style Ajuntament (town hall) and two majestic 19th-century palaces: **Cas Comte** (Palau Torresaura) and **C'an Salort** (admission 2.50€; May–Oct Mon–Sat 10am–2pm). Enter the old town along **2B Carrer Major,** pausing to see the blind-folded figure adorning the portal of Cas Comte. The dignified Gothic **2C** ★★ **Catedral,** with a single high nave and Baroque chapels, was built on the site of a former Moorish mosque in the early 14th century. Down carrer del Roser, head past the 18th- century **2D Església del Roser,** now an art exhibition space. Three 17th-century manor houses are directly ahead: **2E C'an Sintias;** grand, British-built **C'an Saura;** and **Cas Duc (Martorell).** Head east on carrer del Santissim and left on carrer del Seminari, where you'll find the **2F** ★ **Museu Diocesà de Menorca** (☎ 971/48-12-97; 2.50€ with free admission to cloisters every evening; May–Oct Mon–Sat 10:30am–2pm), occupying the 17th-century quarters and cloisters of an Augustinian convent displaying archaeological finds. Behind the museum, on carrer de l'Hospital, is the charming **2G** ★ **Mercat de Peix,** the fish market constructed in 1895. Follow carrer d'Alaior to Sant Eloi and the delightful **2H Plaça d'Alfons III,** full of popular café terraces, on the outskirts of old town.

3 ★★ **Port de Ciutadella.** The slender port isn't nearly as deep as Maó's, although it may surpass it in terms of beauty. The early-evening view from across the port, of the old town and cathedral rising above it on a hill, is magical. Late in the evening, the port—lined with restaurants, bars and

Praça des Born.

clubs—is transformed into the focus of Ciutadella's nightlife. 🕐 *20 min.*

Above the port, from Plaça d'es Born, head northeast along the old city ramparts (and carrer Sa Muradeta).

④ ★★ Museu Municipal de Ciutadella. The museum inhabits 17th-century defence ramparts, the bastion of the old city wall. Inside the collection of archaeological finds from pre-Talayotic to Roman and Moorish eras is handsomely displayed in a vaulted brick space. Some amazing 3,000-year-old remains found in nearby caves are still waiting to be exhibited. 🕐 *1 hr. Pl. Sa Font.* ☎ *971/ 38-02-97. www.ciutadella.org/museu. Admission 2.20 adults, 1.03 ages 13–18, free children under 12 & students. Tues–Sat 10am–2pm & 6–9pm.*

Return to Plaça d'es Born along carrer de sa Muradeta, which rises above the port.

⑤ ★ Sa Fideura. This small, friendly gourmet shop and delicatessen, in a 1930s' pasta factory just around the corner from the fish market, hides a

wonderful surprise. There's a wine-tasting room in the back, where the gregarious owner, Gabi, entertains oenophiles with a nice variety of wines by the glass, always including a few from Menorca, and some snacks. *Castell Rupit, 24, Ciutadella.* ☎ *971/ 38-64-51. $.*

Ancient artefacts in the Museu Municipal de Ciutadella.

Ciutadella's *Festes de Sant Joan*

Citutadella is famed for its unique and spectacular celebration of the feast of Sant Joan (June 23–24), or Saint John, the origins of which date back to at least the 14th century. Leading processions are formally dressed representatives of ancient Menorcan society: nobility, clergy, artisans and farmers. The most spectacular part of the festival is the *Convidada,* which takes place on June 24, when startling (and dangerous) equestrian skills contests, racing and jousting fill Plaça d'es Born with excited crowds. The party ends with a congratulatory fireworks display.

Day Two
8 km (5 miles) south of Ciutadella, along Camí Sant Joan de Missa (veer west at the Son Vivó fork, towards Son Saura beach).

⑥ **Son Catllar.** Before heading to the beach, stop off at this prehistoric settlement, the largest on Menorca. The pre-Talayotic village, still in expansion when the Romans arrived in 123 B.C., was entirely encircled by a massive stone defence wall (900m (3,000 ft) long and originally 3m (10 ft) high). The rather well-conserved wall—the only one of its kind in the Balearics—is the highlight; much of the interior is inscrutable, although you can identify a taula and five ruined talayots. ⏱ *30 min. Sant Joan de Missa. No phone. Free admission and open access.*

The scenic shoreline of Cala Macarelleta.

7km (4 miles) south of (west on) Son Vivó fork, along Camí Sant Joan de Missa.

⑦ ★★★ **Cala en Turqueta.** This enticing cove and beach southeast of Ciutadella is one of the best on the island. It features crystalline waters and sparkling white sands, bordered by large boulders, and is an easy 10-minute walk from the parking area. Although a favourite of Menorcans, it has no services and so it's rare to find a crowd here. ⏱ *2 hr. See also p 162.*

⑧ ★★★ **Cala Macarella/ Macarelleta.** Two of the prettiest beaches on Menorca are these twin coves just east of Cala en Turqueta. The easiest way to get to either is to drive and park just beyond Macarella.

The secluded cove of Cala Mitjana.

But the most adventurous and scenic way is to hike along a path from Cala en Turqueta, indicated by *'Camí Vell'* signs, that rambles for about 30 minutes high above the coast, affording mesmerising views of the Mediterranean. Although not unknown, Macarelleta is referred to as a *platja virgen* (unspoiled beach) and promoted by some as a nudist or semi-nudist beach, although it's usually a mix of clothed and unclothed, very casual and accepting of all sunbathers. The water is crystal-clear and the cove framed by hills and pine trees. Cala Macarella, a 10-minute walk around the bend, is pretty and has a beach bar-restaurant and other services, but it's not as pristine or as photogenic as Turqueta or Macarelleta. ⏱ *2 hr.*

Day Three
8km (5 miles) south of Ferreries along ME-22.

⑨ ★ Cala Santa Galdana. The popularity of this wide, sheltered horseshoe-shaped cove and full-service beach resort, with white sand, turquoise waters and beach bars, isn't difficult to grasp. However, its beauty has led to rife high-rise holiday development and second-home villas and the resort can be crowded during the height of summer. ⏱ *1 hr. See also p 163.*

3km (1.8 miles) east of Cala Galdana.

⑩ ★★ kids Cala Mitjana/Mitjaneta. Another handsome pair of secluded twin coves framed by

Beaches Near Ciutadella

Ciutadella makes a perfect base to explore some of the finest beaches on the island—but those aren't the ones to the immediate north and south of the city on the west coast, which have been desecrated by some of the most prosaic and unappealing *urbanitzaciós* and resorts on Menorca. Avoid Cala en Blanes and Cala Blanca, and head instead to the secluded coves along the southeast coast: **Cala en Turqueta** (p 156, ⑦), **Cala Macarella** (p 156, ⑧) and **Cala Mitjana** (⑩). In some cases you'll have to walk along rustic paths to get there, but you'll be rewarded with the kind of pristine beauty—translucent turquoise waters, white sands, limestone boulders and shady pine trees—that epitomises the Mediterranean.

wooded cliffs, just east of Cala Galdana and easily accessible from Ciutadella or Ferreries. Both are just a short walk from the parking area, although there are no facilities. Mitjana, with a wide strip of sand, occasionally has problems with seaweed.

To get to its smaller cousin, the especially beautiful Cala Mitjaneta, take the wooden stairs above Mitjana and walk 5 minutes east for sweeping views of the coves. ⏱ *2 hr.*

Where to **Stay & Dine**

★★★ Café Balear CIUTADELLA *SEAFOOD* This old-school restaurant is my pick of the bunch in Ciutadella. It specialises in fresh, market-priced seafood and shellfish—not surprising, given that the restaurant owns its own fishing boat. Recommended dishes include *sopa de peix* (fish soup) and *arroz de llagosta* (lobster paella). The midweek lunch menu is an outstanding deal at 18.50€. The interior is classic, with hardwood floors, beams and white tablecloths, but on a nice afternoon or evening you can't beat sitting out on the terrace at the edge of the port. *Pla de Sant Joan, 15, Ciutadella.* ☎ *971/38-00-05. www.cafe-balear.com. Main course*

Café Balear.

14–45€. AE, DC, MC, V. Lunch & dinner Tues–Sun. Map p 152.

★ Cas Ferrer de sa Font CIUTADELLA *MENORCAN/MEDITERRANEAN* A welcoming restaurant serving island and Mediterranean cuisine, some of it with innovative modern touches. It's based in a 17th-century townhouse not far from the cathedral in the old town. Among top dishes are the stuffed squid and roast goat. The garden patio is lovely in good weather. *c/ Portal de sa Font, 16, Ciutadella.* ☎ *971/48-07-84. Main course 15–22€. AE, DC, MC, V. Lunch & dinner Tues–Sun. Map p 152.*

★ kids Hotel Hesperia Patricia CIUTADELLA A smart and conveniently located modern hotel just a short walk from the port and old town, this is a good choice for travellers of all types. With a small outdoor saltwater pool and surprisingly good-looking rooms, it's also a bargain. *Pg. Sant Nicolás 90–92, Ciutadella.* ☎ *971/38-55-11. www. hesperia-patricia.com. 44 units. Doubles 64–118€ w/breakfast. AE, DC, MC, V. Map p 152.*

★★ kids Hotel Rural Sant Ignasi CIUTADELLA Built in 1771, this attractive country manor house, just 4km (2½ miles) northeast of Ciutadella, is surrounded by farmland. A boutique hotel, it has ample rooms decorated in Old World country style, with period antiques, and many have large terraces with

Menorcan *Ensaïmades*

The deliciously flaky and light-as-air spiral pastry that gets carted out of Mallorca by the baker's dozen is also a speciality on Menorca. You can pick *ensaïmades* up at several excellent bakeries in Ciutadella's old town. Although you might simply have to follow your nose, two popular choices are: **Panadería Montaner** (c/ Cal Bisbe, 11; ☎ 971/38-08-32), an ancient bakery with antique ovens and sublime *ensaïmades;* and **Pastissería Ca'n Moll** (c/ El Roser 1; ☎ 971/38-10-85), a local favourite, and just across the square from the cathedral.

Ensaïmades are sold in most bakeries.

far-reaching views. The house has pleasant gardens and a cooling outdoor pool as well as horses for riding. *Ctra. Cala Morell s/n, Ciutadella. ☎ 971/38-55-75. www.santignasi. com. 20 units. Doubles 105–252€ w/ breakfast. Closed Oct–Mar. AE, DC, MC, V. Map p 152.*

★ **La Guitarra** CIUTADELLA
MENORCAN This amiable eaterie tucked down a side street in the old town, near Plaça d'es Born, is a winner for dependable, family-friendly Menorcan fare. Occupying a cellar, it feels like an old rustic tavern, with arched ceilings and stone walls. The *caldereta de llagosta* is cheaper here than on the north coast, and the rice dishes *Fideuá* and *Arrós Brut* are classic and well prepared. *c/ Dolors, 1 (bajos), Ciutadella. ☎ 971/ 38-13-55. www.menorcadigital.com/ laguitarra.htm. Main course 12–35€. AE, MC, V. Lunch & dinner Mon–Sat. Closed Feb. Map p 152.*

★★ **kids Port Ciutadella** CIUTADELLA The sleekest and most modern hotel in Ciutadella, this stylish, well-managed place is outside the old town but close to the sea and an easy 10-minute walk. The contemporary rooms are spacious,

cleanly decorated and built around two levels overlooking the interior patio and large, gleaming pool. The other welcome amenity is the full-service spa and beauty centre with an indoor pool. A good choice for both families and business travellers. *Pg. Marítim, 36, Ciutadella. ☎ 971/ 48-25-20. www.sethotels.com. 94 units. Doubles 80–132€ w/breakfast. AE, DC, MC, V. Map p 152.*

★ **kids Roma Pizzería** CIUTADELLA PIZZA/ITALIAN Hidden down an old side street, this pizzeria, owned by the people behind Café Balear (p 158), is an enjoyable change of pace. It's attractive, with a vaulted ceiling downstairs (non-smoking) and a busier upstairs where all the locals go to smoke. The wood-burning oven kicks out great thin-crust pizzas; I'm partial to the *Menorquí* (with local *sobressada* sausage) and the *Spinaci* (with spinach, pine nuts and Rochefort cheese). Besides pizza, there's an extensive menu of pastas and meats. *c/ Alcántara, 18, Ciutadella. ☎ 971/38-47-18. www.cafe-balear. com. Main course 5–21€. AE, DC, MC, V. Lunch & dinner Tues–Sun. Map p 152.*

Beaches Best Bets

Best for **People-Watching**
★★★ Cala de Binibèquer, *Southeast Coast (Menorca) (p 162)*

Most **Scenic Beach**
★★★ Cala Pregonda, *North Coast (Menorca) (p 163)*; and Cala en Turqueta, *Southeast Coast (Menorca) (p 162)*

Best for **Families**
★★ Cala Santa Galdana, *Southeast Coast (Menorca) (p 163)*; and Son Parc, *North Coast (Menorca) (p 164)*

Best for **Swimming**
★ Cala en Porter, *Alaior/ South Coast (Menorca) (p 162)*; and Cala en Turqueta, *Southeast Coast (Menorca) (p 162)*

Toughest to **Get to But Worth the Effort**
★★★ Cala Pregonda, *North Coast (Menorca) (p 163)*

Best **Sand as Far as the Eye Can See**
Platja de Son Bou, *South Coast (Menorca) (p 164)*

Best **Beach Bar**
★ Cala de Binibèquer, *Southeast Coast (Menorca) (p 162)*

Best **(Sometimes) Nude Beach**
★★★ Cala Macarelleta, *Southeast Coast (Menorca) (p 162)*

Best for **Sun-Worshipping & Partying**
Cala en Porter, *Alaior/ South Coast (Menorca) (p 162)*

Most **Beautiful Secluded Beach Cove**
★★★ Cala Macarelleta, *Southeast Coast (Menorca) (p 162)*; and Cala en Turqueta, *Southeast Coast (Menorca) (p 162)*

Cala de Binibèquer on the southeast coast.

Menorca **Beaches**

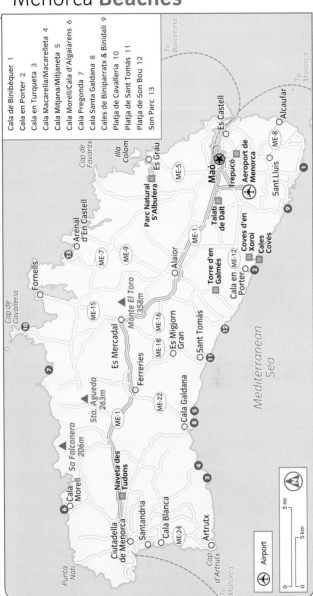

Cala de Binibèquer 1
Cala en Porter 2
Cala en Turqueta 3
Cala Macarella/Macarelleta 4
Cala Mitjana/Mitjaneta 5
Cala Morell/Cala d'Algaiarens 6
Cala Pregonda 7
Cala Santa Galdana 8
Cales de Biniparratx & Binidali 9
Platja de Cavalleria 10
Platja de Sant Tomás 11
Platja de Son Bou 12
Son Parc 13

Menorca Beaches **A to Z**

★ **Cala de Binibèquer** SANT LLUIS/SOUTHEAST COAST This small, sandy cove (also called Binibeca Nou) with a gentle slope and calm, clear turquoise water, is frequented, largely, by those with beach houses in the area. The small *chiringuito* (beach bar) claims to be the only spot you can get a drink with your feet in the water, and is enjoyed by locals and tourists alike. *6km (3½ miles) south of Sant Lluís.*

★ **kids Cala en Porter** ALAIOR/ SOUTH COAST Although this shell-shaped beach is pleasant, Cala en Porter is one of the oldest resorts on Menorca and has long been engulfed in heavy development. Framed by rocky cliffs on either side, the clear waters are perfect for swimming. It's a favourite of British visitors, with plenty of pubs in town. A star attraction along the coast is Cova d'en Xoroi (p 143, ⑪), a night-club carved out of a cave in a sheer

cliff face. *11km (7 miles) south of Alaior along ME-12.*

★★★ **kids Cala en Turqueta** CIUTADELLA/SOUTHEAST COAST This is a splendid beach—one of the prettiest and most protected on Menorca—with crystal-clear waters and fine white sand, bordered by large boulders. It's ideal for swimming. Although secluded, it's still only a 10-minute walk from the car park, and so on summer weekends you may find crowds and the car park overflowing. No facilities or services. *10km (6 miles) south of Ciutadella along Camí de Sant Joan de Missa.*

★★★ **Cala Macarella/Macarelleta** CIUTADELLA/SOUTHEAST COAST This pair of alluring beach coves just east of Cala en Turqueta, are reached either by a 15-minute walk from the car park or scenic but long treks from Cala Santa Galdana

Cala Mitjaneta.

(east) or Cala en Turqueta (west). Cala Macarella is a small U-shaped cove surrounded by high cliffs covered by thick pine trees. It has a beach bar-restaurant, and is only slightly less pristine than its cousin, although it's occasionally very crowded. Macarelleta, a 10-minute walk around the bend, is unspoiled and considered a nudist or semi-nudist beach. The water is crystal-clear and the cove is framed by steep cliffs covered with pine trees. *14km (9 miles) south of Ciutadella along Camí de Sant Joan de Missa. See also p 156,* ⑧.

★★ **Cala Mitjana/Mitjaneta** FER-RERIES/SOUTHEAST COAST   This twin set of secluded coves backed by wooded cliffs is easily accessible from the road to Ferreries and just a short walk from the car park. Mitjana has a wide, sheltered strip of fine-grained white sand and is surrounded by high rocks and thick pine woods. The water is calm and crystal clear. Smaller and even more beautiful, Cala Mitjaneta is reached by a trail behind and above Mitjana (up a set of wooden stairs). It's not uncommon to find nude sunbathers, especially in the off-season. *7km (4 miles) south of Ferreries along ME-22 and then an unpaved road.*

★ kids **Cala Morell/Cala d'Algaiarens** CIUTADELLA/NORTH-WEST COAST   Most easily reached from Ciutadella, Cala Morell is a whitewashed *urbanització* made more interesting by a series of caves, a sprawling necropolis complex from the 6th century B.C., and the breathtaking coastal views from the *mirador* of the promontory jutting out into the ocean. About 4km (2½ miles) east, the wide, sandy cove beach at Cala d'Algaiarens isn't as pretty as Cala Pregonda but offers good sheltered swimming (but no services). *Take the turn-off to the right from the Ronda Norte road to*

Sand dunes, Cala d'Algaiarens.

Cala Morell; after 2km (1¼ miles) there's a car park; the beach is a 5-minute walk.

★★★ **Cala Pregonda** ES MER-CADAL/NORTH COAST   This breath-taking beach has earthy red sand and a collection of seastacks rising out of the bay. Although it's often cited as everyone's top beach, there are surprisingly few crowds because it's a 20-minute hike from the car park. No services or facilities. *10km (6 miles) north of Es Mercadal along Camí de Tramuntana.*

★ kids **Cala Santa Galdana** FER-RERIES/SOUTHEAST COAST   A thriving, popular resort with easy-going development, a lovely cove, a blue-flag beach, sheltered by cliffs and with fine white sand and turquoise waters. This is a good option for families, with shallow waters and water sports rentals. Walkers are drawn to long treks along the coast through pine woods to more isolated beaches. *7km (4 miles) south of Ferreries along ME-22.*

Menorca's Two Coasts

Although just one-fifth the size of Mallorca, Menorca boasts 215km (135 miles) of coastline and at least 75 beaches. The southern coast is characterised by limestone, high cliffs and pine forests, with a number of small, protected coves, but open sea along the middle of the island (south of Alaior). The north coast is much wilder, buffeted by sharp northerly winds, with an abundance of sandstone and reddish, earthy sands and more secluded coves (many of which can be reached only on foot or by boat).

★ Cales de Biniparratx & Binidalí MAÓ/SOUTHEAST COAST
These two attractive small beach coves are found at the end of a narrow sea inlet along the southeast coast, just west of Binibeca Vell. They're sheltered and good for swimming, with fewer people than other beaches. *9km (5½ miles) south of Maó along ME-12 and Ctra. de Binidalí.*

★★ Platja de Cavalleria ES MERCADAL/NORTH COAST
One of the most scenic beaches along the north

Platja de Cavalleria.

coast, heading out to the Cavelleria Cape, this wide curve along a bay features fine-grained, gold-coloured sand. It's a short walk from a car park, but has no services or facilities. *9km (5½ miles) north of Es Mercadal along Cami de Tramuntana.*

Platja de Sant Tomás ES MIGJORN GRAN/SOUTH COAST
Fronting open waters, this popular beach is frequently crowded. The beach is sandy, with rocky areas and thick pine woods, and the water is clear. *5km (3 miles) south of Es Migjorn Gran.*

kids Platja de Son Bou ALAIOR/SOUTH COAST
This beach is the longest on Menorca at 2½km (1½ miles) long, with fine golden sand and calm, clear waters. The blue-flag beach has a gentle, shallow shelf and is safe for children but can be very crowded. There are several snack bars connected by a wooden path and plenty of water sports. *8km (5 miles) south of Alaior.*

kids Son Parc ES MERCADAL/NORTH COAST
This large, white-sand beach has shallow waters, ideal for children. Nearest the resort, the sand has an extremely gentle slope. Facilities include a beach bar and sun loungers, parasols, pedalos and canoes for hire. *14km (9 miles) north of Es Mercadal along ME-7.* ●

The
Savvy Traveller

Before You Go

Government Tourist Offices

In the UK: 79 New Cavendish St, 2nd floor; W1W 6XB London (☎ 0207/317 2010; www.spain.info/uk/TourSpain). **In the US:** 666 Fifth Ave., Fifth Floor, New York, NY 10103 (☎ 212/265-8822). **In Canada:** 102 Bloor St. W., Suite 3402, Toronto, Ontario M4W 3E2, Canada (☎ 416/961-3131). A full list of Spanish tourist offices worldwide can be found at: www.spain.info.

The Best Times to Go

The Balearics are a massive summer destination, and beaches, hotels and restaurants in the high season, July, August and early September (increasingly being stretched a few weeks on either side) are jam-packed and sold out. If you can, go in the shoulder season (April to June and late-September to late-October) or off-season (November to March), which is the best times for walkers and cyclists. The Mediterranean Sea is perfect for swimming from late June to October. If you're not going strictly for the beaches, both islands can be considered year-round destinations, and the weather can be quite mild—pretty warm and sunny even in January, when almond trees blossom spectacularly across Mallorca—even though many coastal resorts essentially shut down in winter. Going outside of high season will get you better airfares, better hotel rates, better service and, best of all, a reprieve from the crowds that overwhelm so much of the Mallorcan coast.

Festivals & Special Events

For a complete list of festivals and events, see www.illesbalears.es.

SPRING. One of the high points across the islands is **Semana Santa (Holy Week)**. The **Good Friday procession (Davallament)** in Pollença, when the body of Christ is symbolically carried down the El Calvari steps, is the emotional and visual highlight. **Sa Fira** is Mallorca's largest traditional agricultural market, held in Sineu on the first Sunday of May, and the next weekend in May is **Es Firó** in Sóller, a colourful reenactment of a pirate siege and battles between Christians and Moors.

SUMMER. The **Festes de Sant Joan** (23–24 June) in Ciutadella, Menorca, is one of Spain's great festivals (see p 156). **Nit de San Joan** (23 June) is a huge party, especially in Palma with concerts, *correfocs* ('fire runs') in streets and all-night festivities on the beach. Fishing villages and coastal towns celebrate the **Festa de la Verge del Carme,** the patron saint of fishermen and sailors, on 16 July. In August, the annual **Festival Chopin** is held in Valldemossa, with a month's worth of concerts of the Polish composer's works (see p 95).

AUTUMN. Binissalem in the Mallorcan interior celebrates the grape harvest and wine vintage with the **Feste d'es Vermar** in late September (see p 33).

WINTER. **Nadal, or Christmas, is** very colourful, especially in Palma and Ciutadella, with events and nativity plays in the preceding weeks. **Día dels Reis (Three Kings Day),** on 6 January, remains the traditional Catholic celebration of Christmas gift-giving. **Carnaval** (just prior to Lent) is celebrated across the islands, with

Previous page: Mallorcan sailing boats.

Useful Websites

www.illesbalears.es: The Balearic Islands' official tourism site, with excellent information in English as well as Catalan and Spanish on all the islands.

www.tourspain.es: Turespaña's website, with helpful primers on leisure, adventure and business travel, as well as a feature of Spanish news from around the world.

www.spain.info: Loads of practical tips on driving, destinations, bringing in pets and even learning Spanish.

www.mallorcabeachguide.com: An official guide to the Balearics' best beaches, this site is amazingly detailed, with up-to-date surf and swimming conditions, transportation information and extensive aerial photos.

parades; the biggest is in Palma, called **Sa Rua**. **Festes de Sant Antoni** (17 January) honours St. Anthony, the patron saint of animals, and in many villages and towns, animals are marched through streets to receive the saint's blessing (the night before sees bonfires and traditional dancing). Palma's patron saint, **Sant Sebastià,** has his feast day on 20 January, celebrated with fires and concerts; Pollença also celebrates the day.

The Weather

The Balearics are blessed with a Mediterranean climate, and spring and autumn are unfailingly pleasant, with sunny skies and moderate temperatures. Even in the winter, days are crisp but not exceedingly cold and often sunny. July and August are very hot and even at night the temperature often only drops minimally. Along the north coasts of both Mallorca and Menorca, a strong wind known as the tramuntana blows, occasionally fiercely.

Car Rentals

Many destinations on both islands are problematic or all but inaccessible by public transportation. Hiring a car is pretty much essential if you want to see much more than Palma or a single resort. Even on relatively large Mallorca, no part of the island is more than a few hours away. The biggest car-rental companies, including Avis, Budget and Hertz, maintain offices in Palma, especially at the airport, in Sóller and the larger resorts on the north and east coasts, as well as Maò and Ciutadella in Menorca. All the major international agencies (and many smaller companies) have offices in both islands, including:

Avis (☎ 0844/581 0147 in UK; ☎ 800/331-1212 in US; www.avis.com);

Hertz (☎ 020/7026 0077 in UK; ☎ 800/654-3131 in US; www.hertz.com);

National (☎ 0870/400 4581 in UK; ☎ 877/222-9058 in US; www.nationalcar.com);

Budget (☎ 0870/156 5656 in UK; 800/472-3325 in US; www.budget.com); and

Auto Europe (☎ 0800 2235555 in UK; 800/223-5555 in US; www.autoeurope.com).

Note that rental agencies don't allow cars to travel from one island to the other on car ferries.

Getting **There**

By Plane

Palma de Mallorca's Sant Joan airport (☎ 902/40-47-04; www.aena. es) is the busiest in Spain, with hundreds of flights arriving daily from mainland Spain as well as the UK, Germany and many other points across Europe, including those of many low-cost carriers and charters. From the airport (8km/5 miles) east of the city centre), there are two ways to get into town: Bus Line 1 (Aeroport-Ciutat-Port) (☎ 971/43-10-24; 2€), leaves every 15 minutes and goes to central Palma, with several stops along the way; abundant taxis (about 15€) leave from outside all terminals.

There are direct flights from the UK to Menorca, though many require stops in Barcelona or Palma. The airport in Menorca is just outside of Maó (4½km/3 miles) southeast) with transport by bus or taxi to Maó and other destinations.

Getting **Around**

By Train

Two train lines operate in Mallorca: the **Ferrocarril de Sóller** narrow-gauge train from Palma to Sóller (7 trips daily; Estació Plaça Espanya, Eusebio Estada, 1 (Palma); ☎ 971/ 75-20-51; www.trendesoller.com; 10€ one-way, 17€ roundtrip); and the modern **Ferrocarril Inca—Manacor** (Estació Plaça Espanya, Palma; ☎ 971/75-22-45), which travels from Palma to Inca and Sa Pobla or Manacor.

By Taxi

Reliable taxi companies in Palma include Fono Taxi (☎ 971/72-80-81) and Radio Taxi (☎ 971/76-45-45. In Menorca: Maó (☎ 971/36-71-11); Ciutadella (☎ 971/38-28-96).

On Island Hopping

Although relatively few people travel to both islands on the same trip, doing so gives you an idea of their very different terrains and rhythms (Menorca is much flatter and less hurried, with smaller coves and beaches), and I recommend it if at all possible, even though logistically it's not the simplest of things to do. The most interesting way to travel between Mallorca and Menorca is by ferry from Port d'Alcúdia to Ciutadella, though it may be simpler to fly from Palma to Maó on Iberia airlines (the only company to fly direct). If you want to take the ferry and begin a tour of Menorca in Ciutadella rather than Maó, ferries depart twice daily from May to September, arriving in Ciutadella about one hour after departure. For more information, contact **Balearia** (☎ 902/16-01-80; www. balearia.net) or **Iscomar** (☎ 902/11-91-28 or ☎ 971/43-75-00; www. iscomar.com).

Street Names

Making your way around Mallorca and Menorca can be confusing, given the predominance of Mallorquín (the island variant of Catalan) and common abbreviations for streets (used in many places, including this text). Although Catalan has been ascendant on the mainland ever since the end of the Franco dictatorship, Castilian Spanish is still spoken widely in Mallorca, and in several places on the Balearics (such as in Palma) is even more prevalent than in Barcelona. Still, your high school Spanish is unlikely to prove much of a guide for street signs that commonly appear in Catalan, such as: *carrer* (c/) or street; *Avinguda* (Avda.) or avenue; and *Passeig* (Pg.) or boulevard.

By Car
Car is the best and really the only practical way of covering many parts of Mallorca and/or Menorca in a reasonable amount of time. See 'Car rentals' earlier in this section.

By Bus
Bus lines criss-cross both islands, but their limited services can make travelling through a region a challenge.

For more information on Mallorcan bus schedules (five lines fan out from Palma to each major coast), visit www.caib.es or call ☎ 971/17-77-77. On Menorca, there are two main lines: Maó-Aeroport and the Ciutadella line, which travels along the west coast of the island. For more information, call ☎ 902/07-50-66 or visit www.e-torres.net.

Fast **Facts**

APARTMENT RENTALS Among the options are **Holidaylettings.co.uk** (www.holidaylettings.co.uk/mallorca-majorca); **Owners Direct** (www.ownersdirect.co.uk/Balearic-Islands.htm); **Engel & Völkers** (www.bestpollensa.com) for villas, houses and apartments along the northwest and north coasts of Mallorca; and **Holiday Home Rentals** (www.holiday-home-rentals.co.uk/europe/spain/rent-menorca.html) for Menorca.

ATMS/CASHPOINTS Maestro, Cirrus and Visa cards are readily accepted at all ATMs. Exchange currency at banks or *casas de cambio* (exchange houses). Most banks offer 24-hour ATMs.

BUSINESS HOURS Banks are open Monday to Friday from 8:30am to 2pm. Most offices are open Monday to Friday from 9am to 6 or 7pm (in July, 8am–3pm.) In August, businesses are on skeleton staff if not closed altogether. At restaurants, lunch is usually from 1:30 or 2 to 4pm and dinner from 9 to 11:30pm or midnight. Major shops are open Monday to Saturday from 9:30 or 10am to 8pm; staff at smaller establishments, however, often still close for siesta in the mid-afternoon, doing business from 9:30am to 2pm and 4:30pm to 8 or 8:30pm.

CONSULATES & EMBASSIES **UK Consulate**, Isidor Macabich, 45 - 1r, Palma (☎ 971/31-54-28); **US Consulate**, c/ Portopí 8, 9º D, (☎ 971/40-39-05).

CREDIT CARDS **Visa's** UK emergency number is ☎ 0800 891725, or +1 (0) 410 581 9994 when abroad. US emergency number is ☎ 800/847-2911, or 900/99-11-24 in Spain. **American Express** UK cardholders and traveller's cheque holders should call ☎ 01273 696 933, or +44 (0)1273 696 933 when abroad. US Travellers should call ☎ 800/221-7282 in the US, or ☎ 902/37-56-37 in Spain. **Master-Card** UK holders should call ☎ 0800 964767, or +44 (0) 20 7557 5000 when abroad. US travellers should call ☎ 800/307-7309 in the US, or ☎ 900/97-12-31 in Spain.

DOCTORS Dial ☎ 061 to find a doctor or ambulance. The main hospital in Palma is **Hospital Universitari Son Dureta**, c/ Andrea Doria, 55, Palma de Mallorca (☎ 971/17-50-00; www.hsd.es).

ELECTRICITY Most hotels operate on 220 volts AC (50 cycles). Some older places have 110 or 125 volts AC.

EMERGENCIES For medical emergencies, dial ☎ 061; for other emergencies, call ☎ 112.

GAY & LESBIAN TRAVELLERS Spain legalised homosexuality among consenting adults in 1978, and in 1995 banned discrimination based on sexual orientation. Marriage between same-sex couples became legal in 2005. The Balearic Islands are major centres of gay life in Spain. The website **www.gayinspain.com** has complete and destination-specific

listings for gay travellers (with links for both 'Mallorca gay' and 'Menorca gay', and **Ben Amics** (c/ Conqueridor, 2, Palma; www.benamics.com) is the local GLBT organisation in the Balearics.

HOLIDAYS Public holidays observed include 1 January (New Year's Day), 6 January (Feast of the Epiphany), March/April (Good Friday and Easter Monday), 20 January (Feast of St. Sebastian), 1 May (May Day/Labor Day), 23–24 June (Feast of St. John), 25 July (Feast of St. James), 15 August (Feast of the Assumption), 24 September (Feast of Our Lady of Mercy), 12 October (Spain's National Day), 1 November (All Saints' Day), 8 December (Feast of the Immaculate Conception), 25 December (Christmas) and 26 December (Feast of St. Stephen).

INSURANCE Check your existing insurance policies before you buy travel insurance to cover trip cancellation, lost luggage, medical expenses or car rental insurance. EU citizens pay a fee for all medical treatment, but must show an EHIC card (UK: www.ehic.org.uk; Ireland: www.ehic.ie). For US travellers travelling overseas, most US health plans (including Medicare and Medicaid) don't provide coverage, and the ones that do often require payment for services upfront. If you require additional medical insurance, try **MEDEX Assistance** (☎ 410/453-6300; www.medex assist.com) or **Travel Assistance International** (☎ 800/821-2828; www.travelassistance.com; for general information on services, call the company's Worldwide Assistance Services, Inc., at ☎ 800/777-8710).

INTERNET Internet access is plentiful, both in cybercafes (*cafés Internet*) and frequently in hotels, many of which offer Wi-Fi. The Azul Computer Group operates an Internet café in Palma at c/ Soledad 4, bajos (☎ 971/71-29-27). To find additional cybercafes, check out **www.cyber captive.com** and **www.cybercafe. com**.

LOST PROPERTY   For objects lost on buses, contact Balearic Islands Transport, ☎ 971/17-77-77. For objects lost at airports, contact **Mallorca airport** (☎ 902/78-94-56) or **Menorca airport** (☎ 971/15-71-08). Call credit card companies the minute you discover your wallet has been lost or stolen and file a report at the nearest police precinct. Your credit card company or insurer may require a police report number or record.

MAIL & POSTAGE   Spanish post offices are called *correos* (koh-ray-os) or *correus*, identified by yellow-and-white signs with a crown and the words *Correos y Telégrafos*. Main offices are generally open Mon–Fri 9am–8pm and Sat 9am–1pm. The Central Post Office is at c/ de la Constitució, 6, Palma.

MONEY   The single European currency in Spain is the **euro**. At the time of going to press, the exchange rate was approximately 1€ = £0.90 (or US $1.49). For up-to-the minute exchange rates between the euro and the pound or dollar, check the currency converter website **www. xe.com/ucc**.

PASSPORTS   No visas are required for UK, US or Canadian visitors to Spain providing your stay doesn't exceed 90 days. Australian visitors do need a visa. Most EU countries need only their national ID cards, but UK citizens must travel with their passports. If your passport is lost or stolen, contact your country's embassy or consulate immediately (see 'Consulates & Embassies'). Make a copy of

your passport's critical pages and keep it separate from your passport.

PHARMACIES   Pharmacies *(farmà-cies)* operate during normal business hours and one in every district remains open all night and on holidays. The location and phone number of this *farmàcia de guàrdia* is posted on the door of all the other pharmacies. A central pharmacy is Plano, c/ de la Volta de la Mercè, 4 (☎ 971/22-88-88).

POLICE   The national police emergency number is ☎ 091. For local police, call ☎ 092; c/ Son Dameto, 1, Palma (☎ 971/22-55-00).

SAFETY   Violent crime in the Balearics is a rarity but pickpockets frequent tourist areas and major attractions such as restaurants, hotels, beach resorts, train stations, airports and ATMs. Exercise care with your belongings around major tourist sights and on beaches. **Turisme Atenció** (Tourist Attention Service), La Rambla, 43 (☎ 932/56-24-30) has English-speaking attendants who can aid crime victims in reporting losses and obtaining new documents. The office is open 24/7.

TAXES   The value-added (VAT) tax (known in Spain as *IVA*) is 7–33%, depending on the commodity being sold. Food, wine and basic necessities are taxed at 7%; most goods and services (including car rentals) at 13%; luxury items (jewellery, all tobacco, imported liquors) at 33%; and hotels at 7%. Non-EU residents are entitled to a reimbursement of the 16% IVA tax on most purchases worth more than 90€ made at shops offering 'Tax Free or Global Refund' shopping. Forms, obtained from the store where you made your purchase, must be stamped at Customs upon departure. For more information see **www.globalrefund.com**.

TELEPHONES For national telephone information, dial ☎ 1003. For international telephone information, call ☎ 025. You can make international calls from booths identified with the word *Internacional*. To make an international call, dial ☎ 00, wait for the tone and dial the country code, area code and number. If you're making a local call, dial the two-digit city code first (**91**) and then the seven-digit number. To make a long-distance call within Spain, the procedure is exactly the same because you must dial the city prefix no matter where you're calling.

TIPPING More expensive restaurants add a 7% tax to the bill and cheaper ones incorporate it into their prices. This is *not* a service charge, and a tip of 5–10% is expected in these establishments. For coffees and snacks most people just leave a few coins or round up to the nearest euro. Taxis don't expect tips. Tip hotel porters and doormen 1€, and maids about the same amount per day.

TOILETS Public toilets are called *aseos*, *servicios* or *lavabos*, and are labelled *caballeros* for men and *damas* or *señoras* for women.

TOURIST INFORMATION There are tourist information offices (OIT) scattered across both islands, beginning with the Sant Joan airport in Palma

(☎ 971/78-95-56), Passeig des Born, 27, Palma (☎ 902/10-23-65); and Can Bordils, c/ de l'Almudaina, 9 Palma (☎ 971/22-59-63). Other offices are in Valldemossa, Sóller, Pollença, Port d'Alcúdia, Cala Ratjada, Portocolom, Colònia de Sant Jordi and other resorts along the east and south coasts. On Menorca, there are OITs at the airport in Maó, downtown Maó, Fornells on the north coast and Ciutadella. Find a full list of OITs at www.illesbalears.es.

TRAVELLERS WITH DISABILITIES Some newer hotels are more sensitive to the needs of persons with disabilities and more expensive restaurants are generally wheelchair-accessible. However, because most places have very limited, if any, facilities for people with disabilities, you might consider taking an organised tour specifically designed to accommodate such travellers. **Flying Wheels Travel** (☎ 507/451-5005; www.flyingwheelstravel.com) offers escorted tours to Spain ('Spanish Symphony'), and **Access-Able Travel Source** (☎ 303/232-2979; www.access-able.com) has access information for people travelling to Barcelona. TMB (the public transportation system for both bus and Metro) has a help line for disabled travellers (☎ 934/86-07-52), and ECOM is a federation of private disabled organisations (☎ 934/51-55-50).

The Balearic Islands: A Brief History

7000 B.C. First evidence of human existence in the Balearic Islands.

1400–120 B.C. Prehistoric Talayotic culture reigns, especially in

Menorca; named after the stone structures they built.

700–400 B.C. Carthaginians conquer Balearics, and colonise the region.

500 B.C. Phoenicians settle along coast of Mallorca.

123 B.C. Romans invade, conquering Carthaginians; they name the islands Balearis Major (Mallorca) and Balearis Menor (Menorca).

120 B.C.–A.D. 400 Romans found cities of Pol·lèntia (modern-day Alcúdia) and Palmaria (Palma), and Port Magonum (Maó) on Menorca.

A.D. 426 Vandals storm Balearics, prompting the abandonment of Pol·lèntia.

711 Moors invade southern Spain and rule most of the country for the next 8 centuries.

848–903 Moorish Caliphs impose Islamic rule in Balearics, which lasts 300 years.

1075 Mallorca made an independent kingdom (*taifa*).

1229 Christian army under leadership of King Jaume I of Aragón sack Palma, seize Mallorca and end Moorish rule.

1349 Jaume III killed in battle when forces of Pedro IV of Aragón invade city, putting end to the independent kingdom of Mallorca.

1492 Spain united under Ferdinand and Isabella.

1708 Menorca seized by Britain.

1773 King Carlos III decrees end of discrimination of Jewish populations.

1802 Menorca ceded back to Spain.

1838 Frédéric Chopin and mistress George Sand spend winter in Valldemossa.

1900–2 Most of Palma's medieval walls sacrificed for urban expansion.

1912 Inauguration of Palma-Sóller railway to facilitate transport of produce.

1936–39 Spanish Civil War; Mallorca seized by Nationalist (Franco) forces; Menorca declares itself in support of the republic.

1960s–70s Beach tourism and construction explodes on Mallorca; tourism income raises per capita income for region to one of the highest in Spain.

1983 As a democracy (after death of Franco in 1975), Spain allows regional autonomy status (similar to Catalonia) for Balearic Islands.

1986 Spain enters European Community (today EU).

1990s–2000s Local environmental groups resist further coastal development but experience setbacks.

Useful Phrases: **Spanish & Catalan**

Useful Words & Phrases

ENGLISH	SPANISH/CATALAN	PRONUNCIATION
Good day	Buenos días/Bon dia	*bweh-nohs dee-ahs/ bohn dee-ah*
How are you?	¿Cómo está?/Com està?	*koh-moh es-tah/com ehs-tah*

ENGLISH	SPANISH/CATALAN	PRONUNCIATION
Very well	Muy bien/Molt bé	*mwee byehn/mohl beh*
Thank you	Gracias/Gràcies	*grah-thee-ahs/ grah-see-uhs*
You're welcome	De nada/De res	*deh nah-dah/duh ress*
Goodbye	Adiós/Adéu	*ah-dyos/ah-deh-yoo*
Please	Por favor/Si us plau	*por fah-vohr/see yoos plow*
Yes	Sí/Sí	*see*
No	No/No	*noh*
Excuse me	Perdóneme/Perdoni'm	*pehr-doh-neh-meh/ per-don-eem*
Where is. . . ?	¿Dónde está. . . ?/ On és. . . ?	*dohn-deh es-tah/ ohn ehs*
To the right	A la derecha/A la dreta	*ah lah deh-reh-chah/ ah lah dreh-tah*
To the left	A la izquierda/ A l'esquerra	*ah lah ees-kyehr-dah/ ahl ehs-keh-ra*
I would like. . .	Quisiera/ Voldría	*kee-syeh-rah/ vohl-dree-ah*
I want. . .	Quiero/Vull	*kyeh-roh/boo-wee*
Do you have. . . ?	¿Tiene usted?/Té?	*tyeh-neh oo-sted/teh*
How much is it?	¿Cuánto cuesta?/ Quant és?	*kwahn-toh kwehs-tah/ kwahnt ehs?*
When?¿Cuándo?/Quan?	kwahn-doh/kwahn	
What?	¿Qué?/Com?	*Keh/Cohm*
There is (Is there. . . ?)	(¿)Hay (. . . ?)/Hi ha? or Hi han?	*aye/ee ah/ ee a hn*
What is there?	¿Qué hay?/Que hi ha?	*keh aye/keh ee ah*
Yesterday	Ayer/Ahir	*ah-yehr/ah-yeer*
Today	Hoy/Avui	*oy/ah-wee*
Tomorrow	Mañana/ Demá	*mah-nyah-nah/ deh-mah*
Good	Bueno/Bon	*bweh-noh/bohn*
Bad	Malo/Mal	*mah-loh/mahl*
Better (Best)	(Lo) Mejor/ Millor	*(loh) meh-hohr/ mee-yohr*
More	Más/Mes	*mahs/mehss*
Less	Menos/Menys	*meh-nohs/meh-nyus*
Do you speak English?	¿Habla inglés?/ Parla anglès?	*ah-blah een-glehs/ pahr-lah ahn-glehs*
I speak a little Spanish/Catalan	Hablo un poco de español/Parlo una mica de Catalá	*ah-bloh oon poh-koh deh es-pah-nyol/ pahr-loh oo-nah mee-kah deh kah-tah-lah*
I don'tNo entiendo/ understand	noh ehn-tyehn-doh/ No comprenc	*noh cohm-prehnk*

ENGLISH	SPANISH/CATALAN	PRONUNCIATION
What time is it?	¿Qué hora es?/ Quina hora és?	keh oh-rah ehss/ kee-nah oh-rah ehss
The bill, please	La cuenta, por favor/ El compte, si us plau	lah kwehn-tah pohr fah-vohr/ehl cohmp-tah see yoos plow
the station	la estación/ la estació	lah es-tah-syohn/ la esta-cyo
a hotel	un hotel/l'hotel	oon oh-tehl/ehl ho-tehl
the market	el mercado/el mercat	ehl mehr-kah-doh/ ehl mehr-kaht
a restaurant	un restaurante/ un restaurant	oon rehs-tow-rahn-teh/ oon rehs-tow-rahn
the toilet	el baño/el lavabo	ehl bah-nyoh/ ehl lah-vah-boh
a doctor	un médico/ un metge	oon meh-dee-koh/ oon meht-jah
the road to. . .	el camino a/ al cami per	ehl kah-mee-noh ah/ ahl kah-mee pehr
to eat	comer/menjar	ko-mehr/mehn-jahr
a room	una habitación/ un habitació	oo-nah ah-bee-tah-syohn/oon ah-bee-tah-syohn
a book	un libro/ un llibre	oon lee-broh/ oon yee-breh
a dictionary	un diccionario/ un diccionari	oon deek-syoh-nah-ryoh/oon deek-syoh-nah ree

Numbers

NUMBER	SPANISH	CATALAN
1	uno (oo-noh)	un (oon)
2	dos (dohs)	dos (dohs)
3	tres (trehs)	tres (trehs)
4	cuatro (kwah-troh)	quatre (kwah-trah)
5	cinco (theen-koh)	cinc (sink)
6	seis (says)	sis (sees)
7	siete (syeh-teh)	set (seht)
8	ocho (oh-choh)	vuit (vweet)
9	nueve (nweh-beh)	nou (noo)
10	diez (dyehth)	deu (deh-yoo)
11	once (ohn-theh)	onze (ohn-zah)
12	doce (doh-theh)	dotze (doh-tzah)
13	trece (treh-theh)	tretze (treh-tzah)
14	catorce (kah-tohr-theh)	catorza (kah-tohr-zah)
15	quince (keen-seh)	quinza (keen-zah)
16	dieciséis (dyeh-thee-says)	setze (seh-tzah)

NUMBER	SPANISH	CATALAN
17	**diecisiete** *(dyeh-thee-syeh-teh)*	**disset** *(dee-seht)*
18	**dieciocho** *(dyeh-thee-oh-choh)*	**divuit** *(dee-vweet)*
19	**diecinueve** *(dyeh-thee-nweh-beh)*	**dinou** *(dee-noo)*
20	**veinte** *(bayn-teh)*	**vint** *(vehnt)*
30	**treinta** *(trayn-tah)*	**trenta** *(trehn-tah)*
40	**cuarenta** *(kwah-rehn-tah)*	**quaranta** *(kwah-rahn-tah)*
50	**cincuenta** *(theen-kwehn-tah)*	**cinquanta** *(theen-kwahn-tah)*
60	**sesenta** *(seh-sehn-tah)*	**seixanta** *(see-shahn-tah)*
70	**setenta** *(seh-tehn-tah)*	**setanta** *(seh-tahn-tah)*
80	**ochenta** *(oh-chehn-tah)*	**vuitanta** *(vwee-tahn-tah)*
90	**noventa** *(noh-behn-tah)*	**noranta** *(noh-rahn-tah)*
100	**cien** *(thyehn)*	**cent** *(sent)*

Freephone Numbers & Websites

AER LINGUS (MALLORCA ONLY)
☎ *902/50-27-37 in Spain*
☎ *01/886-8844 in Ireland*
☎ *0871 718 5000 in the UK*
☎ *800/474-7424 in the US (NOT TOLL-FREE)*
www.aerlingus.com

ALITALIA
☎ *+39 06 2222 when outside UK*
☎ *800/223-5730 in the US*
☎ *08714 241424 in the UK*
www.alitalia.it

AMERICAN AIRLINES (MALLORCA ONLY)
☎ *902/11-55-70 in Spain*
☎ *0207 365 0777 in the UK*
☎ *800/433-7300 in the US*
www.aa.com

BMI BABY
☎ *902/10-07-37 in Spain*
☎ *0905 8282828 in the UK (NOT TOLL-FREE)*
☎ *+ 44 845/ 810- 1100 in the US*

BRITISH AIRWAYS (MALLORCA ONLY)
☎ *902/11-13-33 in Spain*
☎ *0870 850 9850 in the UK*
☎ *800/247-9297 in the US*
www.british-airways.com

EASYJET
☎ *807/ 26-00-26 in Spain No US number*
☎ *0905 8210905 in the UK (NOT TOLL-FREE)*
www.easyjet.com

IBERIA
☎ *902/40-05-00 in Spain*
☎ *0870 609 0500 in the UK*
☎ *800/772-4642 in the US*
www.iberia.com

ICELANDAIR (MALLORCA ONLY)
☎ *932/17- 91-42 in Spain*
☎ *0844 811 1190 in the UK*
☎ *800/223-5500 in the US*
www.icelandair.is

LUFTHANSA (MALLORCA ONLY)
☎ *800/645-3880 in the US*
☎ *0180-5-838426 in Germany*
☎ *0871 945 9747 in the UK*
www.lufthansa.com

RYANAIR (MALLORCA ONLY)
☎ *807/18-18-81 in Spain*
☎ *0871 246 0000 in the UK*
www.ryanair.com

Index

day BY day™

Get the best of a city or region in 1, 2 or 3 days

Day by Day Destinations include:

Europe

Amsterdam
Athens
Barcelona
Berlin
Brussels & Bruges
Budapest
Cornwall
Dublin
Edinburgh & Glasgow
Florence & Tuscany
Lake District
Lisbon
London
Madrid
Malta & Gozo
Moscow
Paris
St Petersburg

Prague
Provence & the Riviera
Rome
Seville
Stockholm
Valencia
Venice
Vienna

Canada and The Americas

Boston
Cancun &
the Yucatan
Chicago
Honolulu & Oahu
Los Angeles
Las Vegas
Maui

Montreal
Napa & Sonoma
New York City
San Diego
San Francisco
Seattle
Washington

Rest of the World

Bangkok
Beijing
Hong Kong
Melbourne
Shanghai
Sydney
Toronto

Frommer's®

Available wherever books are sold

Photo **Credits**

Front Matter Credits: i: © Shutterstock.

All images: © Neil Edward Schlecht with the following exception:

Courtesy of Hotel Alcaufar Vell: p145 bottom.